Ban

ABOUT THE AUTHORS

David Brandon is a university lecturer in social history and author of twelve history books. He lives in Peterborough.

Alan Brooke has taught in further and higher education for many years and has a particular interest in the history of crime. He lives in Peterborough.

Bankside

London's Original District of Sin

DAVID BRANDON
& ALAN BROOKE

AMBERLEY

Cover illustrations: Front: Bankside, detail from Anthonis van den Wyngaerde's pen and ink drawing of *c.* 1544. © Jonathan Reeve JR1095b20p952-3 15001550. *Back inset colour image:* Claes Visscher's *View of London* c. 1616 © Stephen Porter. *Back, background:* Bankside as depicted on the plan of London included in Georg Braun and Franz Hogenberg's *Civitatis Orbis Terrarum* (1572). © Jonathan Reeve JR1107b21p429 15501600.

First published 2013

Amberley Publishing
The Hill, Stroud,
Gloucestershire, GL5 4EP

www.amberleybooks.com

British Library Cataloguing in Publication Data.
A catalogue record for this book is available from the British Library.

ISBN 978 1 4456 1384 0 paperback
ISBN 978 1 4456 0962 1 ebook

Typesetting and Origination by Amberley Publishing
Printed in Great Britain

CONTENTS

Introduction

The intention of this book is to provide a thematic introduction to the history of Bankside. While there is no official definition of exactly what constitutes Bankside, most people would probably agree that it certainly includes that part of the south bank of the Thames which lies between Blackfriars Bridge and London Bridge. The authors, however, felt that for the purposes of this book to concentrate simply on this small quarter would be to take Bankside out of its context. The Borough and Bankside run into each other seamlessly so that it is impossible to say where one ends and the other begins. We believe that Bankside can only be understood and appreciated as an integral part of the historically very rich area of transpontine London which developed on the south side of the Thames at the foot of London Bridge and is conveniently, if misleadingly, referred to as 'Southwark'. It is this bridge foot that is the historic core of Southwark, which was contiguous with the Borough and Bankside. Modern Southwark is a borough created in 1965 by merging the metropolitan boroughs of Southwark, Bermondsey and Camberwell. The modern Borough of Southwark extends as far south as the Sydenham Hill and Crystal Palace area, which historically has little in common with old Southwark. It also includes Bermondsey and Rotherhithe to the east. These districts have their own very rich history. So we have taken Bankside as synonymous with the historic core of Southwark. It is the area encompassed by Blackfriars Road on the west, Southwark Street, Southwark Bridge Road, Marshalsea Road,

Long Lane, Bermondsey Street and Tooley Street to London Bridge. Occasionally we mention places and associations just outside this immediate area. The bridges across the Thames, for example, have a massive presence. London Bridge has had an absolutely formative effect on the district, and its history must be sketched.

Sometimes described as London's oldest suburb because it was here that the Romans built the first bridge over the Thames with a settlement on the south side of the bridge, Bankside has always been at the centre of things and yet, curiously, away from them as well. This is because of the daunting physical barrier presented by the Thames. Even today, London south of the river seems an alien, unknown place and somewhere apart to those Londoners firmly domiciled north of the Thames who are thoroughly convinced that the real London is only to be found on their side of the river. A commonly uttered joke is that you need a passport to cross the Thames into South London. We are not keen to become involved in these issues. We admit to feeling that there is a strong sense of difference between the atmosphere of London north and London south of the river, although we cannot explain exactly why this is so. However we are not partisans. We simply love and revere London, north and south, and we hope that this feeling can be sensed in the pages that follow.

The Bankside district has been fought over for almost as long as London and its first bridge have existed. When attacks from the south have been made on the Metropolis, inevitably Southwark and London Bridge have born the brunt. The bridge was fortified and the works involved gave the name 'Sudwerka' or 'South Work' to the district. The name 'Borough' recalls the fact that here was located a defensive 'burgh' intended to protect the south end of the bridge. The Bishops of Winchester played a major part in the history of the area. They had a palace and controlled the Bankside area which was known as the 'Liberty of the Clink'. This became a criminal 'sanctuary', attracting all manner of fugitives from the law, scallywags and chancers. Historically, it would not be unfair to say that Southwark has been considered as the City of London's disreputable underbelly. Being outside the jurisdiction of the City of London, it was renowned as a place of raffish recreation with its cockpits, theatres, brothels, its bear garden and its bawdy taverns and alehouses. Symptomatic of the role it carved out for itself or that was thrust upon it, the area had what seems to be an undue concentration of prisons. It was almost as if, at least as far as the City of London was concerned, anywhere south of London Bridge was, thankfully, mostly out of sight and as far as possible out of mind.

Many travellers from overseas gained their first impressions of London as they came up from Dover and passed along what is now Borough High Street. If they arrived late in the evening, they often had little option but to stop over for the night before the final stage of their journey when they crossed London Bridge and passed into the City. The gates on the bridge closed at night. Additionally, stagecoaches and large wagons were not allowed to cross London Bridge while it still had houses on it, and so the Borough was the southern transport terminus of London. A sense of transience was always a feature of this part of Southwark with many travellers and strangers passing through but also with substantial communities of immigrants making their homes around the district and often living in the direst poverty at first. Subsequent generations frequently made good and moved on. Dutch and Flemings arrived in the sixteenth and seventeenth centuries, German and Irish in the nineteenth, and Cypriots, Caribbean, south Asian and Africans in the last fifty years. Southwark expanded very rapidly in the nineteenth century as huge numbers of large and small industrial and commercial concerns opened up operations to add to the existing long-standing industrial activity characteristic of the district. These new arrivals added to a growing population of indigenous English who had migrated from other parts of the country. It often took time for these various incomers to learn how to live with each other and there were racial tensions. The Irish, for example, were strongly resented because they were prepared to accept low wages and were said to be particularly dirty. What the newcomers nearly all had in common was the experience of being crammed into some of London's most noxious and notorious slums.

This workforce was engaged in an enormous range of industrial activities – it is often forgotten that London was a hub of the Industrial Revolution. These industries polluted and blighted the district with their filthy effluents. The overcrowding of industry and housing – the two were closely intermingled – was exacerbated by the coming of the railways on viaducts that carved cruel swathes through the district and created areas of no man's land. Immediately east of London Bridge Station they continue to do so even to this day. The area was heavily bombed in the Second World War, and it remained one of London's least regarded districts as it suffered the blight of industrial decline, poor housing and deprivation. It was somehow symbolic of Southwark's Cinderella status that the cathedral, albeit while still a parish church, was allowed to be squeezed too close both to busy but forbidding warehouses and the Borough Market and then visually browbeaten by a railway viaduct on one of the busiest stretches of line in England. In order to build this railway, the fine Lady Chapel was demolished and the retrochoir or extreme eastern end nearly followed suit. Even today the cathedral is seen by vast numbers of commuters but probably not actually noticed. Tourists flock in huge numbers around the locality and many, we suspect, are surprised to find a cathedral there at all. Ask people to name ten British cathedrals and the odds are on that Southwark would not be among them. Southwark's history has been one of ups and downs. It seems now to be on the up.

In the last two decades, the riverside area between Blackfriars and Southwark Bridges in particular has undergone a remarkable renaissance. This is based on the discovery in 1989 of the remains of the Rose Theatre. This focused interest in the theatrical past of Bankside and led to the building of a recreation of the seventeenth-century Globe Theatre. The revival was spurred on by the conversion of Sir Giles Gilbert Scott's post-war Bankside Power Station into the Tate Modern Art Gallery. The Millennium Bridge, although initially something of a fiasco, has brought Bankside and St Paul's closer and carries a steady traffic of pedestrians, large numbers of whom are tourists. This was the first completely new bridge across the Thames in London since the opening of Tower Bridge over one hundred years earlier.

The last decades have seen a dramatic reduction in the commercial and industrial activity which was such a feature not only on the south bank but also of this part of the Thames. Gone from Bankside or changed out of all recognition are the grimy wharves, cranes and warehouses of an earlier, very different era, yet one that seems so recent because it can be remembered by people aged in their fifties. Whatever happened to the characteristic 'dirty British coaster with its salt-caked smokestack' that loaded and unloaded its seemingly mundane cargoes amidst a frenzy of labour-intensive human activity at Pickle Herring Wharf or St Olave's Wharf? H. E. Popham in a quaint little book called *The Taverns of London* (Popham, 1928) neatly encapsulates the sense of Bankside as it was at the time:

> To get the correct atmosphere of the locality it is as well to walk along the side of the river from Blackfriars Bridge – not along modern Southwark Street – but close to the water, by the wharves, under the cranes, over the ropes, and round the barrels, stumbling over a chain every hundred yards, and incidentally getting a glorious view of St Paul's Cathedral. Although we are almost in hail of the Bank of England, yet we have in spirit left it far behind, and are now down at the heart of things, where the actual work is done, and connection established between the Mother City and every other part of the world. Not on paper but in stern reality; where the things that you actually touch have been or will be handled by some stevedore at Valparaiso or Sydney or Tokyo. Silk hats and patent boots are not for Bankside nor Bankside for them. Coats off here, for there's heaving to be done.

Popham would be amazed were he to visit this part of Bankside today. Since his time Bankside has continued in its distinctive way, which involved considerable continuity and interaction with its past yet also reflected the wider economic, social and cultural changes brought about by the decline in Britain's manufacturing base and the seemingly unstoppable growth of the tertiary or service sector of the economy. The pace of change in this formerly very characterful part of London is accelerating enormously. Moving in are international corporate solicitors and chartered accountants, media and publishing companies

– the sunrise industries. Bankside could be said to be gaining a new character, but it is one that is inevitably far less distinctive. Bankside and the Borough have now been 'discovered' and are seen as ripe for exploitation. What is happening is striking evidence of the massive power of corporate business to transform the function, culture and appearance of a district. Glitzy offices, riverside apartments at prices beyond the comprehension of most of the longer-standing local residents, cafés, bars and bistros are the music of the moment. Rich pickings are to be had but Bankside is in danger of going on to look exactly the same as every other similar area of honeypot development across the globe. Even many of the tourist attractions of Bankside, in attempting to emphasise the unique historic character of the area, are part of a powerful thrust that is actually destroying it. Is there any real necessity for Shard London Bridge? Yes, it will certainly be striking and distinctive but it is corporate one-upmanship, deliberately intended to be higher than anything at Canary Wharf. How long before another consortium comes along and promises to build the Tower of Babel because it will be even higher? Perhaps every era has to have its icons. These icons tell us much about the mores of the age.

1

From Roman to Norman Times

Man has left such an imprint on London that it is very difficult for us to visualise the previous natural landscape. London stands on an uneven bed of gravel, clay, sand and chalk, sedimentary rocks laid down when the London area was covered by the sea. It clusters on either side of the Thames in a depression or basin formed by the northern heights around Muswell Hill, Highgate and Hampstead and the high ground around Streatham, Dulwich and Forest Hill to the south. Where it flows through London, the Thames has formed an alluvial floodplain through which it makes its way in a series of great sweeping curves. The Thames changed its course about 500,000 years ago when the glaciers of the Ice Age forced the river to take a more southerly route – basically the one it takes today. Prehistoric people were attracted to the fertile soils of the floodplain and archaeologists have found and studied artefacts from the primitive culture they developed. In particular, large numbers of flint implements have been unearthed, although not necessarily in situ. They suggest that hunting, scavenging and foraging took place. Remains of creatures such as the woolly rhinoceros and the mammoth have also been discovered and indicate that periods of glaciation were interspersed with other periods only relatively warmer.

As the glaciers finally retreated around 6500 BC, Britain broke away from the European mainland. The Thames where London now stands was considerably wider and slower-flowing than it is today. The north bank, apart from a narrow marshy margin, was probably densely wooded while the southern side was lower-lying, muddy and marshy and it may have been difficult to establish the exact meeting place of land and river. It was often flooded by high tides. London was a natural place for permanent settlement. It was the lowest point at which the Thames could feasibly be bridged. It was forty miles from the sea, but the river was perfectly navigable for oceangoing vessels this far inland. A variety of pre-Roman artefacts and evidence of dwellings have been found in the Southwark area. They provide evidence of early ploughing and of burial mounds. Fresh water would have been available along with abundant timber, fishing and fertile soil for simple agricultural activity. Inland there would have been plenty of game on offer. Perhaps pre-Roman Londoners built their homes on piles on the south side of the Thames, which was shallow and experienced far fewer tidal differences than today.

Although the Romans under Caesar had made initial forays in the London area in 54 BC and apparently crossed the Thames, possibly on pontoons, they did not stay and headed back to more hospitable surroundings and balmier climes. However, in AD 43 they returned under Claudius and settled, if not permanently, at least for almost four centuries and went on to stamp their imprimatur firmly on the country they controlled. It is likely that they surveyed the scene and decided that the north bank of the Thames was an ideal place for a major settlement. It was above the likely level of flooding and was flattish and well drained. On the west there was a natural moat provided by the considerable valley carved out by the River Fleet. The steep slopes down to the edge of the Thames also assisted defence. Plenty of fresh water was available in numerous springs that could be tapped through the gravel and could also be taken from the small stream called the Walbrook. The Thames itself was navigable and the building of a port would be comparatively easy. Shallow the Thames may have been, but it was also wide and a formidable barrier to communication. It had to be bridged.

The campaign to subjugate the native population of eastern and south-eastern England was a hard-fought one. London was by no means the focus of their military activity and the main centre of native resistance at first was Colchester. The Romans landed at Richborough, on the east coast of Kent. The Thames estuary and even the river where London was eventually sited were formidable obstacles to the movement of troops and supplies. A bridge was essential. The Romans were great civil engineers, and it may well be that Southwark was a hive of activity as it became the bridgehead and depot for the formidable project of crossing the wide river.

Archaeologists have unearthed evidence of a bridge at Southwark which they believe could not possibly have been built before AD 50. Before that time it is likely that there was a ferry where the great Roman Watling Street crossed the Thames. It was natural that a settlement would develop around the landing place for the ferry. Little is known of this first bridge – of its method of construction and materials. It is likely that it had foundations on stone piles. It was situated around fifty yards east of the present London Bridge. It quickly became of strategic importance as the new roads made by the Roman army from the Kent coast and other parts of the south to London and Camulodonum (Colchester) converged on this bridge. One major road was from Chichester; the other, Watling Street, was from the coast of Kent. Clearly the importance of these roads meant that the south bank of the Thames at the bridge foot found itself very much at the centre of things. However, typically, it was not destined to remain as such when the Romans established their capital on the other side of the river at Londinium. In fact, Southwark may have been the earliest occupied part of Roman London in the sense that there was a substantial military encampment there defending the new crossing before much of the town on the other side had been built. Southwark was already cast in its role as a satellite or suburb, but it was clearly seen as being important enough for Boudicca's warlike followers to make their way across the Thames and put it to fire and the sword in AD 61. The inferno created by the attackers was such that coins found on both sides of the river had been fused by the heat. It should be mentioned that the Thames could be forded in the Westminster area where the gravel bottom of the river allowed it to be crossed at low tide.

The settlement, although virtually razed to the ground, was quickly re-established, and what is now Borough High Street was the major artery along which traffic to and from London moved. It would have been busy and such bustle attracted tradesmen retailing food and other necessities and also those providing vital services, such as farriers and blacksmiths. Warehouses developed along the bank, which had been stabilised by the Romans and strengthened by ingenious wooden retaining walls in the construction of which simple piledrivers had been used. Although very much subsidiary to the huge town that developed on the north bank, Southwark seems to have been favoured by some Romans of substance as a desirable residential suburb. Traces of a hypocaust which provided underfloor heating have hinted at a degree of luxury which must have at least partly offset what would have been regarded by the newcomers as a fairly barbaric climate. As Tony Aldous (1980) wittily commented, 'Southwark was evidently to *Londinium* what Gerrard's Cross and Virginia Water are to modern London' – in other words, desirable suburbs.

Archaeologists have been able to establish many details about what the Romans ate. They seemed to have a liking for seafood if the number of recovered oyster shells is anything to go by. Interestingly, fragments of a Roman boat were recovered from the site of Guy's Hospital, evidence that some of what was probably a maze of creeks in the area were large enough to be navigable. It is known that they used shallow and flat-bottomed barges, which would have been well-suited to such waterways. As with so many things, the Romans were effective and efficient boatbuilders. They built very sturdy vessels, the hulls of which were joined by mortises and tenons rather than being nailed to ribs, a method which required the seams to be caulked. This we know was done with slithers of hazel twigs. London became a major port, as it made much more sense to move goods by water than lug them laboriously along what passed for roads at the time.

A number of archaeological discoveries have been made in the Southwark area which shed some light on life in Roman times. One of these was a jug inscribed 'London, at the shrine of Isis'. It is thought that it was used for carrying holy water. Isis was a god of Egyptian origin popular throughout the Roman Empire. Amphorae were two-handled earthenware jugs used in large quantities, especially for carrying olive oil and wine. One amphora found in Southwark contained mackerel bones and had an inked inscription that it belonged to a merchant engaged in shipping fermented fish sauce. A similar vessel was used for carrying green olives. It is evident that seagoing trade was supplying London with foodstuffs particularly from Gaul but also from Spain, Tunisia and Turkey. Imports and exports required efficient warehousing, and a wooden industrial building has been discovered in the Southwark area that was partly underground so that commodities could be stored under cool conditions.

Southwark also housed a fishing community. This had previously been on the opposite side of the river, but that side was becoming built up with quays, houses and various primitive industries. Consequently, a declining amount of space was available for them to hang out their nets for drying and mending and to carry out the various tasks involved in the processing of their catches. It seemed that riverside Southwark, being less developed, offered them more secure living and working prospects. The increasing amount of human activity on the north bank of the river, the Middlesex Shore, was driving away the fish and the waterfowl that provided their living. The river was of course considerably wider then, and so the Surrey shore, being quieter, continued to attract large amounts of wildlife which could be trapped or caught. It seems almost inconceivable, looking at Bankside now, that among the feral creatures then finding the wherewithal for life were beavers. Another factor drawing fishermen and their families to settle in the area was the trade that could be attracted by setting up fish and game stalls around what is now Borough High Street with its bustling traffic, including many hungry travellers. There were still families in Southwark obtaining their living from fishing on the river as late as the 1830s.

The story of the decline and fall of the world the Romans had created has been told many times and very successfully. What followed the departure of the Romans in Britain was not exactly the 'Dark Ages'. Schoolchildren used to be given the impression that there was some kind of regression to total savagery and barbarism as hoards of violent uncouth invaders ran amuck, their way of life the very antithesis of the cultured civilisation supposedly associated with the Romans. In reality, of course, the natives had absorbed much of the Roman culture. The various invaders did things differently from the Romans and their culture was therefore a very different one. Generally speaking, they had little time for towns and based their way of life on nomadic foraging and later settled agriculture. The trade to and from the Continent, which had formed the basis of life in Roman London, vanished, and it is likely that the city became almost a ghost town and that Southwark declined as a consequence. It is unclear what happened to the bridge at this time, but it is likely that people and goods had to be ferried across the river between the two banks, which were for some of the time in different kingdoms hostile to each other. In this situation, it is likely that the fortunes of Southwark were in the doldrums. However, the idea of a sudden cataclysmic collapse of an established way of life was a false one. In AD 410 the Roman Emperor Honorius proclaimed that henceforth the inhabitants of Britain would have to fend for themselves. Shortly after that, the remaining Roman troops were withdrawn. However, in AD 429, when Germanus visited Britain, he commented that Britain was still largely Christian and was resisting invaders. In 457 Britons evacuated London in the face of attacks from the Saxons, who then took control for several centuries.

Sporadic warfare continued for 150 years or more as the Anglo-Saxons tried to conquer those parts of the British Isles which appealed to them, but from around 600, large numbers of them were settling permanently. London was becoming the most important town in the country. Commerce returned to the Thames, the economy starting to grow again and things would have been looking up for Southwark, in London's shadows and largely dependent on its prosperity. In 730,

Bede described London as 'an emporium for many nations'. The dominance of the Anglo-Saxons was challenged from around 800 with the first appearance of marauding Norsemen. In 842, Norsemen attacked London but were repelled. In 851 they returned and seized it. They destroyed it and massacred its people. Nationally, periods of uneasy peace were interspersed with resistance by the natives under inspirational leaders such as Alfred, who in 886 wrested control of London back from the Norsemen. In 892 a Danish fleet sailed up the Thames intent on taking London but was repelled, and Londoners felt confident enough to counter-attack, destroying enemy ships on the river. In 994 another Danish attack was fought off. This was led by Sweyn, King of Denmark. In 1013 and 1016 London was besieged, again by Danish forces, and on the latter occasion the Danes were successful. Led by Cnut, who was not sure that a direct attempt on the bridge was a practical possibility, they dug a channel through the muddy and marshy ground on the Surrey shore, probably from Rotherhithe to the Battersea area. This was no mean feat. It was wide and deep enough to allow them to haul their vessels past the bridge, whereupon they were ready to launch an attack on the City side of the river. Negotiations took place which avoided too much death and destruction, the outcome being that Cnut became King.

The name 'Southwark', incidentally, seems to be mentioned first of all about 920. It is referred to then as 'Suthringa Geweorche'. This can be rendered as 'the Surrey folk's defence-work'.

Returning to the chronological outline, the Danes held sway in England from 1014 to the death of Hardicanute in 1042 when the Anglo-Saxons resumed power. In 1066, of course, the Normans under Duke William arrived on these shores. Determined to seize the crown which a few years earlier had been promised to him, he wasted little time in taking London. But only after he had laid waste to Southwark in December 1066.

2

London Bridge

The first London Bridge was built by the Romans, and its successors remained the only crossing in central London until 1750 when Westminster Bridge was built. A bridge at this point has played a leading role not just in the history of London but in the history of the nation for nearly 2,000 years. The first bridge was probably a wooden one erected shortly after the Romans had conquered most of Britain in AD 43. This bridge was of major strategic importance, as roads from Richborough and Chichester converged on it, crossed over it and then proceeded to Camulodonum, which the Romans at that time made their capital. A small settlement was created at what is now Southwark on the south side of the river and a major settlement on the north, which they called Londinium. Further major roads, to Chester and York, were built from Londinium and the bridge then became even more important, as traffic from the south used it before heading northwards into the provinces.

The first London Bridge was short-lived, becoming the victim of Boudicca's vengeance on the Romans for the scourging they had inflicted on her and for their raping of her daughters. Her forces sacked and destroyed Camulodonum and then Londinium and put anyone they could find to the sword. The Romans rapidly retaliated with their brutally efficient war machine and slaughtered Boudicca and her forces. They moved their capital to Londinium and probably rebuilt the bridge but there is absolutely no documentary evidence to confirm it.

Archaeological evidence exists of a wooden bridge a short distance downstream from the present-day bridge. This was probably built about AD 80–90 and had a drawbridge to allow ships to pass through. Iron-tipped wooden piles have been discovered and large numbers of Roman coins have been found on the bed of the river – these were probably votive offerings. It is not known what happened to this bridge when the Roman forces left in 410. It is likely that it was left to decay, and London may have been bridgeless for several centuries. On the other hand, there may have been wooden bridges during some of this period.

Some kind of bridge had certainly come into existence in the ninth or tenth century according to documentary evidence. The bridge has a long history of suicides or of people thrown from it. One widow and her son were found guilty of witchcraft. The son disappeared but his mother paid the full penalty. She was thrown off London Bridge and drowned. An often-told story concerns the second decade of the eleventh century. By this time the Danes occupied London, much to the chagrin of the Saxon King, Æthelred. Allying himself with Olaf, King of Norway, he made plans to recover the capital from the upstarts who had seized it. A combined force sailed up the Thames until they reached the bridge, on which Danish soldiers stood, brandishing weapons and mouthing insults. Quite how the Saxons and Norwegians did the next bit has not been satisfactorily explained. Somehow, they managed to tie ropes round the wooden piers of the bridge and then bend their backs for all they were worth as they rowed back downstream (with the flowing tide helping them). Their efforts were rewarded. They pulled the bridge down and precipitated large numbers of Danes, no longer shouting insults, into the river where they drowned. This event is almost certainly the origin of the well-known children's nursery rhyme 'London Bridge is Falling Down'.

The bridge was rebuilt but, being wooden, it proved vulnerable to tidal surges on the river and also to fire. In the City of London, most of the buildings were timber-built, and between 1077 and 1136 no fewer than eight major fires broke out in the City and on each occasion the bridge was affected. In 1091 the bridge collapsed in one of the worst storms London ever experienced. In 1093 the Thames froze over, and when the thaw came, the bridge was nearly destroyed by ice floes. The decision was made to build a masonry bridge, not least because London was growing in wealth and importance and needed a bridge of a more durable and permanent nature. The building of this bridge was a daunting prospect given that the river had fierce tides and was approaching 1,000 feet wide at this point. The supervisor of the building of the new bridge was Peter de Colechurch, who was a priest. This is not surprising, because the building of bridges was regarded as a religious duty in medieval times and major bridges frequently had chapels on them, often constructed and funded so that prayers would be said for the souls of those who provided them. The chapel built on the new bridge was dedicated to St Thomas Becket, the furore over his murder in Canterbury Cathedral in 1170 still being fresh in people's minds. Colechurch died before the bridge was completed. This was in 1209. The fact that the bridge took so long to build suggests that it was a difficult task. An estimated 150 workmen died during this time. However, it can be said that a good job was done because the bridge served for more than 600 years. The difficulties experienced by the builders attempting to drive piles and create firm foundations while working from floating barges on the fast-flowing tideway can scarcely be imagined. When the bridge was demolished in 1832, some excitement was caused by the fact that a number of bones were found in the undercroft of the chapel. It was said that these were the remains of Colechurch, but in fact close examination showed that only one of the bones was actually that of a human and there was no proof whatever that it had ever belonged to the revered Colechurch.

Much of the funding required for the building of the bridge came from a tax on wool, which had already become England's major industry and a source of considerable wealth. An old saying was that London Bridge was built on woolpacks. As is so often the case on such occasions, other money came in from people who wanted publicity for their wealth and munificence. Bridge House Estates was established in the 1280s to take over the care and maintenance of the new bridge which, rather confusingly, historians now call 'Old London Bridge'. This organisation is still in existence and undertakes the maintenance of all the bridges from Blackfriars to Tower Bridge.

Old London Bridge had twenty arches, one being a drawbridge. These arches were irregular in width and shape, although all had pointed arches with the exception of the drawbridge. The length of the bridge has been given as between 880 and 936 feet. There were massive structures described as 'starlings', but which we today would probably call cutwaters, and these were designed to give the bridge sound foundations and to provide protection for the piers.

There were many hazards that could befall those using the river and needing to pass under London Bridge. The public and private latrines on the bridge discharged through the air and into the river. Their users made no attempt to ensure that the coast was clear, as it were, before they urinated or defecated. The latrines were housed in little boxes protruding from the back of the buildings on the bridge. There was a public facility on the bridge, which collapsed in 1481; five people who had the misfortune to be using it at the time fell into the river and drowned. However, an ultimately more serious hazard was the fact that the arches and particularly the starlings channelled and concentrated the flow of water in the river. The water rushed through the arches with tremendous and, under certain tidal conditions, terrifying force. The bridge in effect acted as a weir. At high tide the starlings were submerged and the water passed through the arches in a fairly tranquil fashion, but it was a different matter when the tide ebbed. The bridge effectively banked up the water on the upstream side and there could be a difference in height of up to six feet between the water on either side.

Many people refused to pass under the bridge and disembarked on one side and walked or rode to the other side where they would try to engage another conveyance. Cardinal Wolsey was a regular traveller on the river to and from Hampton Court and Greenwich Palace. He was always scrupulous in ensuring that he did not pass under the bridge, leaving the risks to the servants who manned his sumptuous vessel. The Revd John Ray, a seventeenth-century man of wit and wisdom, wrote in 1670 that 'London Bridge was made for wise men to go over, and fools to go under'. There were always headstrong men, usually young, who wanted to show off their derring-do by 'shooting the bridge' as the act of folly became known. Over the years, substantial numbers paid the price. They included in 1290 a ship full of Jewish people who were being deported from England on the orders of Edward I. Some say that their ghostly woeful cries and agonised screams can still be heard from time to time.

John Lyly was a travel writer who published prolifically during the reign of Elizabeth I (1558–1603) and he was greatly impressed when he said the following:

> ... among all the straung and beautifull showes me thinketh there is none so notable, as the Bridge which crosseth the Theames, which is in manner of a continuall street, well replenished with large and stately houses on both sides, and situated upon twentie [sic] arches whereof each one is made of excellent free stone squared.

In 1581 a Dutchman by the name of Peter Morice erected a waterwheel on the most northerly arch to raise water from the river and pump it to a cistern. Residents of the City who paid a subscription could then access the cistern for their water supply. Morice had met with some opposition when he first proposed to install his contraption, but he silenced those who thought it was simply impracticable when he gave a demonstration and directed a jet of water over the steeple of the Church of St Magnus the Martyr. The wheel was made of wood and Morice employed considerable ingenuity in employing a system of pulleys so that it was automatically raised or lowered depending on the state of the tide. Morice's device proved very successful. Four more wheels were built at the northern end and two at the Southwark side. These enterprises, however, had the effect of further constricting the flow of the river and channelling it through the central arches, which consequently became even more difficult to navigate. By partially blocking the flow, the wheels made it more likely that the river would freeze over in the very cold winters being experienced at this time.

Old London Bridge had a drawbridge, sited towards the middle. The intention was that, when it was raised, cargo vessels with tall masts could pass the bridge to and from the quay at Queenhythe. The other purpose of the drawbridge was a defensive one. It could be raised to prevent enemy forces crossing the bridge. In fact the bridge had quite a formidable defensive capability. There was a stone tower with a stout gate at the Southwark end and a wooden gate known as the Drawbridge Gate at the north end as well as the drawbridge. It is clear that the City authorities thought that a potential enemy would approach the City from the south and so they made sure that they themselves were all right. It is typical of the Cinderella status of Southwark, however, that the City was presumably prepared for its neighbour on the far side of the Thames to be laid waste as long as its own integrity was not seriously threatened.

The Drawbridge Gate was used for the display of the severed heads of people found guilty of treason. The first head to adorn the bridge was that of William Wallace in 1305. He was the Scottish patriot who led a campaign against Edward I. After being captured, he was hanged, drawn and quartered. This involved him being partially hanged and then, while he was still conscious, he was cut open, eviscerated and his entrails were burned in front of him. After he had expired – and this couldn't come soon enough – he was decapitated and his body was divided into quarters. These were despatched to places in the north and in Scotland where they were displayed publicly to act as deterrents to any other people considering a rebellion against the King. His head, meanwhile, was parboiled and tarred to preserve it and then placed on a spike on the Drawbridge Gate.

The heads of traitors being treated in this way was common practice, and other locations such as Temple Bar usually had a head or two on view, but display on London Bridge was reserved for special celebrities – posthumous recognition and honour as it were. The heads of many interesting historical figures made their debuts on the bridge over the years. They included that of Sir Thomas More. Foolishly and fatally as it turned out, he refused to acknowledge Henry VIII as the supreme authority over the Church of England. He only had to mutter a few contrite words and he could have escaped his fate, but he was a stubborn man and so his head in due course appeared on the spike on the bridge. A story is told that his daughter, understandably distressed by the fate of her father, prayed to the Almighty that his head might fall off into her lap. It did indeed fall and she managed to get hold of it but those who do not believe in Divine Intervention instead thought, a trifle cynically perhaps, that she bribed someone to take it down. Another man who died for his faith was Bishop Fisher. His head was put up on the bridge whereupon, instead of deteriorating in the exposed position as the heads tended to do, it apparently grew fresher looking with every passing day. As a contemporary observer stated, '… it could not be perceived to waste nor to consume … but daily grew fresher and fresher, so that in his lifetime he never looked so well; for his cheeks being beautified with a comely red, the face looked as though it had beholden the people passing by and would have spoken to them.' The gullible immediately flocked to see what they believed was a miracle. This annoyed the authorities, who responded by throwing Fisher's head into the river – out of sight and out of mind. In doing so, they also helped to relieve the quite appalling traffic congestion caused by those who came to gaze in awe at the martyr's head. Not many heads that were formerly attached to females appeared on spikes but one that did was that of Elizabeth Barton, the 'Holy Maid' of Kent. She was a visionary who rather unwisely made a public prophecy that if Henry divorced Catherine of Aragon and married Anne Boleyn, he would die a villain's death. She could not expect to get away with that one. Normally the heads remained in place until time and weather had done their work and they simply rotted, fell down and were then thrown into the river.

The Drawbridge Gate was demolished in 1577 but all was not lost. The impaling and displaying of heads was simply moved to the Great Stone Gate at the Southwark end of the bridge. These were troubled times and religious bigotry, persecutions and executions provided a steady supply of the heads of those arraigned for treason on the grounds of practising their Catholic religion and therefore denying the Queen's role as Head of the Church. These gruesome trophies accumulated in substantial numbers. A fascinated German visitor to London counted thirty-four in 1592. Particular celebrities whose heads appeared on the Great Stone Gate were many of the conspirators who took part in the Gunpowder Plot of 1605. Had people had to pay to look at the heads, these would have been a sell-out. The most distinguished of the heads to make it onto a spike at that time was that of Guy Fawkes. After the Restoration of the Monarchy in 1660, the heads of some of those who had signed the death warrant of Charles I were placed on the bridge.

All good things come to an end. In 1678 the last head to be spiked on London Bridge was that of William Stayley. He was executed after perjured evidence had been submitted by that egregious and odious little toad Titus Oates. He was making a name for himself inventing Popish plots to restore Catholicism in England. After this, traitors' heads were spiked at Temple Bar, much to the annoyance of Dr Johnson, who spent much time frequenting taverns in nearby Fleet Street. A giant white spike on the current bridge recalls the practice.

London Bridge has had a history of finding itself at the centre of things. In 1216 the barons became so disillusioned with King John that they invited Louis, the Dauphin of France, to seize the throne. Understandably excited at the prospect, he led a force which landed in Kent, marched up-country, through Southwark and over London Bridge. Louis received a rapturous welcome which proved to be short-lived. King John chose this moment to die, just having lost the Crown Jewels and in his misery dining on an injudicious meal of peaches washed down by copious quantities of cider. Possibly the food was poisoned deliberately. Anyway, no sooner had the barons heard the news of John's death than they suddenly got very cold feet about the idea of being ruled by Louis. They may have been half French themselves, but he was wholly French and it would never have done to have him on the throne. England would have become part of France! They had a whip-round, thanked Louis for his interest in the post, paid him off and sent him back to France. Actually he didn't want to go and he put up some military resistance before realising that he was fighting a lost cause. A return to reassuring normality was achieved when John's son became King. Henry III, as he was styled, was only a boy of nine at the time, and the barons looked forward to being able to bend him to their wills.

Henry was, on balance, not a successful monarch. Just like his father, he found himself in conflict with the barons, who, in 1264, marched on London, led by Simon de Montfort. The rebel force occupied Southwark but the King's forces on the other side of the bridge reckoned they had outwitted the rebels when they barred the gates, raised the drawbridge and – a masterstroke this – threw the keys into the Thames. However, the rebels had many supporters among the London citizenry, who, notwithstanding the loss of the keys, wrenched open the gates, lowered the drawbridge and let de Montfort's forces cross the bridge and seize control of London.

There is nothing new about the ordinary people being forced to pay taxes to help meet the cost of a war they do not support. In 1381 the anger at the imposition of a poll tax to finance war with France, combined with a far-reaching list of other grievances, led to the rebellion known as the Peasants' Revolt. A force largely consisting of angry countrymen from Kent converged on Southwark. They found the drawbridge raised against them, but Wat Tyler, their leader, then threatened to set fire to the houses at the Southwark end of the bridge. Many ordinary Londoners sympathised with the peasants and even those who didn't thought it expedient to lower the drawbridge and allow them to cross into the City. Wat Tyler's men were joined by another rebel force from the eastern counties and together they proceeded to settle accounts with some of those who they thought of as their worst oppressors. Among these was Simon Sudbury, who combined the roles of Archbishop of Canterbury and Lord Chancellor. His severed head soon appeared on a spike on the Drawbridge Gate. The Revolt failed for reasons beyond the scope of this book, and Wat Tyler's head replaced that of Sudbury on the selfsame spike shortly afterwards. Frightful vengeance was wreaked on the rebels by the forces of 'law and order'.

In 1450 the people of Kent rose up once more, taxation again on their list of grievances. Led by Jack Cade, a force of about 30,000 men marched up from the country and converged on Southwark. There they made camp while Cade tried to negotiate passage of the bridge. This took some time, but he was successful and he and his followers crossed into the City peacefully enough. However, violence quickly broke out and the rebels embarked on an orgy of rape and rapine. This annoyed the locals, and the rebels wisely withdrew over the bridge to Southwark once more. They were followed by the catcalls and taunts of the Londoners, who then proceeded to close off the bridge. This incensed the rebels and a pitched battle broke out lasting several hours through the night. Both sides suffered losses, but many of those who lived on the bridge were caught up in the fracas and died when their homes were set on fire. When morning dawned, the bridge was a complete shambles and the rebels were making their way back home. Cade was quickly captured and he was decapitated. More alert readers may hazard a guess where his head ended up. It was impaled on the Drawbridge Gate, of course.

In 1528 Cardinal Campeggio, the Papal Legate, rode with an impressive entourage across the bridge to put the Pope's side of things to King Henry on the small matter of the latter's wish for a divorce from Catherine of Aragon. Large crowds came to cheer him, and Henry put on an impressive show of hospitality for him. They failed to reach an accord. Campeggio's return across the bridge was less auspicious.

Enough of all this misery and mayhem; let's have a happier story just for once. In the 1530s there lived on the bridge one William Hewet, who was a wealthy cloth-worker. He had an infant daughter called Anne. Lodging in the Hewets' house was Edward Osborne, who was an apprentice in the cloth trade. One day in 1536 Anne fell out of one of the windows overlooking the river and plummeted into the waters below. As luck would have it, her fall was spotted by the doughty young Osborne, who, without a thought for himself, plunged into the torrent and succeeded in rescuing the little girl. We can almost hear our readers, if any, purring with pleasure. However, even better was to follow. Hewet grew wealthier and wealthier and in 1559 became Lord Mayor of London. Anne, meanwhile, had grown into a most toothsome young lady with many suitors. Her father was an exceptionally rich man and she was an only child. The authors would hate to imply that any of these surely very worthy swains had ulterior motives. Doubtless Anne's beauty and personal charms greatly outweighed whatever financial benefit might come by way of a dowry upon marriage to the young lady. Osborne, despite an assiduous attention to his duties in learning the trade, must have despaired of his chances given that among others bent on wooing her was a real young sprig of the aristocracy in the form of the Earl of Shrewsbury. He need not have worried. Hewet kept his beady eye on what was going on and eventually uttered the immortal words, 'Osborne saved her and Osborne should enjoy her.' We hope that he meant that Osborne should indeed enjoy Anne but only after undertaking the sacred and legal rituals associated with the Holy Sacrament of marriage. On hearing Hewet's declaration and presumably giving the matter a bit of thought, Osborne proposed to Anne and was overjoyed when she accepted. He was probably even more overjoyed when he heard of the dowry that Hewet had settled on her. The wedding took place in 1562. This fable about the virtue of being in the right place at the right time becomes even more exemplary when we can reveal that the worthy Edward Osborne went on to become a Knight of the Realm and Lord Mayor of the City of London.

In 1642, early in the Civil War, both sides knew that control of London was imperative to their cause. Parliament stole a march on the King's supporters. General Fairfax led a strong Parliamentary force on London via Southwark and London Bridge and did so without opposition because the ordinary folk of London, although not necessarily all of the rich and powerful, supported the struggle against the King.

It was not all war and violence. The bridge saw its share of pageant. For example, in 1357 the Black Prince crossed it to a hullabaloo of huzzahs from cheering crowds. He had disembarked on the Kent coast and made his way through the countryside up to London, passing Southwark and crossing the bridge, having shortly before completed an extraordinary victory over a much larger French army at the Battle of Poitiers. Even better, he brought with him John, the captured French king. In 1390 a joust was held on the bridge attended by Richard II. Sadness was combined with celebration in 1396 when Richard passed over the bridge accompanied by his bride. She was his second wife, Isabella, the daughter of the French king. The girl was a mere child of six and the marriage was for reasons of political expediency. It was never consummated. Unfortunately, in the crowd, nine people were crushed to death.

Others who passed this way in triumph were Henry V after his sensational victory at Agincourt in 1415, Catherine of Aragon in 1501 on her way to marry Prince Arthur, the future Henry VIII's older brother and heir to the throne, and on 29 May 1660 Charles II re-entered London at the Restoration of the Monarchy, passing through jubilant cheering crowds.

The bridge obviously evolved through its long and complex history, and as it grew older so its appearance reflected change. Probably its most obvious feature for much of this time was that it was lined with buildings. These, with the exception of St Thomas's Chapel, were built of timber. From time to time there were fires. Ice and various objects floating down the river damaged the bridge. Sometimes individual buildings needed replacement. The result was that, over the centuries, the bridge became a hodgepodge of mixed styles but, rather like the hammer with three heads and five handles, it remained the same bridge. The buildings were all of three storeys. At street level they consisted of shops or other businesses and above that they provided residential accommodation. Passing over the bridge was rather like traversing a gloomy canyon, albeit a constantly bustling and rather claustrophobic one. The roadway was only twelve feet wide and many of the buildings shored each other up with beams that ran across the street and formed extensions of the houses. The only gap was that provided by the drawbridge. In 1460 a list of shops on the bridge would consist of a glover, a goldsmith, a cutler, a jeweller, a fletcher and a tailor. By the seventeenth century, most of the shops sold clothing or books. The word 'picturesque' had not been invented in the seventeenth century, but by that time the bridge was attracting much interest, especially from visitors to London, who might have described it as 'quaint' or 'curious'. The idea of an inhabited bridge was itself an attraction but by this time people were becoming aware that the bridge was a structure that both witnessed and encapsulated much of London's history. Inhabited bridges were by no means uncommon in Europe, but London Bridge was by far the longest and it was generally regarded as one of the wonders of the world. The spiked heads drew the visitors too.

Most visitors would have taken in St Thomas's Chapel. This was built of stone. It stood on the east or downstream side of the bridge and access could be made not only from street level but also from the river by boat. The original chapel was in the Early English architectural fashion of the twelfth century, but in the late fourteenth century it had a makeover and re-emerged in the modish Perpendicular style. It was dissolved in the 1530s during Henry's religious changes and became what would now be called a 'retail outlet'.

A newcomer to the bridge appeared in 1577 – Nonsuch House. This curious title reflected the slightly hyperbolic name given by Henry VIII to Nonsuch Palace. He started building this hugely overblown and never fully completed hunting lodge and grandiloquent statement about himself in the 1530s. It was near Cheam in Surrey. Nonsuch House was shipped over from Holland in pre-fabricated pieces. Timber-built, it was decorated to resemble masonry, and with its turrets it looked like a scaled-down version of a Tudor mansion with very extensive use of glass. It immediately became an attraction for sightseers and the most expensive and sought-after dwelling on the bridge. Prestigious addresses mattered even in those days. A curious point commented upon in the sixteenth century was that those who dwelt on the bridge tended to be much healthier than their contemporaries who lived either in Southwark or on the north side of the river. This was hardly surprising. They were away from the stench of the cesspits and inefficient drains, the overcrowding and the mounds of ordure, offal and other filth which lay in the streets.

The northern end of the bridge suffered a serious fire in 1633, but in September 1666, London Bridge suffered damage in the Great Fire which destroyed so much of London itself. Some houses and the waterwheel at the City end burned down. It was the turning point for the bridge as a place to live. The rebuilding of the City and developments close by provided many new and more desirable residential quarters and the bridge fell out of favour. No longer was there an appeal in the gimmick of living on a bridge across a large tideway. The constant roar of the water, the bawdy shouts of uncouth watermen and the bedlam caused by those trying to make their way along the most congested street in London had long been constants in the life of those who lived on the bridge. Now they became seen as reasons for not living there.

In 1722 vehicles crossing the bridge had to pay tolls for the first time. In an attempt to tackle the total chaos which was the almost permanent state of the traffic attempting to pass over the bridge, men were employed to enforce a 'keep left' rule on the bridge, almost certainly the first time this was required anywhere in England.

Old London Bridge was tired and becoming ever more decrepit. One observer described its appearance as 'exceedingly disagreeable'. Those using it to cross the river with wheeled vehicles were increasingly vociferous in their complaints about having to pay tolls for the privilege of fighting their way through what would now be described as traffic gridlock. A rising crescendo of voices demanded one or more new bridges. The watermen did not contribute to this demand. Their business, which involved moving people and things along and across the river, prospered as the shortcomings of the bridge became more manifest. In the face of their outright hostility, Westminster Bridge, some way upstream, opened in 1750. It was not just that this broke the monopoly of London Bridge as a road crossing in central London but it looked so much more modern and efficient by comparison. Pressure began to develop for a modernisation of London Bridge or even for a new bridge at the same location. An obvious if controversial suggestion was to knock the houses down as a means of widening the carriageway and thereby easing the chronic congestion. This proposal became law in 1756 and work started building a temporary wooden bridge to be used while the buildings were demolished. Among those who opposed the knocking down of the buildings on the bridge were, of course, those who lived in them. One night in 1758 the temporary bridge burned down, and there were many who pointed fingers of suspicion at the displaced residents or at the watermen who obviously did not want an improved bridge. Guilt was not established but a guard was put on the new temporary bridge on which work quickly restarted. The final house on Old London Bridge was pulled down in 1762.

The Great South Gate was demolished in 1760. On it was the coat of arms of George II. This was taken down and placed on the frontage of a new house in Axe Yard, off Borough High Street. The cipher was altered to indicate George III. In 1879 Axe Yard became Newcomen Street, and the building, which became a pub, displays the arms to this day. There was a bridge house and yard in Tooley Street just to the east of the bridge. It acted as a store and maintenance depot for the bridge. It was a substantial structure because banquets were sometimes held there and the premises contained a bakery in which ship's biscuit for the Royal Navy was produced.

The traffic may have moved more quickly but somehow, without the buildings on it, London Bridge had lost its soul. Despite that, the amount of traffic using it continued to build up. On one day in the summer of 1811 a census took place. It recorded 89,640 pedestrians, 769 wagons, 2,924 carts and drays, 1,240 coaches, 485 gigs and 764 horses. This level of usage took its toll. In 1801 structural weaknesses had been discovered and this provoked a crescendo of calls for a new bridge. There was no shortage of people who came forward eager to gain fame and fortune by designing a replacement bridge, but none of them appealed to Bridge House Estates. Along with the predictably eccentric and entirely impractical designs submitted by a variety of understandably unknown architects, grandiloquent but also possibly impractical designs were put forward by better-known men such as Ralph Dodd and the eminent Thomas Telford. A particularly interesting proposal was that of George Dance the Elder. This was for two parallel bridges each with a drawbridge in the middle. These would allow the passage of ships with high masts and rigging to sail past the bridge but to avoid undue road congestion, one bridge would remain open to vehicular and pedestrian traffic while the other had its drawbridge raised to allow the ship through. Much property on either side of the bridges would have been knocked down to make way for two elegant piazzas. However, no progress was made until 1823, when Parliament sanctioned the building of a new bridge and chose a design in granite. This was the work of John Rennie Senior, who was the man of the moment because the nearby Southwark Bridge, which he had also designed, had just been completed. Rennie actually died before the decision to adopt his design had been made, and in the event it was his son John, later Sir John, who superintended the building of the bridge. This bridge required the demolition of many buildings at the north end of Borough High Street.

The ceremonial laying of the foundation stone took place on 15 June 1825. The new bridge was completed on 1 August 1831. It was over one hundred yards upstream from the bridge it replaced. King William IV (often referred to contemptuously as 'Silly Billy') and Queen Adelaide performed the grand opening, which was made an occasion for great ceremonial. Technology was moving forward rapidly in the 1820s and 1830s, and the builders had various new methods and techniques at their disposal which made the task quite a bit simpler than it would have been even fifty years earlier. Despite using the new technology, the construction of the new bridge was hazardous and forty workers lost their lives while the operation was taking place. Viewing the progress of the new works became a popular activity both for Londoners and visitors. Some of the regulars must have been quite bereft when the bridge was open to traffic. At least they could then look at the demolition of the old bridge. This started on 22 November 1831 and took over a year, ending with the removal of the starlings. The timbers of these ended up as souvenirs.

The bridge was 2,350 feet long, including the approaches, and the total cost of construction was over two and a half million pounds. The bridge unquestionably looked good, but structural faults were quickly discovered and the proud boast that it would last 1,000 years proved to be a mistake. Over the course of its relatively short life, the traffic on the bridge became increasingly heavy and put it under considerable stress. In 1836 London Bridge Station opened, and as the railway network south of the river expanded, the station generated completely unforeseen amounts of traffic both vehicular and pedestrian. The number of passengers using the station doubled, for example, between 1850 and 1854 alone. Large numbers of them were commuters travelling every working day and almost all of them crossed the bridge by one means or another. In 1859 a traffic census counted 20,498 wheeled vehicles and 107,074 pedestrians crossing the river in a 24-hour period. The river was being intensively used as well and a pier at the Southwark end known as the 'Surrey Side' provided cheap boats carrying commuters and pleasure-seekers. The pressure on the bridge led to it being widened in the 1900s.

On 22 June 1861 London Bridge provided an ideal viewing point for the great night-time fire in the warehouses in Tooley Street, Southwark. This event attracted large numbers of spectators from right across London. It was just getting dark on the evening of 13 December 1884 at a time when homeward-bound commuters were hurrying across to London Bridge Station, eager to catch their trains to the suburbs. A loud and powerful explosion shook the bridge. A bomb had exploded under the second arch on the downstream side of the bridge. Perhaps surprisingly, given the volume of noise, little damage was done and there were only a few minor injuries. It was never established how the explosive device had been detonated or even where it had been placed, but it was generally agreed that it was the work of the Fenian Brotherhood of Irish Nationalists.

In the 1920s it became clear that some settlement of the structure had taken place. Cracks began to appear in 1962, and in 1967 Parliament was once again called upon to give its approval for the building of a new bridge. This bridge has three pre-stressed concrete arches faced in granite, the outer ones of 260 feet and the central one 340 feet. It officially opened in 1973.

Most of the fabric of Rennie's bridge was sold to an oil-rich American corporation who had it transported to Lake Havasu City, a new city being constructed in the Arizona desert. They wanted the bridge to act as a major tourist attraction. Demolition began in November 1967. The stones were carefully numbered – all 10,246 of them – and exported under the collective description of a 'large antique'. London Bridge rose again in its new home. An artificial stretch of water was created so that it could be a bridge in its new location. Doubtless the Americans would have preferred the Thames itself, but it was not for sale. An opening ceremony was conducted by the then Lord Mayor of London on 10 October 1971 in front of large crowds, who heard many speeches emphasising the spirit of amity between the two great English-speaking nations.

One arch of Rennie's bridge remains on the Southwark side of the river and can be viewed from the narrow stairs known as Nancy's Steps. These have Dickensian associations. A feature of the declining years of Old London Bridge was a number of half-domed alcoves which provided a refuge for hard-pressed pedestrians from the incessant vehicular traffic. One of these can be seen in the grounds of Guy's Hospital and two more are in Victoria Park in the East End. Some stones from the bridge are in the churchyard of St Magnus the Martyr. In Gilwell Park, Chingford, is a section of balustrade which almost certainly came from Old London Bridge.

In July every year, the race with the quaint name of Doggett's Coat and Badge is staged on the Thames starting from London Bridge and covering the four and a half miles to Chelsea. This event has its origins with an Irishman by the name of Thomas Doggett who was a comedian and theatre manager. Doggett intended the race to be a celebration of the accession to the throne of George I, and he left money for the Worshipful Company of Fishmongers to organise the race and to present the coat and badge to the winner. This is the oldest contested race in the English sporting calendar and is no pushover because the rules require the race to be held when the adverse tide is running at its fastest. The winner received an orange-coloured coat and breeches, a cap with the badge of liberty and a rather outsized silver badge with the rampant White Horse which was the insignia of the House of Hanover. It is worth mentioning that Doggett's enthusiasm for the Hanoverian monarch was shared by few other people. This was hardly surprising. George I hated England, spent all his time pining for Hanover and never took the trouble to learn English.

Commuters still cross the river daily in large numbers, rather like a tidal ebb and flow – in one direction in the morning and in reverse after work. To take the tidal analogy a little further, there is little undertow; few people crossing against the flow. Those who walk across the bridge are cosseted – the pavements have what in effect is underfloor heating to keep them free of ice in cold weather. Commuters have on more than one occasion been likened to herds of sheep. Once a year, a flock of real sheep crosses the bridge. This is an enactment of the right of all the Freemen of the City of London to drive their sheep across the bridge free of charge.

For those who like 'pop' history, under the southern end of the bridge is the 'London Bridge Experience' where, with a fair amount of visual and verbal gimmickry and also some actual artefacts, the history of the bridge can be traced.

3

Other River Crossings

Bankside owes its existence to the Thames. A navigable river attracted settlers, and the lowest point at which the river could be crossed fixed the place. These two factors have been intertwined for two thousand years. 'Old Father Thames keeps rolling along' with its massive presence while the uses that humankind makes of it have evolved and changed over the centuries. Boats go up and down; boats go across; people have swum from one side to the other. In former times, the Thames was fordable in the Westminster area. The Thames has been constricted and embanked. It has been bridged. Men, like moles or perhaps more like the Teredo, or shipworm, have tunnelled under it. People have fallen into the Thames and it has often taken their lives. Others have used it to commit suicide – perhaps by jumping off a bridge – in order to end their blighted existence. Meanwhile the river, 'liquid history', has simply and nonchalantly continued to ebb and flow with the tides, contemptuous of the puny efforts and activities of mere mortal men. The river has been used, it has been regulated but it has never been tamed. It is far too independent.

Millions cross and re-cross the river as part of their daily routine. On trains and buses few give the river a second look. They are vaguely aware that it is part of their lives. Walking commuters probably do not spare the Thames a thought but dull indeed of soul would be the tourist and visitor to London who remains unmoved by the sight of the river 'gliding at its own free will' as Wordsworth put it. In tube tunnels the Thames is so close yet thankfully it does not make its presence felt. The regular travellers, especially the commuters, can do their best to ignore the river but somehow by simply just being there it still manages to exercise influences on their everyday lives.

The Thames bred its own races or sub-species of humans. Watermen, lightermen, bargees and ferrymen all used their special skills to obtain a living from the need for goods and people to be transported along or across the river. Conflict has been inevitable between those who move up and down the river and those who need to cross it. However, the men who worked on the river were a breed of their own. What they had in common was vehement opposition to the building of new bridges. They were determined to maintain the lucrative income that resulted from the Thames being London's main highway – the easiest and quickest way, for example, to get from the City to Westminster. The City Livery Company known as the Watermen and Lightermen of the River Thames was established in 1555, and in the seventeenth century it had something like 20,000 members. There were innumerable ferries and ferryman's stairs, all now consigned to the history books.

The bridges of Bankside have not been built according to any master plan. They tend just to have happened. Londoners have rarely regarded them as adequate because they have tended to lag behind demand and to play a catch-up game. That was true until the Millennium Bridge. This seems to have created its own demand and appears to be used and already to be accepted, and even loved, far beyond the planners' expectations – at least since the teething problems have been ironed out.

The first stone-built London Bridge was London's only bridge for over five centuries, and despite continuous grumbling by large numbers of the citizenry, the building of additional bridges was held back by the efforts of powerful vested interests. Some people may be reassured to know that such groups are not just a product of modern British politics. This bridge was replaced by Rennie's structure, which lasted for about

135 years. Its replacement opened for business in 1972. It has not solved the problems of traffic congestion even in the sector it serves, let alone been part of any greater scheme to deal with the permanent mayhem of gridlock on central London's streets.

The tunnels used by Underground trains beneath the Thames in this area obviously have little visual impact on London's cityscape but without them the traffic problems would be infinitely worse. There are, however, two largely forgotten tunnels of considerable historical significance. The first to be built was the Tower Subway which was opened in 1870 from Tower Hill to Vine Lane, off Tooley Street. This passes almost directly under HMS *Belfast*. Of the Tower Subway, more will be said later. Use is still made of the Tower Subway, although not as a public facility. A genuine 'ghost' tunnel is that which houses the stretch of the former City & South London tube railway that ran between London Bridge and King William Street.

Today the traffic on the river is largely confined to pleasure craft. Britain is no longer a major manufacturing economy. The way that imports and exports are handled has changed out of all recognition and the Pool of London and the docks that had such a massive presence downstream are no more. The former hustle and bustle of commercial activity among the riverside wharves and warehouses close to Tooley Street has gone. It has been replaced by the shining glass of offices, riverside apartments, cafés and bars and the other trappings of a twentieth-century consumer society, which is good for those who, in material terms, are successful. No more than a stone's throw away is a terrain of bleak high-rise flats and drab streets for those who, in material terms, are not.

A large Dominican monastery called the Blackfriars, dissolved in the reign of Henry VIII, was formerly sited close to what is now the north-east end of the bridge which takes its name, Blackfriars Bridge. Almost all physical traces of this monastery have disappeared with the exception of a small section of wall in Ireland Yard, EC4. A magnificently eccentric, wedge-shaped art nouveau pub called The Blackfriar at the bottom end of Queen Victoria Street commemorates the brethren and their activities in a delightfully mocking way. The pub stands very close to where the River Fleet enters the Thames. The Fleet is now little more than a subterranean storm sewer but a walk north towards Holborn Viaduct will bring an appreciation of the substantial valley which the Fleet has carved out for itself in this area. In 1756 the Corporation of the City of London submitted a Bill to Parliament to give it powers to cover the lowest section of the Fleet and to build a bridge across the Thames. Westminster Bridge had opened shortly before, and the Corporation was concerned that if another bridge was not built in the area under its jurisdiction, it might lose business to the Charing Cross and Westminster areas. Although it excited some controversy, the Bill with various amendments became law. Some public money was to be provided. Otherwise the cost was to be defrayed by levying tolls on those who used the bridge until the income raised allowed the loan that had been required to be paid off.

With a bridge legally authorised, the submission of designs was invited. Gaining the contract to design any bridge to cross the Thames, particularly where it flowed past London, was seen as a real 'plum'. Some heavyweight architects of the time put forward their designs. Among them were George Dance and John Smeaton. In the event, the contract went to a little-known architect called Robert Mylne (1734–1811) who was then appointed as surveyor and engineer. The various illustrious architects whose designs were rejected were most put out by Mylne's success. They considered him a mere parvenu. Also seething with barely suppressed rage was the cantankerous Dr Johnson. He fulminated about the potential weakness of the elliptical arches which were a feature of Mylne's design. Johnson may have been known as 'The Great Cham of Literature' but a total lack of knowledge of architecture and constructional engineering principles was no obstacle to his holding forth at great length on the shortcomings of the design to which he had taken such great exception. Some people mischievously said that the root of his protests was that Mylne was a Scotsman. Dr Johnson was notorious for his antipathy to the Scots, but he denied that this had anything to do with it. He was actually a good friend of John Gwynn, who was among those submitting an entry in the competition.

The ceremonial laying of the first stone took place on 31 October 1760. The usual fulsome speeches were made including paeans of praise for the Prime Minister of the time, William Pitt the Elder (1708–78). His conduct of the various wars in which Britain was engaged was so meritorious, it was said, that the public had indicated that they wished the bridge to be known as the 'William Pitt Bridge'. *Sic transit gloria mundi!* When the bridge opened to all traffic in 1769, it was known as 'Blackfriars Bridge'. By this time the tax burden of paying for the wars was so heavy that Pitt was more likely to be burnt in effigy than to have a bridge officially named after him.

Many problems were encountered during the building of the bridge. Technical problems with the caissons around the piers were difficult to eliminate while the outpourings into the Thames from the River Fleet proved troublesome. The contents of the Fleet were not just river water but also sewage and untreated effluents from the homes, businesses and industries that drained into it. The presence of this filth made working conditions on the project particularly unpleasant. In the winter of 1762/63, the Thames froze solid and work had to be abandoned for the duration of the cold snap.

In June 1780 the bridge found itself caught up in the Gordon Riots, which sparked off in Southwark. The ostensible cause of the riots was vehement anti-Catholic feeling but many of the rioters probably forgot what had brought them together in the first place, when, gaining numbers as they went, they surged across Blackfriars Bridge and towards the City. As they went, they vented their spleens on the tollhouses on the bridge. The tolls payable for crossing the bridge were widely resented and so the rioters broke into the tollhouses, seizing any money they could lay their hands on and destroying anything easily destructible, including the account books.

There were problems at the southern end of the bridge in the St George's Fields area because of the complexities of landownership. The original intention was that a road would be built along the south bank connecting Blackfriars to London and Westminster Bridges, but the legal and financial wrangles involved with this project would probably have proved insuperable. Instead a road was built connecting the bridge foot with St George's Circus where existing roads from Westminster and London Bridges came together.

Only about thirty years after the bridge opened, concerns were being expressed about the wear and tear from which the surface of the roadway was suffering. The potholes became notorious. The fabric of the bridge was also deteriorating, partly because the tides in the river were flowing so much more rapidly after the removal of Old London Bridge. The main structure of the bridge was composed of Portland stone, which, while being easy on the eye, is rather soft, and the piers were suffering damage from ice floes and minor collisions with barges on the river. Not just Blackfriars but also Waterloo and Westminster bridges were suffering badly from scouring around the base of the piers. Things muddled on until 1860 when the decision was taken to replace the bridge. In 1863 authority was given for the demolition of the old bridge and its replacement by a bridge of five spans designed by Joseph Cubitt. The foundation stone of this new bridge was laid on 20 July 1865 and the construction work on the second Blackfriars Bridge was expedited much more quickly because it was ready for the official opening by Queen Victoria on 6 November 1869. She was deeply unpopular at the time because she had become a reclusive widow after the death of Prince Albert. This was one of her very rare appearances in public in those years. Strong republican feelings were developing in Britain, and the Queen had to run the gauntlet of considerable abuse and derision as she passed through the streets.

The bridge had five wrought-iron spans and displayed ponderous-looking polished red granite columns and columns carved with plants and birds to be found along the river. The River Fleet has its outfall into the Thames directly underneath the bridge, but there is normally little flow to be seen unless there has been persistent heavy rain and then only at low tide. At the end of the first decade of the twentieth century, the bridge was widened, partly to allow the passage of electric trams.

This is the widest road bridge in London. Under the arches of the south end of the bridge are a number of mosaics which trace the history of the bridge.

It was under Blackfriars Bridge early on the morning of 18 June 1982 that the dead body of a man was found hanging from scaffolding. The pockets of his clothes contained bricks and stones – there were even some inside the trousers – and they were clearly intended to weigh him down. There was a large amount of money in his pockets and an expensive watch adorned his left wrist. The deceased was identified as Roberto Calvi, a wealthy and powerful Italian banker with links to the Vatican and to the Mafia. His nickname was 'God's Banker'. His extensive and lucrative operations on behalf of these and other clients had destructively imploded after years during which he had both enriched himself and made huge amounts of money for those who had entrusted their investments to him. He had been convicted of fraud and jailed but was out of prison pending an appeal. The initial conclusion was that he had committed suicide. Later investigations showed that the circumstances of his death rendered suicide impossible. Calvi was in Britain in disguise and with false papers, accompanied by two or three louche characters on whom suspicion immediately fell. Certainly Calvi had reasons to commit suicide. He was disgraced, terrified of the prospect of returning to prison and, perhaps more pertinently, he knew that those whose funds he had badly mismanaged were anxious to meet with him and impress upon him personally their grave displeasure at what, charitably, might be seen as incompetence or, at worst, deliberate deception. The case has never come to any satisfactory conclusion. In 2005 a number of men were tried for Calvi's murder but they were acquitted on the grounds of insufficient evidence. Explanations of what actually happened on a postcard, please, to the authors, who will pass on information received to the authorities. Discretion and anonymity are, of course, guaranteed.

The London, Chatham & Dover Railway opened a temporary station in 1864 called 'Blackfriars Bridge'. This was on the south bank of the Thames and it acted as a terminus for various services originating in Kent.

The LCDR had ambitions. Its intention was to cross the Thames and thereby become the first company from south of the river to enter the City and build a station there. If this was not enough, it also intended to link up with the Metropolitan Railway at Farringdon and with other companies who had lines north of the river with extensive access to the provinces. This could make the line a very important one not only for passengers but for carrying coal and general merchandise. In December 1864 the LDCR opened its bridge across the Thames. The bridge was built by Joseph Cubitt, a member of an extensive and successful dynasty of engineers. It ran parallel with and close to Blackfriars Bridge, which was also his work. The new bridge consisted of five wrought-iron lattice girders supported by very substantial cast-iron columns. Observers at the time refused to be carried away by this bridge as they were by so many engineering structures associated with the railways, and it was widely denounced for its perceived ugliness.

A station was built on the north bank at Ludgate Hill, and the LCDR was required to run what were known as 'workmen's trains' into this station. These ran at peak periods in the morning and evening with very cheap fares. They were legally required because large numbers of working-class dwellings had been demolished when the LCDR built its viaduct through the densely built-up districts just south of the river. Large numbers of people had been displaced and had been forced to move home. Since many of them worked in the City or elsewhere north of the river, the cheap fares and special trains were some attempt to compensate them for the inconvenience they had suffered.

Later, a second railway bridge was built by the LCDR, and Cubitt's effort was largely rendered superfluous. It went out of use in 1971 and the superstructure was removed with some difficulty in 1985 with the aid of a massive floating crane. The gaunt remnants of Cubitt's bridge can still be seen. These are the cast-iron columns on which the girders once stood but, while ugly in themselves, they catch the eye because of the huge LCDR coat of arms on them which has been restored and brightly painted.

The London, Chatham & Dover Railway built a second bridge which opened in 1886 across the river to a station initially called St Paul's. The bridge was designed by John Wolfe Barry, noted for his work at Tower Bridge, and Henry Marc Brunel, second son of the immortal Isambard Kingdom Brunel. It was completed in 1885 and had five spans on piers aligning with those on the earlier bridges to the west. The ironwork was provided by the foundries of the Thames Ironworks & Shipbuilding Company of Blackwall, a reminder of the heavy industry that could once be found along the Thames below the Pool of London. This bridge is still in use carrying, among other services, trains currently operated by First Capital Connect linking Bedford and Luton with a variety of destinations south of the river; in fact, they run as far south as Brighton. St Paul's station is now Blackfriars.

The Millennium Bridge opened amidst great jubilation in June 2002. Was it not the first entirely new bridge to be built across the Thames in central London for over one hundred years? Did it not link St Paul's Cathedral, the icon of London's spirit of resistance in the Blitz to a newer icon – Tate Modern, the state-of-the-art gallery in a converted coal-fired power station which was helping to inject new life into a formerly neglected and run-down part of London? Did it not symbolise the hopes and aspirations of a new century? All these and various other mantras were advanced as great cause for celebration. Most of all, we were told that this striking and unquestionably modernistic bridge contributed to that conveniently abstract and inchoate concept known as the 'feel-good factor'. Two days later it had to be closed because there was a possibility that those crossing it in such huge numbers would be precipitated into the river. When this announcement was made, the feel-good factor evaporated within minutes as people shrugged their shoulders and, relapsing quickly into their normal cynicism, made disparaging comments to the effect that planners, engineers and others couldn't organise a booze-up in a brewery.

Extraordinary though it may appear, a bridge at this point had first been proposed as early as 1854. In 1911 a road bridge was authorised. Money was spent acquiring property that stood in the way of the projected approach roads but the scheme was abandoned in 1931. It would have been known as St Paul's Bridge. However the idea was taken out and dusted down once more in the 1990s. The south bank of the Thames opposite St Paul's was becoming run-down as the wharves and warehouses fell into disuse. The striking Bankside power station, itself modernistic in its time, went out of operation and the whole area, so close to the prestigious glass and steel monoliths of corporate finance capitalism, was in danger of becoming an intrusive eyesore and unwelcome reminder that economic change could bring with it decay and dereliction. The decision was taken to regenerate the south bank, and the idea of a new bridge, albeit now a pedestrian one only, was back on the agenda. This idea was taken up with considerable enthusiasm, and there were suggestions that the residential aspect of Old London Bridge should be reprised and that the bridge should be lined with houses. Well, not exactly houses, but luxury apartments for the ultra-wealthy who would happily part with a king's ransom in order to occupy what would unquestionably have been among the most sought-after addresses in the whole of London.

Reviving memories of a common practice in Victorian times, a competition was held for those who wished to obtain the prestigious contract. There were no less than 227 entries. The winner was announced in December 1996. It was for a design submitted by a consortium composed of Norman Foster and Anthony Caro with Ove Arup & Partners providing the engineering expertise. They submitted a design for a suspension bridge which was intended to be eye-catching while also being light enough to add to rather than detract from views along the river, to St Paul's. It obviously needed to provide sufficient headroom for what was left of the rivercraft on the Thames to pass underneath. The Queen performed the official opening ceremony on 9 May 2000. The bridge was to be opened for public use on 10 June. Hordes of people rushed to cross the bridge anxious to say that they had done so on the first day. It took some pounding because of the numbers crossing, and the bridge shook and wobbled quite violently. Most of those crossing thought this was great fun and some even jumped up and down in order to enhance the unexpected movement.

Such antics were watched with horror by coveys of engineers and health and safety people, and the decision was taken that the wobble was a potentially serious problem and that, while it was investigated, the bridge needed to be closed to the public. The media naturally and understandably had a field day. The wobble, we were told, was the result of 'synchronous lateral excitation'. This phenomenon has long been a well-known property of suspension bridges, even if those actual words were unfamiliar to the general public. They were more likely to call it 'stress'. Just along the river, the Albert Bridge had for years displayed a notice requiring troops to break step when crossing the bridge. It seems extraordinary that professionals who were paid vast amounts of money to bring their expertise to bear on the design of this bridge had either ignored, forgotten or made insufficient allowance for this factor. In the inevitable stampede among all those responsible to exculpate themselves, there was even an attempt to blame the public for walking across the bridge in the wrong way or in numbers that were more than the bridge was designed for!

Repairs cost £5 million and involved the installation of large numbers of what, in effect, are shock absorbers. These had to be incorporated without affecting the appearance of the bridge, which did not reopen until 22 February 2002. Although the fiasco around the wobble will never be forgotten, the bridge is proving to be an immensely popular means of crossing the river and has become an accepted and valued part of London's riverscape. It is an unashamedly modern bridge. Most people would also say that it has a certain beauty.

From a bridge that created great excitement and drew huge crowds we move on to one that has never attracted a great volume of traffic, Southwark Bridge. By the eighteenth century, London Bridge was synonymous with traffic congestion and consequently also with what we now call road-rage. It simply could not cope effectively with the amount of traffic needing to cross the river. Bankside and the Southwark area in general were changing in character. Now it was much less the place where Londoners went for entertainment, often of a dubious character, and instead it was developing as a substantial enclave of working-class housing. Large numbers of the people living in the area worked north of the river and it was partly the additional pressure they put on London Bridge that led to an increasing crescendo of calls for a new bridge.

In 1811 the Southwark Bridge Act was passed and John Rennie Senior was taken on as engineer. Although he was already engaged in the building of Waterloo Bridge, by common consent a very handsome structure, he produced a very different design for Southwark Bridge. This had three cast-iron arches. The centre one, at 240 feet, was at the time the widest ever erected in this material. Difficulties involved in transporting the huge granite blocks with which the piers were encased and in casting the massive bridgeworks were overcome and the bridge opened for public use, without ceremony and in fact almost coyly, at midnight on 24 March 1819. The Jeremiahs of the time were proved right in their gloomy prognostications that few people would use the bridge because of the tolls that were being levied and that it would prove to be a financial fiasco. It did not help that there was a steep gradient on the bridge which caused problems for horse-drawn traffic. Even the freeing of the toll did not lead to greatly increased usage and the bridge continued its quiet and humdrum existence almost totally ignored by artists and those writers who went into paeans of praise for various of the other bridges in London.

In 1913 work started on a replacement bridge which would not contain the hump that was such an irksome feature of the existing structure. The bridge was officially opened on 6 June 1921. For nearly thirty years trams ran over the bridge. It is hard to escape the feeling that Southwark Bridge is the Cinderella among the river bridges in central London. Ask people to list those bridges and the odds are that at least some would forget this one. It is not really ugly but neither is it beautiful, striking nor of particular historical interest. Even to this day, it does not carry a great volume of traffic. It has been described as a bridge from nowhere to nowhere.

Under the arches at the Bankside end of the bridge are a series of mural pictures depicting the Frost Fairs that used to be held on the frozen river during the numerous bouts of extremely cold weather that were a feature of the past.

Cannon Street Railway Bridge is barely 150 yards east of Southwark Bridge. The bridge and the railway over it were built by the South Eastern Railway, the deadly rival of the LCDR, who had already gained a foothold in the City courtesy of Blackfriars Railway Bridge. In 1861 the SER gained authorisation for a bridge across the Thames and for an extremely imposing station significantly nearer the centre of the City than that of the LCDR. In the studied and ruthless one-upmanship that was railway politics of the nineteenth century, this was a major coup. The SER's effort to impress went much more into the resulting station than into the bridge. The latter was a fairly utilitarian structure which had five wrought-iron spans supported by clusters of ponderous cast-iron piers. The bridge and the station opened in 1866 and initially it had a pedestrian path on which tolls were charged. The footway was closed in 1877.

Traffic, almost exclusively provided by commuters at peak hours, expanded almost exponentially and the bridge had to be widened in order to accommodate ten running lines. These made it, some people claimed, the widest railway bridge in the world.

In addition to finding ways over the Thames, Victorian engineers were exploring the idea of travelling under it. The Tower Subway was the second tunnel under the Thames and work started on building it in February 1869. The first was the Thames Tunnel between Rotherhithe and Wapping for whom Sir Marc Brunel was largely responsible. The Tower Subway made use of a circular tunnelling shield invented by Peter William Barlow, resident engineer to the South Eastern Railway, and further improved by his assistant, James Greathead, both machines being a development of the ingenious device used by Brunel at Rotherhithe. The Greathead Shield, as it became known, was eight feet six inches in diameter and enabled three teams of men working eight-hour shifts to advance the tunnel an average of ten feet every twenty-four hours. Each section was lined with cast-iron segments behind the miners while the space between the lining and the surrounding earth was filled with liquid cement. The whole 1,350 feet from Tower Hill under the river to the junction of Tooley and Vine Streets was completed in five months. A narrow gauge railway was laid through the tunnel and two stationary steam engines at each end and a system of ropes and pulleys enabled a small passenger carriage to complete the journey in less than two minutes. That at least was the theory, but the 'sub-aqueous omnibus service', as it was rather pompously called, kept breaking down and the carriage could not hold a viable payload of passengers. Having opened in 1870, after a few months it was withdrawn. With a little revamping, the tunnel was converted to a pedestrian subway. In its new role it was quite successful. A million or more pedestrians used it annually despite the fact that it was somewhat claustrophobic, echoing and poorly ventilated. Tower Bridge opened in 1894 and most of its regulars decided they preferred the fresh air.

The Tower Subway closed to the public in 1897, but it survives as a conduit for a water main and a spaghetti of pipes and cables. The small circular entrance structure still exists in Vine Lane. While its purpose and indeed the existence of the Tower Subway are now largely forgotten, the Greathead Tunnelling Shield went on, metaphorically, to scale the heights. It was used in the building of the deep-level tunnels of the London underground railway system and, enlarged and considerably modified, remains the inspiration for heavy-duty tunnelling across the world.

The first underground railway in London was opened in 1863. It ran from Paddington to Farringdon and was a great success. It was a sub-surface railway constructed, where possible, on the cut-and-cover principle with rolling stock built to the main line loading gauge. It was designed primarily to tackle road congestion in the district through which it ran, and its success sparked off plans for more lines of the same sort. Haulage was by steam locomotives with condensing apparatus to minimise emissions. Smoke simply dissipated on those stretches of line open to the elements.

The Tower Subway had proved that it was possible to build a small tunnel under the river at a cost markedly less than that of a bridge at the same point. Thoughts were turning to building railways under the Thames but what kind of power could be used for haulage? The stationary steam engine and its associated ropes and cables had not been a success. No one had mastered the atmospheric system of traction, and steam locomotives were out of the question in the confines of deep underground tube railways. Electric traction seemed to offer a viable alternative.

The development of the railways in the Bankside and Southwark area is dealt with elsewhere. Here, suffice it to say that two tube railway tunnels run under the Thames from the Bankside area. One is disused and contained the City & South London's line, which ran under the river from London Bridge to King William Street. The other is the present-day City Branch of the Northern Line. Additionally, there are deep-level tunnels containing cable communications systems which pass under the river to the east of Blackfriars Bridge.

The Thames where it passed London and Southwark produced strange breeds of men – watermen, lightermen, bargemen and ferrymen who plied their skills on the river and gained their living from it. The southern bank of the river had many ferrymen's stairs until alternative means of crossing the river came into use. The stairs have mostly vanished, leaving only ghostly traces, often in street names. The stairs survived long enough to feature with some frequency in the novels of Charles Dickens, who clearly had a great fondness for them.

The River Thames was the main thoroughfare of London, and a case could be made for saying that it acted likewise for the English nation given the dominant presence of London in the country's affairs. The roads to places like Windsor, Greenwich, Westminster, Richmond and Hampton Court were poor and often impassable in bad weather. Footpads and highwaymen lurked in the thickets. It is small wonder that those who could afford to use river transport made use of this alternative. Although not without its hazards, it was quicker, safer and generally more reliable. For those in the Westminster district, for example, wanting to travel to Bankside or the Borough, it made sense to use a short crossing of the river rather than the tedious journey along the north bank and across the bridge. No one knows when watermen first plied their trade on the river, but their importance in the life of the capital is confirmed by the fact that their activities have been regulated since time immemorial. With only the one bridge in London until the eighteenth century, a great burden fell on the bulging muscles of those who pitched their brawn and their skills against what could be a highly capricious and even spiteful tideway. Their rewards could be considerable and some went on to become rich men.

We do know that, before Old London Bridge was built, a ferry operated from Southwark to Churchyard Alley, near the Church of St Magnus the Martyr in the City. The authorities of the City rented out the right to operate the ferry and we will see elsewhere how the miserly John Overs enriched himself. It is evident that complaints had been made from early times about the conduct of the watermen, and in 1193 the City Corporation started licensing boats. In 1514 an Act was passed to regulate the fares charged for journeys on the river. Watermen were well-known for haggling with prospective customers over the fares. Once a fare had been agreed, it was by no means uncommon for the fare suddenly to be unilaterally revised by the waterman when the boat was in mid-stream. It was never revised downwards. A threat to tip the fare into the river usually did the trick and there were cases when those that refused were literally forced to swim for their lives – or sink like a stone, presumably. On other occasions watermen fought each other for fares.

It was as a result of this sort of thing that in 1555 a governing body known as the Company of Watermen was established. It consisted of senior and highly respected watermen who had the job of supervising and disciplining their fellows and also carrying out the training of new entrants. The training was rigorous because the work was highly skilled. Provisional licenses to operate would be issued after a period of apprenticeship to a master and an examination. The full licence might require up to seven years training during which the apprentice would have to satisfy his betters not only on his knowledge and his skills but also on his character – rather like London cabbies today. Licensed watermen had to have their boats numbered and were also required to display a list of the agreed charges. The establishment of the Company of Watermen did not necessarily lead to root-and-branch improvements of the services they offered. In 1603, for example, Parliament had to legislate to ban the carrying of passengers on the vessels manned by apprentices under eighteen years of age after too many lives had been lost through their inexperience or incompetence.

Lightermen also worked the river but on cargo boats rather than passenger vessels, and in 1700 they joined with the watermen to form the Company of Watermen and Lightermen. They proved to be solid in their opposition to the building of new bridges across the river but they have adapted to changed times. Very few vessels now ply the river past Bankside carrying commercial cargoes, although there are many refuse lighters. However, the men who work them and handle all the apparently ever-growing numbers of pleasure vessels on the river have to be licensed Thames Watermen. The systematic opposition of the watermen to road traffic and new bridges was voiced by John Taylor (c. 1580–1653), who was known as the 'Water Poet':

Carroaches, coaches, jades, and Flanders mares,

Doe rob us of our shares, our wares, our fares:

Against the ground we stand and knock our heeles,

Whilest all our profit runs away on wheels ...

The men who work the river have had their moments. St Mary Overie's Stairs, which was the Southwark or Bankside terminal of the ferry, were also used by people travelling along the river. An example was the occasion in 1428 when a large party led by the Duke of Norfolk embarked on a dark November evening to travel downstream. However, the watermen misjudged the currents and collided with one of the starlings. The Duke himself and a few others managed to leap for dear life onto a starling from which they were rescued but the others were swept away to their deaths when their boat overturned in the torrential force of water passing through between the piers of the bridge. In spite of the known hazards, there were watermen who boasted of their prowess at 'shooting the bridge'.

One thing that Parliament could not really legislate against was the argot or slang speech known as 'water language' employed by the watermen. Like Cockney rhyming slang it could be used to maintain conversation between those who were 'in the know' and exclude those who were not. The utterings of the watermen were liberally punctuated with remarkable oaths and scathing abuse of those who used their services and, with probably more justification, politicians and other public figures. However, in the absence of their being fully able to comprehend what was actually being said, passengers who may have guessed were still not quite certain enough to make an effective protest. Anyway, most passengers out in midstream felt at a disadvantage when in the hands of a truculent waterman. Even John Taylor, mentioned above, had to admit that many of his fellows were rude and uncouth. Some people found the repartee of the watermen highly entertaining. César de Saussure was a young Frenchman visiting London in 1725 and he wrote, 'Most bargemen are very skilful at this mode of warfare using singular and quite extraordinary terms, generally very coarse and dirty and I cannot possibly explain them to you.'

The Frost Fairs held on the Thames are mentioned elsewhere but they were one of the occupational hazards facing the watermen. Long-lasting and heavy freezing of the Thames was a feature of the period between the thirteenth and the eighteenth centuries. The freezes could last for weeks during which time no one had need of the normal services provided on the river. In 1762/63 the icing of the river was so prolonged that distress among the watermen reached levels severe enough that a relief fund was raised by public subscription.

Not only did the building of the various bridges diminish the work available for the watermen but so also did the appearance of and growth in the use of river steamers, both the regular scheduled services and pleasure trips. At first the watermen found reasonable business in rowing passengers to and from the steamships, but the operators of these vessels found it more economical and convenient to use riverside piers. Additionally, the turbulence on the river which was produced by steamships using paddles meant that the traditional watermen lost business as timorous passengers thought their smaller and lighter vessels were likely to capsize. In 1850 the social observer Mayhew reckoned that there were only about 1,500 watermen left on the river, although he mentioned that there were still seventy-five stairs from which they were operating. He specifically mentioned how few there were plying for trade in the neighbourhood of Blackfriars Bridge. John Stow in his celebrated *Survey of London*, published in 1598, made a rough estimate that there were 40,000 licensed watermen on the Thames.

4

The Outlaw Borough:
The Shaping of Bankside's Reputation
from Conquest to Restoration

From the Norman Conquest the fortunes of Bankside and Southwark were closely tied to those of the City of London, whose rulers often tried to exert their authority over the inhabitants of the autonomous manors and lordships that made up 'Southwark'. From 1295 Southwark was a parliamentary borough and sent representatives to assemblies. It also gained a reputation for lawlessness and as a haven for prostitutes, brothels, criminals and workers hoping to escape the vigilance of London's craft authorities. By the mid-sixteenth century, when Southwark came under the jurisdiction of the City, it was seen as the most disreputable quarter of London. Both the King and the City authorities made frequent attempts to ensure that law and order were maintained there, but their efforts met with only limited success.

Nonetheless this image should not obscure the fact that throughout most of the early Middle Ages, Southwark's reputation was anything but notorious. The borough was also known for its inns, public garden, vast open spaces, and as a fashionable place of residence. At the end of the thirteenth century a number of town houses of great ecclesiastics and other magnates were established by the riverbank, which provided an easy means of access to Westminster. In fact Southwark's importance was due to its proximity to the southern end of London Bridge and subsequently the High Street in which three Roman roads were concentrated. This provided an important means of communication for visitors, kings returning from the Continent, and for pilgrimages.

In her article 'Wrong Side of the River: London's disreputable South Bank in the sixteenth and seventeenth century', Jessica A. Browner explains the transformation of Southwark from a seemingly upper-class retreat to a place of disorderly resort by the sixteenth century as a result of two particular factors. The first was the jurisdictional anomalies of the borough and the other was the persons, professions, and pastimes which these jurisdictional anomalies attracted.

Medieval Bankside, which was mainly low-lying marshy ground and subject to flooding, particularly during times of heavy rain, consisted of five manors. Bridgehead (the area around London Bridge) belonged to the Crown and, by the fourteenth century, became better known as Guildable Manor. To the east of London Bridge was the Archbishop of Canterbury's manor, known by the sixteenth century as the Great Liberty. The Liberty of the Clink was to the west of London Bridge. The most westerly manor was that of the Templars, which later became known as Paris Garden. To the south-east was the Prior of Bermondsey's manor, or the King's or Queen's manor. The three manors that spanned specifically the area of medieval Bankside are briefly summarized below.

The Guildable Manor was the original 'Town of Southwark' and is almost certainly coterminous with the original Bridgehead settlement. In the Domesday Book of 1086 it is described as an estate with taxable revenues, a landing place and bridge crossing, with the interests shared between the king and the local earl. A 1327 charter refers to it as 'the town of Southwark' and the charter of 1550 as 'the town and borough of Southwark'.

The name 'Guildable' was first recorded in 1377 to distinguish this part of Southwark from all of the other neighbouring manors which were referred to as 'in Southwark'. In the first parliament that called 'burgess' representatives in 1295, Southwark had two MPs, which suggests its formal recognition as a 'borough'. The reasons for the City wanting control over Southwark were mainly twofold. The first concerned the difficulties of judicial process and the arrest of miscreants who could escape to the south side out of the City's reach, and the second was the potential of Southwark for becoming a competitive alternative to the City markets. An extract from the 1327 Charter of Edward III stated,

> ... [the] parliament at Westminster have given us to understand that felons, thieves, and divers other malefactors and disturbers of the peace, who, in the aforesaid city and elsewhere, have committed manslaughters, robberies, and divers other felonies, secretly withdrawing from the same city, after having committed such felonies, flee to the town of Southwark, where they cannot be attached by the ministers of the said city, and there are openly received; and so for default of due punishment are emboldened to commit more such felonies.

From 1327 Southwark had expanded beyond the original area of the Guildable Manor, thus heightening the problems of law enforcement and unregulated trade. In 1550 the final step in the extension of the City's power over Southwark was taken when Edward VI granted to the Corporation all waifs and strays, treasure trove, goods of felons and fugitives and escheats (a common law that ensures property is not left in limbo and ownerless) and forfeitures in the parishes of St Saviour, St Olave, St George, St Thomas, and elsewhere in the borough and town. He also gave, as his predecessors had done, the execution of writs, the power to arrest felons and other malefactors and to take them to Newgate. The Mayor of the City, the recorder and all aldermen who had held the mayoralty became justices of the peace in Southwark, with all powers exercised by other justices in Surrey. The charter also gave the City the right to appoint the Southwark Coroner, whose administration was at that time in the hands of the City, even though it was physically on the other side of the river. Being appointed by an independent corporation rather than being elected by the county, these coroners were known as 'franchise coroners'. For many years it was usual to appoint the same person to be both Coroner of the City and Coroner for Southwark. Originally coroners were elected in each county to look after local matters in which the King has a financial interest and they also had certain ministerial functions. In addition there were the Courts and Prisons of Royal Prerogative based in the Borough, the Marshalsea and King's Bench, which eventually became gaols for debtors and closed in 1842. Not surprisingly, the citizens regarded this charter as a complete annexation of Southwark to London, as an extension of the City boundaries.

It was in the early in the twelfth century that the Abbey of Bermondsey granted to the Bishop of Winchester and his successors a stretch of land extending from the precincts of St Mary's Church on the east to the Manor of Paris Garden on the west, for a payment of eight pounds a year. This land became known as the Bishop of Winchester's and by the 1470s the Clink Liberty with its notorious prison. This in turn gave rise to conflicts of jurisdiction, most notably with the Magistrates of Surrey, who also operated in the Borough.

The manor covered an area extending to Maiden Lane in the south and was composed mainly of fields and meadows long after the Reformation. A partial description of the manor in the mid-fifteenth century is contained in a lease from Bishop Waynflete. He observed that the meadows on the west side had been customarily mown for the use of the bishop's household, with the 'profits of the fisheries and the loppings of trees'. There was also a plot of ground on the bank of the Thames called le Wharf, which was 60 feet long and 40 feet wide. A particularly impressive house was that of the Bishop of Winchester described by John Stow in his 1598 *Survey of London* as 'a very fair house, well repaired, and hath a large wharf and landing-place, called the bishop of Winchester's stairs'.

It is believed that Winchester House was built by William Giffard, Bishop of Winchester from 1107 to 1129. The earliest reference to Winchester House is by William FitzStephen in the late twelfth century, who records Archbishop Thomas Becket on his last visit to London going in procession to the abbey church of St Mary in Southwark and receiving hospitality in Winchester House before he met his death in Canterbury in 1174.

The Manor of Paris Garden, the most western part of Bankside, belonged respectively to the Bishops of Winchester and the Templars (then after 1324 the Hospitallers). It was bounded on the north by the river and on the other three sides by a stream or open sewer which ran in a wide loop round the manor from the Old Barge House Stairs, south to what is now Surrey Row, and north again to the river. It became known as Paris Garden from the fifteenth century after being called Parish Garden. It comprised a little less than 100 acres and had various appurtenances, including a mill (later known as Pudding Mill). In 1629 the millpond was railed off at a cost of six pounds for the safety of the 'poor people of this liberty many of whom have been endangered and some there drowned' (*The accounts of the overseers of the Poor of Paris Garden, Southwark*, P. Norman, 1901).

In 1489 the tenants of the manor were ordered to put crosses on their houses, which was expected of tenants living in the prior of St John of Jerusalem. However the prior and knights of the order do not seem to have occupied a house in Paris Garden.

Bankside riverfront was several feet below high-water level and this continued to remain a problem for centuries, often giving rise to flooding and complaints of dampness in the nearby houses. In 1809 the Surrey and Kent Sewer Commission obtained powers by Act of Parliament to build new main sewers in 1809 to deal with the problem but later Parliamentary Commissions still recorded problems of flooding. In the early medieval period the whole area was largely uninhabited and, according to Martha Carlin (*Medieval Southwark,* 1996), Bankside became the site during Elizabeth's reign for clandestine meetings of foreign ambassadors and their agents. Carlin records how in 1578 William Fleetwood, recorder of London, wrote to Lord Burghley, Secretary of State, of secret political meetings held in Paris Garden between the French Ambassador and the Bishop of Ross.

Records of trial offences (the Court Leet) throw some light on the conditions of the manor and its inhabitants in the fifteenth and sixteenth centuries. For example, most of those presented for misconduct were women, common scolds, whores, or hucksters who gave short measure.

Men were indicted mainly for offences connected with property such as failure to repair buildings or wharves, or to cleanse the sewers. There are a number of references to the cage, the cucking stool, and the stocks as instruments of punishment. In 1632 Donald Lupton in his *London and the countrey carbonadoed and quartred into severall characters* (1632), described Paris Garden as 'better termed a foul den than a fair garden'. He added that it was frequented by 'the swaggering Roarer, the cunning Cheater, the rotten Bawd, the swearing Drunkard, and the bloody Butcher'. By the late seventeen century Paris Garden was built over and began to bear little resemblance to its earlier and more residential days.

Comparing the City side of the river with Bankside, Edward Walford in *Old and New London* (vol. 6, 1878) commented,

[The] London side, high and well built, thickly studded with spires and public edifices, and resounding with all the noise of the operations of a various industry; the Southwark and Lambeth side, low and flat, and meanly built, with scarcely an edifice higher than a wool-shed or timber-yard, and a population with a squalid, dejected, and debauched look ... The situation of Southwark upon the low swamp is, no doubt, one cause of the unhealthy appearance of the dwellers on the south side of the Thames; but the dissolute and rakish appearance of the lower orders among them must be otherwise accounted for. From a very early age, if the truth must be told, Southwark and Lambeth, and especially the former, were the great sinks and receptacles of all the vice and immorality of London. Down to the year 1328 Southwark had been independent of the jurisdiction of London—a sort of neutral ground which the law could not reach—and, in consequence, the abode of thieves and abandoned characters of every kind.

From the late eleventh century to the beginning of the fourteenth century Southwark grew rapidly. This was evident by the creation of manors, parishes, drainage networks, houses and shops. The growth was also made possible by industries such as lime-burning, water mills on the river bank, and windmills on inland sites from the thirteenth to the seventeenth century. These industries entailed occupations and institutions the City did not want such as the noxious lime-burning and tanning, prostitution, and hospitals for the poor. There were also markets, which gave occasion for disputes between the City and Southwark. After one such dispute in 1541 the King granted to the City in 1550 liberty to hold a market in Southwark on every Monday, Wednesday, Friday and Saturday. A proliferation of inns and drinking houses sprang up in great numbers along the High Street to accommodate the flow of traffic, visitors and locals.

The fourteenth century saw the establishment of the two royal prisons, King's Bench (1368) and Marshalsea (1373), and of course the 'stews' (brothels) for which Bankside became famous and which will be dealt with in another chapter. A growing metropolitan population meant there were many who searched for pleasures whether they were in the form of acrobats, actors, ballad-singers, clowns, fencers, puppeteers, fairs, balladeers or bear-baiting and dog fighting. Many of these entertainments were to be found around Bankside and London Bridge. The diarist John Evelyn recorded a visit to Bankside on 16 June 1670:

> [He went with] some friends to the bear garden, where there was cock-fighting, dog-fighting, bear and bull-baiting, [and] all these butcherly sports, or barbarous cruelties. The bulls did exceedingly well, but the Irish wolfe-dog exceeded, which was a tall grey-hound, a stately creature indeed, who beat a cruel mastiff. One of the bulls tossed a dog full into a lady's lap, as she sate in one of the boxes at a considerable height from the arena. Two poor dogs were killed, and so all ended with the ape on horseback, and I, most heartily weary of the rude and dirty pastime, which I had not scene, I think, in twenty years before.

Southwark provided the gateway for foreign people – both friend and foe – for some two millennia. The Roman invasion of Britain in AD 45 saw people from all parts of the Roman Empire come to live and work in Southwark. They brought with them imported goods such as wine and olives from Spain and Italy and Samian ware pottery from Gaul (France). When the Romans arrived in London, the River

Thames was wider and shallower and the Roman city of Londinium was built on the higher north side of the river. Roman Southwark was mainly a small settlement around the present-day Borough High Street and excavations from the 1970s, particularly the recent Jubilee Line extension, have revealed remains of a settlement that was probably viewed as an extension of Roman London. Some buildings located around Borough were large, prestigious stone structures with mosaic floors, heating systems and elaborate painted wall frescoes.

After the Romans left, Southwark was abandoned for over 400 years until the Saxons from northern Germany settled in the eighth century. The monk and English historian Bede (673–735) described London as 'a market for many peoples coming by land and sea'. This was certainly true, as the Saxon settlements came under attack a century later by Viking raiders sailing up the Thames and then invading Normans conquered the Saxons in 1066.

It was during the fifteenth century that Flemish emigrants, mostly poor artisans, flowed into Southwark. A succession of immigrants had come into the area from at least the thirteenth century and included drifters, seamen and mercenaries. However, it was the 'Doche', people from Germany and the Lowlands, especially Flanders that arrived in greater numbers. These people were fleeing from religious persecution. They included brewers, tailors, jewellers, sawyers, goldsmiths, dyers, and hatmakers. Many brought crafts with them but were excluded by the City of London as they were not members of a trade guild. Dutch settlers began making Delftware (blue and white pottery made in and around Delft in the Netherlands) in Southwark, which became popular. These skills had been added to by the sixteenth century with the Flemings working as leatherworkers, alehouse keepers, builders, shoemakers and joiners. There was also a Flemish burial ground in St Olave's parish. Another popular import was bears, which were imported from northern Europe for the sport of bear-baiting.

During the sixteenth and early seventeenth centuries, the population of London and its immediate suburbs grew much more rapidly than the population of the country as a whole, attracting immigrants from the rest of England as well as from a continent damaged by religious wars. Between 1550 and 1700 immigrants flocked to the suburbs of London. Early maps show the rapid urban growth, particularly in places along the South Bank. The population of Southwark grew threefold in the century after 1550 and the area of Borough and Bankside was, by the later seventeenth century, more densely populated than the growing suburbs of East London. In 1600 Southwark contained approximately 10 per cent of the entire population of the City of London. This figure increased over the next century to around 13.5 per cent.

During the sixteenth century London merchants and shipowners initiated many of the great voyages of discovery, and from this a huge expansion of trade developed. London's worldwide trading links were very much a result of the activities of the joint stock companies. As global trade expanded, new facilities were needed to load and unload ships and the building of new quays followed. In 1588 twenty 'legal quays' were located in the short distance between London Bridge and the Tower and financial institutions were built across the river in the City such as the Royal Exchange.

As overseas trade expanded during this period so did Southwark's docks. It became a hive of activity as tea was landed from India and China as well as silks, cotton and spices. Sugar came from the Caribbean and tobacco was imported from the new territories of Virginia in North America. Timber came from Scandinavia and Russia. Fur and animal skins came from Quebec and rubber from plantations in Sri Lanka and the Belgian Congo.

By the sixteenth century we have the advantage of more information and records, particularly maps which show a growing urbanisation of closely knit houses, and alleys with names such as Fishmongers, Ram's, Rose, Mermaid, Bear, etc., as well as wharves, river traffic and ferrymen. The previously sparse area of Paris Garden witnessed a sprouting of houses and an expanding population. Tooley Street in particular became an enclave for large houses. People wanted pleasures and these were provided in the form of bowling alleys, bear gardens, theatres and tennis courts. However, urban growth brought with it pressures and problems relating to burial grounds, sanitation and the increase of rubbish. In response to the increase in crime, public punishments – pillories, cucking stools, lock-ups (cages) – were installed.

Southwark's reputation for lawlessness was both reinforced and facilitated by the existence of its many prisons (the Clink, the Compter, the King's Bench, the Marshalsea, and the White Lion, which were notoriously overcrowded, unsanitary and many of the inmates were often near to starvation), the supposed 'liberties and sanctuaries' (areas which offered the criminal an escape from justice), the expansion of London generally, a particular type of migrant shift to south of the Thames, and, compared with the City, a weaker administration.

However, there is a danger of assuming that the area offered a free licence as a sanctuary and a haven for criminals of all shades. There were cases of sanctuary being offered by the Knights Hospitaller's in Paris Garden, but from the fifteenth century those escaping from a criminal action could only seek refuge in the manor as long as they registered their presence and obeyed the rules. Paris Garden and the Clink were known as 'bastard sanctuaries' because they were a combination of both lay and ecclesiastical franchises, which by charter claimed independence from royal justice, thus allowing them to shelter criminals and debtors. However, the 'privileges' of sanctuary were very much in decline by the early seventeenth century.

The City continued in its efforts to try and exert its control over Southwark and as mentioned above they did this by buying rights of administration in 1327 and 1406. In 1550 the City purchased the full rights of the Crown in Southwark, including the King's manor, the Great Liberty Manor, and the lands of the Duke of Suffolk and the Archbishop of Canterbury, for the sum of £647. Although this gave the City the rights of criminal jurisdiction in the Guildable manor and beyond, we should not exaggerate the amount of power that was actually exerted.

Was the desire to bring Southwark under control of the City because of the fears of criminal activity? The answer is uncertain but there was clearly some substance behind this claim. The concern that roguish bands of a hundred or two hundred at a time rowed from Bankside to do their robbing in Westminster and the City caused great alarm for residents and the authorities. The Lord Mayor and aldermen ordered that a watch be kept upon the bridge at nights to prevent such activity. It might be that the image of Bankside thieves rowing in their hundreds was a case of scaremongering and moral panic, but there is no doubt that robbers took to their boats at midnight and rowed up the river, landing at Westminster to embark upon their criminal deeds. The magistrates of London expressed their concern and requested that King Edward III (1312–77) act. In 1326 the King ordered that, 'whereas malefactors of London fled to Southwark after they had committed offences in order to escape attachment by ministers of the City, the bailiffs of the franchise of Southwark should be intendent to their capture and the mayor and sheriff should make daily inquiry as to such evildoers and their allies and maintainers'.

Although Southwark was created the twenty-sixth ward (Bridge Ward Without) and retained its manorial status, it was denied representation in the Court of Common Council or the power of electing its own aldermen. Disputes arose between the JPs for Surrey and the City government about their respective spheres of duty as justices, and for a century after the 1550 Charter the jurisdiction of the City extended over only a part of the borough, the rest being subject to the county. Friction between the City and Southwark occurred on a number of occasions. As Jessica Browner has pointed out, 'Southwark's reputation as a radical suburb was not enhanced by the memory of the part it could and did play with its vital command of the Bridgehead in times of civil disorder.'

In 1594 the Lord Mayor, Sir John Spencer, described places south of the river as the 'very nurseries and breeding-places of the begging poor', a number he estimated at 12,000. The Lord Mayor went further and asked that such beggars be prevented from crossing London Bridge. It was a fact that Southwark was poorer than the City, Westminster and most other metropolitan parishes. The growth of tenements and houses teeming with poor people not only led to overcrowding but also to fears of disorder and vagrancy.

Tudor governments perceived the problem of vagrancy (which often equated with villainy) as a real threat to law and order. In light of the religious changes during that century, rumours of conspiracy, real and imagined, were rife. This fear was reflected in a series of royal proclamations. In 1596 the Court of Aldermen appointed a Marshal for Southwark with the task of arresting rogues, beggars, idle and vagrant persons. In 1580 a proclamation attempted to check the extent of building within three miles of the City. By 1603 demands went further when a proclamation called for the destruction of houses in the suburbs for fear that they were breeding grounds for plague as well as for criminals and idle beggars. Much of this was true with regard to Southwark and was borne out with periodic outbreaks of plague between 1577 and 1641. Given the social composition of those living in Southwark, it was no surprise that the City authorities viewed it as a dangerous and lawless place rife with thieves and rogues of every type. What added to that perception was the proliferation of 'base' entertainments such as bear-baiting, gambling, theatres, brothels and what John Stow described as the 'many fair inns for receipt of travellers'. However, this did not stop many visitors from the other side of the river from making regular excursions to partake in those entertainments and keeping the ferrymen in business. An example of a ferryman's seat can be seen along Bankside at the corner of Bear Gardens. The seat was constructed for the convenience of Bankside watermen who operated ferrying services across the river. The plaque states that the seat's age is unknown but that it is thought to be of ancient origin.

London apprentices were never far from disturbances and they often gave cause for alarm. The continuing growth of London's population saw an eightfold increase in vagrancy in the period 1560–1601. The Elizabethan government, concerned by the threat posed by vagrants and masterless men, issued the proclamation in 1595 'Enforcing Curfews for Apprentices', which reflected deep anxieties about disorder and potential revolt and placed the responsibility for control on the apprentices' masters. In June 1595 there were twelve popular disturbances in which apprentices were responsible for starting riots against the Lord Mayor and against food prices. Winchester Yard (which occupied the place of the courtyard of the old Westminster Palace) witnessed great brawls taking place between the cardinal's servants and the citizens at the Bridge Gate.

Apprentices and servants made up nearly half of the workforce in London. It is estimated that between 1640 and 1660 apprentices numbered twenty thousand in London and domestic servants exceeded that number several times. Apprentices added to Southwark's reputation for lawlessness, although some of their activities can genuinely be described as 'high spirits'. In 1582 the authorities were asked to look into the actions of a number of lewd persons who ran up and down Southwark streets at night almost stark naked making loud noises with their swords drawn 'to the great disquiet of the inhabitants'. True to their tradition, apprentices were also involved in street fights, vandalising property and attacks on foreigners. When the Long Parliament was called in 1640, apprentices played an active part in congregating around Westminster, intimidating MPs and bishops. Many of these apprentices worked in trades of Southwark, as tanners and brewery workers, for example.

Puritans in the sixteenth and seventeenth centuries viewed alehouses as the 'nests of Satan', threats to public order and breeding grounds for sedition. Most of these claims were exaggerated but Southwark, with its reputation for a great number of inns, was ripe for such criticism, and this only added to the borough's image of lawlessness. In March 1631 Surrey JPs recorded 228 alehouses in Southwark and Kent Street alone. During this period many alehouse keepers were prosecuted in Southwark for selling beer without a licence, keeping a disorderly house or permitting 'unlawful activities' such as dice, card games and playing bowls, which invariably involved gambling.

Southwark Fair was a further addition to the carnivalesque atmosphere of the Borough.

When John Evelyn visited Southwark Fair, he offered a reason for the suppression of puppet shows: 'The dreadful earthquake in Jamaica, this summer [1692], was profanely and ludicrously represented in a puppet play, or some such lewd pastime, in the fair at Southwark, which caused the Queen to put down that idle and vicious mock show.' Southwark Fair provided both a venue and a diversion for thieves. In 1678 Margaret Smith was charged with stealing 'plate, and goods, to a very great value, and Money' during the time of Southwark Fair. Her sentence was that she be carried from 'hence to the place from to hence you came, and from thence be dragged [and] tied to a Carts-rail through the streets'. Her body was to be stripped 'from the Girdle upwards', and be whipped till her body bled. In 1683 Roger Smithers was tried for Coining and 'uttering false Farthings'. He had gone into an alehouse and bought a drink with six counterfeit farthings. He also tried to exchange them in Southwark Fair. Mary Dorril, who was arrested in Southwark Fair, was whipped for stealing a silk gown. Thomas Bostock was transported for stealing a handkerchief and added in his defence that he had been at Southwark Fair, and was drunk.

As many Londoners looked across the river to the borough of Southwark, they saw a place of pleasure as well as danger. By the sixteenth and seventeenth centuries the combination of a growing population, particularly of dissolute masterless men, inns, entertainments, brothels and prisons assured Southwark's reputation as the most disreputable quarter of London.

5

Markets & Frost Fairs

Originally called 'Our Lady's Fair', Southwark Fair was established after a charter had been granted by Edward VI in 1550. The charter had cost about £650, which was a huge amount by the standards of the time, and the money was put up by the local burghers, who knew that a fair would generate a large amount of money for the local economy. Since the lord of the manor and the King also gained financial rewards from the granting of charters for markets, we can only presume that all concerned thought that the idea was a good one. A fair was in effect a seasonal market, much bigger than the regular markets and having an additional recreational aspect.

Initially the fair was arranged to be held annually on 7–9 September, centred on the feast of the Nativity of the Virgin. In time it became one of England's three major annual fairs, to stand alongside Bartholomew Fair at Smithfield and Sturbridge Fair at Cambridge. It was opened with august ceremony by the Lord Mayor and attracted vast crowds right across the social classes but, as might be expected, it was often marked by disorder and violence.

John Evelyn, in his diary dated 13 September 1660, wrote,

I saw in Southwark, at St Margaret's Fair, monkeys and asses dance and do other feats of activity on the rope, they were gallantly clad a la mode, went upright, saluted the company, bowing and pulling off their hats; they saluted one another with as good a grace as if instructed by a dancing master. They turned heels over head with a basket having eggs in it, without breaking any; also with lighted candles in their hands and on their heads, without extinguishing them ... I also saw an Italian wench dance and perform all the tricks on the tight rope to admiration; all the court went to see her. Likewise, here was a man who took up a piece of cannon of about 400 lb weight, with the hair of his head only.

Hogarth famously portrayed the goings-on in his picture *Southwark Fair* in 1732, by which time the fair lasted no fewer than fourteen days. Hogarth depicts the fairground in the distance, while in the foreground are a mass of performers and spectators. Tragedians and comedians posture and rant beneath banners or painted boards advertising their repertoire. As usual with Hogarth there is a symbolic and satirical element counterposing the sublime and the ridiculous, the rich and the poor, and there is also the portrayal of characters from life, often those of whom Hogarth disapproved (a group of considerable size). On the left of the picture a performance of 'The Fall of Bajazet' is violently interrupted when the temporary staging collapses. A woman selling china from the booth under the stage flees desperately to escape being crushed to death. Close by, dice players are so engrossed in their game they do not realise they are about to be crushed. On the right is a well-known travelling exhibition of the time consisting of waxworks portraying the people who made up the French Court. Violante, who was a notable rope-dancer, swings gracefully above the crowd. Cadman, 'the famed Icarus of the rope', can be seen descending on a rope from the church tower. Only recently a 'flying man' had fallen to his death when sliding down from the steeple of Greenwich church and Hogarth is saying that you may do it this time but ultimately you are powerless if the Fates decree that your time is up. The futility of achievement it might be said. A bald man astride a pony is the well-known James Figg, a showman who called himself the 'Atlas of the Sword' and who performed various remarkable tricks with that weapon. In the centre is an attractive girl who is beating a drum while being followed by a large coterie of admirers. On an earlier occasion, Hogarth had witnessed the leader of the troupe of entertainers to which she belonged strike her viciously and he had waded in, giving the man a hiding he was unlikely to forget for a long time. Those who bought reproductions of the works of Hogarth like this would have recognised many faces in the crowd and the topicality of the subject.

The fair closed permanently in 1762 or 1763. Interestingly, the booth keepers used to collect money for the relief of the prisoners in the Marshalsea. Perhaps some of them had been inmates or thought they might well be in the future.

A food market has existed in the Bankside area possibly since Roman times and certainly from the eleventh century. The busy traffic going to and fro across London Bridge provided lots of potential customers and attracted all manner of traders but particularly those selling grain, fish, vegetables and livestock. Such brisk business was done that the rather informal market became a great nuisance as far as the authorities were concerned because it greatly added to what was already a highly congested area at the foot of London Bridge. In the thirteenth century (probably in 1276) the traders were relocated to the area just to the west of what is now Borough High Street. There has been a market in and around this spot ever since with just one short gap. In 1550 the King granted a charter for the holding of a market every Monday, Wednesday, Friday and Saturday. In 1755 the market was closed down by Act of Parliament. It had spilled over into the High Street and was the constant cause of congestion and general frustration. This angered many people locally and the result was that a fund was set up to buy land for a new market. This was close by on a plot known as The Triangle, which was where the churchyard of St Margaret's had been. This church had been closed down at the Reformation since which time it had had many secular uses before eventually being demolished.

This became known to all and sundry as Borough Market, and it became an important wholesale and retail market for fruit and vegetables in particular. The manner in which business was conducted was robust and full of character and it was always regarded (excuse the pun) as somewhat downmarket, a poor man's market much in keeping with the locality. The new location was inconvenient and trade languished somewhat until the coming of the railways enabled supplies to be brought in quickly and easily from growers in the southern counties. From the 1970s, activity declined somewhat because of competition from supermarkets and congestion in the streets of this inner-city area. The fruit and vegetable wholesale market still operates but the last few years have seen the development of a remarkably successful gourmet food market, currently operating three days a week. This is a big draw for foodies and tourists. The diverse range of smells, tastes and the variety of exotic food on display is an assault on the senses. It may be the case that there is little that could not be bought elsewhere in the Metropolis for less money, but Borough Market has the advantage of providing an exceptionally wide range of food in one particular area and a visit there will be well rewarded. Bargains can be had if the visitor can cope with the dense crowds that pack in, particularly on the Saturday sessions. This vibrant and bustling market is very much in keeping with the process of regeneration typical of much of the district.

Widespread disruption is expected with the Thameslink Programme, which is set to increase the capacity of the railway line westwards from London Bridge. This is one of the busiest and most congested sections of railway in the United Kingdom and the programme involves the laying of additional tracks after widening the viaduct. Part of Borough Market will disappear and there will be much demolition around Tooley Street on the north side of London Bridge Station.

Despite the gloom-ridden prognostications of today's Jeremiahs, there is nothing new about extreme and unpredictable weather conditions in Britain. Evidence of these is provided by the frost fairs and other activities that were held on the River Thames in the Bankside and Borough neighbourhood over many centuries. The period from the mid-fourteenth to the nineteenth centuries has in retrospect been called 'the Little Ice Age' because of the many severe winters.

There is an unconfirmed report that there was extensive icing on the Thames in 923, but although there are mentions of extensive and lengthy freezing of the river before 1309–10, it was in the latter winter that reference is made for the first time to frolicking on the ice. On this occasion a large fire was ignited on the solid ice, there was dancing and even hare-coursing. During the thaw of 1433, large ice floes seriously damaged five arches of London Bridge. Henry VIII is said to have travelled all the way from Westminster to Greenwich in a sleigh on the ice in the winter of 1536. In 1564 there was an extremely cold snap over the Christmas and New Year period and people swarmed onto the ice in huge numbers to take part in various sporting activities. They also found that being on the ice in the middle of the river provided a new and enjoyably novel aspect to the seasonal celebrations. They even roasted an ox. Somehow the festivities were even more fun than normal because they were in the middle of the frozen tideway. Elizabeth I walked on the ice with her retinue and was cheered by large crowds. In January 1608 an exceptionally cold period not only saw sporting activities on the ice but the retailing of all manner of goods from stalls. A barber, for example, did a very brisk trade simply because men wanted to be able to tell their grandchildren that they had had a shave in the middle of the Thames.

The winter of 1683/84 was one of the coldest on record. The Thames froze over for ten weeks and the ice in some places was an estimated eleven inches thick. The ice proved to be an irresistible draw to Londoners and visitors, and the most sophisticated retail frost fair yet did roaring business. An enterprising printer called Croom sold souvenir cards produced on his press on the ice and printed on them the name of the purchaser and the date. It was said that he was earning about £5 a day, which was a small fortune at the time. As Peter Ackroyd (2000) says, the city spawned its own replica, 'with all the characteristics of its own turbulent life'. A joker coined the name 'Freezeland Street', for what a modern property developer with less romance in his soul would call 'a retail park', because that is what the river became.

Someone penned the following quaint little verse about the printing phenomenon on the Thames:

To the print-house go,
Where men the art of Printing soon do know,
Where for a Teaster, you may have your name
Printed, hereafter for to show the same:
And sure, in former Ages, ne'er was found
A Press to print, where men so oft were droun'd!

The diarist John Evelyn (1620–1706) described lines of booths like a city street and Croom's printing press. He also commented on the numbers of people on the ice. There were tens of thousands, he thought, along with innumerable coaches and carts. He described bull-baiting taking place and noted that the various activities covered such an area and attracted so many people that it was possible to hire a hackney carriage to move between the various parts of the fair.

... sleds, sliding with skates, a bull-baiting, horse and coach races, puppet plays and interludes, cooks, trifling and other lewd places, so that it seemed to be a bacchanalian triumph, or carnival on the water.

One gets the impression that Evelyn is something of a curmudgeonly fellow who feels that the spectacle is unusual enough that he ought to record it but he is rather sniffy about much of what is going on. He extends his rather morose musings to the effect that the cold spell is having on the Capital: 'London, by reason of the excessive cold of the air hindering the ascent of the smoke, was so filled with the fuliginous steam of the sea coal ... that one could scarcely breathe.'

In 1715–16 another even more prolonged if perhaps slightly less severe icing on the river is remembered by numerous printing presses being set up. This was tantamount to a licence to print money since there were apparently inexhaustible numbers of people who were prepared to part with good money so that they could carry away a souvenir which declared that it had been printed on a press set up on the frozen Thames. A frost fair began on Christmas Day in 1739 and continued until the middle of February. However, on 21 January there was a partial thaw which provided those who lived on the bridge with a very strange sight. As the *Universal Spectator* commented,

> The inhabitants of the west prospect of the bridge were presented with a very odd scene, for on the opening of their windows there appeared underneath on the river a parcel of booths, shops and huts of different forms, but without any inhabitants. Here stood a booth with trinkets, here a hut with a Dram of Old Gold, in another place a skittle frame and pins, and in a fourth 'The Noble Art and Mystery of Printing'.

The ice had partly broken up overnight and the stalls were floating around in a mixture of water and ice. No one was killed, little property was lost and the temperature dropped once more. Now the problem was to separate the various stalls which had been fused into an icy mass. One of the many who ventured onto the ice was William Hogarth. He could not resist patronising a printer selling souvenir sheets. In the space reserved for the name of the purchaser, he put the name 'Trump'. This was his soul-mate, a bull-terrier. Mischievous people said that, when confronted by Hogarth and his dog, it was difficult to tell which was which. The dog, in fact, was smaller.

From November 1785 through to January 1786, activities on the frozen river took place all the way from Putney Bridge to Rotherhithe, a greater distance than ever before. In 1795 a long, harsh winter provided a gruesome sight for observers on London Bridge as the corpse of a man thought to have fallen into the Thames upstream, floated towards, under and then downstream of London Bridge. Witnesses described it as being encased in ice and only attributable as a dead human because its head and arms were visible. A ship in the Pool of London was hit by blocks of floating ice coming up the river on the tide. The ice cut the ship's anchor-cable and it then floated up the river, out of control until it reached the bridge. Its mast was carried away when it hit the arch but the hull continued some way upstream.

The winter of 1813/14 saw the last great frost fair on the Thames where it passed through the middle of London. For sixteen days a huge mass of thick ice blocked the river between Blackfriars and London Bridges and so, as was their wont on such occasions, huge crowds went onto the ice to enjoy the novelty of sports, games and amusements as well as eating, drinking and shopping from the wide range of stalls retailing all manner of goods. These gave an appearance of semi-permanence and some wag dubbed this stretch 'City Road'. An elephant was led around on the ice close to Blackfriars Bridge, a spectacle which attracted much attention. An enterprising wide boy roasted sheep, called it 'Lapland Mutton' and sold slices of meat at a shilling a time. A contemporary observer commented, 'Merry-go-rounds, skittles, bowls, donkey derbies, dancing, book stalls, toy sellers. Many people charged more for items which had the words "bought on the Thames".' From Three Crane Stairs across the river to Bankside there was almost what amounted to a thoroughfare. It was strewed with ashes and safe but difficult walking because of hard lumps of solid ice protruding from the surface. When the thaw came, massive chunks of ice flowed up and down the Thames on the tides and destroyed large numbers of river craft. As always there were foolhardy people who ventured out onto the ice when it was beginning to thaw, ignoring the warnings of those who knew better. Many paid with their lives.

Genuine frost fairs were to be no more. The Thames did not freeze over just because of consistently colder winters but also because the river was considerably wider and shallower, not having been embanked. Generally its flow was therefore more sluggish. Also crucial was the presence of London Bridge with its numerous piers protected by starlings or cutwaters. As these were repaired over the years, they tended to get bigger and it meant that the bridge had the effect of a partial dam. When temperatures dropped, ice tended to accumulate first of all around the starlings.

The Londoners whose lives were most disrupted by the icing-over of the Thames were those who obtained their living from the river in its normal liquid form. On the earlier occasions on which frost fairs or other activities took place on the ice, it seems that the watermen tried to prevent people getting onto the ice in the first place. The various riverside stairs were the obvious place to gain access and the watermen, who seemed to think that they owned the river, demanded money from those wanting to go on the ice as if they were fares that they were ferrying on the river. As might be expected this led to many ugly scenes. On later occasions, the watermen broke the ice in the vicinity of the stairs and then charged people for assistance in getting across the gap!

Icing on the river and the frost fairs in particular were therefore not welcomed by the watermen but seemed to have been events for rejoicing on the part of every other Londoner and equally by visitors. The novel experience of walking, being entertained, eating and drinking and competing in games on the ice in the middle of this great river seemed to have the effect of lowering the boundaries between the classes. Just for once the so-called great and good set aside the deference they expected from the lower orders and everyone seemed determined to have fun irrespective of social differences. Therefore leg-pulling and practical jokes that at other times would have been intolerable were de rigueur and apparently accepted by most with equanimity.

There is now an annual Bankside Winter Festival that is often referred to as the 'Frost Fair'. It has market stalls, entertainment and various events. It does not have ice and it is not on the river.

In the foot tunnel that runs under the south end of Blackfriars Bridge, there is an engraving by a local sculptor. It is composed of five slabs of grey slate and depicts a stylised view of a frost fair. The frieze bears an inscription:

Behold the Liquid Thames frozen o're
That lately Ships of mighty Burthen bore
The watermen for want of Rowing Boats
Make use of Booths to get their Pence and Groats
Here you may see beef roasted on the spit
And for your money you may taste a bit
There you may print your name, tho' cannot write
Cause numb'd with cold 'tis done with great delight

And lay it by that ages yet to come
May see what things upon the ice were done.

A surviving artefact of the frost fairs is a mug on display in the Victoria & Albert Museum. This has an inscription to the effect that it was bought from a stall on the ice in 1584, and it is thought that the engraving of the mug was probably carried out on the ice.

The last time the Thames froze in the vicinity of Bankside was in the exceptionally harsh (by modern standards) winter of 1962/63. If anyone had thought of replicating the frost fairs of the past, they wisely did nothing about it.

Brothels, Stews & Bear-Baiting

The diarist John Evelyn (1620–1706) went by 'water to the Bear Garden' at Bankside on April 1669 to see a prize fight between a soldier and a country fellow. He enjoyed the spectacle, noting that the countryman 'did soundly beat the soldier, and cut him over the head'. When Evelyn went the following year to Bankside to witness the animal 'sports', he clearly did not like what he saw and was too disgusted to go there again. In his diary on 16 June 1670 he recorded that he went with some friends to the 'Bear Garden, where there was cock-fighting, dog fighting, bear and bull baiting' which he called 'butcherly sports, or rather barbarous cruelties'. The sight of the bulls tossing a dog into a lady's lap as she sat in one of the boxes made him most 'heartily weary of the rude and dirty pastime'. Bankside was also notorious for another type of pleasure and one that had a longer tradition – its many stews or brothels.

Prostitution on Bankside can be traced from the Roman settlement when slave girls and independent whores known as 'night-moths' frequented the area. The busy riverside opposite the City attracted cookshops and quayside inns, which were popular with the crews of ships. In 1162 Parliamentary Ordinances were issued regarding 'the government of the Stewholders in Southwark, under the direction of the Lord Bishop of Winchester'. It appeared there was an attempt to restore some order there, according to the 'olde customs that hath been used and accustomed time out of mind'. The City had driven out prostitutes in the 1270s and again in the 1380s.

Southwark's tolerance of prostitutes was enshrined in a complex code of regulations which attempted to restrict the practice whilst not actually banning it outright. The regulations stated that no single woman was to be kept against her will, no stew-holder was to keep any woman that 'hath the perilous infirmity of burning' (the pox), constables, bailiffs and others were required each week to check on every stew-house and to make sure that the doors were not kept open on Sundays and other holidays. If the holders of the houses broke these 'wholesome rules', they were committed to the Clink prison. All sorts of schemes were resorted to in order to dodge the intrusion of the law including leaving open back doors and windows to escape from, trap doors in the floor in which to hide and many beadles and watchmen were bribed to turn a blind eye to the brothels.

Many women were variously forced into prostitution through kidnap, deception or rape. Many could find no other alternative employment, while there were also those who chose to work as prostitutes. As in any age the women were vulnerable to exploitation by ruthless pimps and brothel and alehouse keepers. Prostitution was associated with vagrancy and deemed to be an act of idleness. This perception was reinforced because prostitution was a common trade of female vagrants. In Southwark and Bankside, prostitutes also worked the streets and alleys as well as the brothels and prices varied accordingly, a point made by Thomas Nashe when he wrote of 'sixe-penny whoredomes' as well as half-a-crown being 'the sette pryce of a strumpets soule'. In 1584 one account records that a young man might have to part with 40 shillings or more in a brothel for 'a bottle or two of wine, the embracement of a painted strumpet and the French welcome [syphilis]'. As well as the streets and stews, prostitutes could be found in other places of amusements, particularly the theatres. The poet John Dryden (1631–1700) commented that 'the playhouse is their place of traffic, where Nightly they sit to sell their rotten ware'.

The practice of prostitution did not prevent those of the upper and well-to-do classes from being involved in the business. They not only frequented brothels but also profited as landlords from such establishments as well as taking part in such 'idle entertainments'. Sir Horatio Palavicino, a leading financier in London and adviser to Lord Burghley, asked the pimp Gilbert Periam to secure a virgin, to which Periam reported (probably tongue in cheek) that there was no available virgin in the entire City. In the 1570s brothel keeper John Hollingbrig wore the livery of Ambrose Dudley, Earl of Warwick.

Bankside properties such as fish ponds, shops, gardens and brothels were very lucrative. The wealth generated by these brothels gave rise to a statute passed by Parliament in 1433 designed to curb the influence of those 'suddenly come to great riches'. Many of the properties and the land on which they were located were owned by a number of eminent people. The Bishop of Winchester's holdings have been well documented but there were other eminent landowners involved in such properties. For example, Edward II owned a suburban residence in Southwark called 'la Rosere'. E. J. Burford in his *Bawds and Lodgings* (1976) suggests that this house in later years became a brothel known as the Little Rose and was despoiled by Wat Tyler and his army in 1381. The house was also owned or held under lease by the Lord Mayor William Walworth. Some historians have suggested that Walworth killed Tyler out of rage for destroying this house more than out of any desire to protect the King. This is pure supposition. There may be some confusion with regard to this property as there was another area of land called the Rose on which was located a brothel by the same name. In fact the nuns of Stratford-at-Bow owned substantial property in this area, and there were at least four brothels on their land known as the Rose. Lord Hunsdon, Elizabeth I's Lord Chamberlain, was enriched by the brothels in the manor of Paris Garden, which the Queen had granted him. When Philip Henslowe took out his lease on the Rose, it was a known brothel. The word 'Rose' had a number of other references including a street term for a prostitute and Rose Alley was believed to be a euphemism for taking a quick pee – plucking a rose. The sign of the Rose was one of many colourful Bankside signs.

Bankside brothels continued to flourish, especially from the fifteenth century when seven stew-houses were recorded in 1381, increasing to eighteen by 1506. There had been an attempt to close them down in 1504 because of the fears related to the spread of syphilis but this ban only lasted for a year. They were finally suppressed in 1546 when Bankside was proclaimed, by 'sound of Trumpet, no more to be privileged, and used as a common Bordell, but the inhabitants of the same to keep good and honest rule'. The proclamation enjoined Henry VIII's subjects 'to avoid the abominable place called the Stewes'. The suppression meant that it became more difficult to operate a brothel openly, so many prostitutes turned to working in alehouses or what Phillip Stubbes (1555–1610) described in *The Anatomie of Abuses* as 'the blockhouses of the Devil'.

Only four years after the proclamation Robert Crowley wrote that the bawds of the stews and taverns might still 'be founde'. Public brothels and prostitution continued to do business and contemporaries such as John Taylor believed that things had got worse: 'The Stewes in *England* bore a beastly sway, Till the eight *Henry* banish'd them away: And since these common *whores* were quite put down, A damned crew of private *whores* are grown, So that the devil will be doing still, Either with public or with private ill.' John Stow mentions two Bankside brothels, the Cardinal's Cap and the Bell, as surviving into the seventeenth century. Elizabethan poet and satirist Thomas Nashe (1567–1601) commented in his treatise *Christs Teares Over Jerusalem*, in 1593, that the metropolitan suburbs were little better than 'licensed stews operating with the connivance of magistrates'. Nonetheless it did not stop celebrated people from visiting them. Both Philip Henslowe, a well-known theatre impresario, and his son-in-law Edward Alleyn, the actor, found that owning a brothel was a very profitable activity. The Cardinal's Cap and the Bell were favourite haunts of Edward Alleyn. Edward Alleyn's wife (Henslowe's step-daughter) may have been a partner in the brothel that Henslowe and Alleyn had a financial interest in. In 1593 she suffered the punishment of a captured prostitutes when she was drawn through the streets of Southwark in an open cart. Samuel

Bankside brothels continued to flourish, especially from the fifteenth century when seven stew-houses were recorded in 1381, increasing eighteen by 1506. There had been an attempt to close them down 1504 because of the fears related to the spread of syphilis but his ban only lasted for a year. They were finally suppressed in 1546 when Bankside was proclaimed, by 'sound of Trumpet, no more to be privileged, and used as a common Bordell, but the inhabitants of the same to keep good and honest rule'. The proclamation enjoined Henry VIII's subjects 'to avoid the abominable place called the Stewes'. The suppression meant that it became more difficult to operate a brothel openly, so many prostitutes turned to working in alehouses or what Phillip Stubbes (1555–1610) described in *The Anatomie of Abuses* as 'the blockhouses of the Devil'.

Only four years after the proclamation Robert Crowley wrote that the bawds of the stews and taverns might still 'be founde'. Public brothels and prostitution continued to do business and contemporaries such as John Taylor believed that things had got worse: 'The Stewes in *England* bore a beastly sway, Till the eight *Henry* banish'd them away: And since these common *whores* were quite put down, A damned crew of private *whores* are grown, So that the devil will be doing till, Either with public or with private ill.' John Stow mentions two Bankside brothels, the Cardinal's Cap and the Bell, as surviving into the seventeenth century. Elizabethan poet and satirist Thomas Nashe (1567–1601) commented in his treatise *Christs Teares Over Jerusalem*, 1593, that the metropolitan suburbs were little better than 'licensed stews operating with the connivance of magistrates'. Nonetheless it did not stop celebrated people from visiting them. Both Philip Henslowe, a well-known theatre impresario, and his son-in-law Edward Alleyn, the actor, found that owning a brothel was a very profitable activity. The Cardinal's Cap and the Bell were favourite haunts of Edward Alleyn. Edward Alleyn's wife (Henslowe's step-daughter) may have been a partner in the brothel that Henslowe and Alleyn had a financial interest In 1593 she suffered the punishment of a captured prostitutes when was drawn through the streets of Southwark in an open cart. Samuel

6

Brothels, Stews & Bear-Baiting

The diarist John Evelyn (1620–1706) went by 'water to the Bear Garden' at Bankside on April 1669 to see a prize fight between a soldier and a country fellow. He enjoyed the spectacle, noting that the countryman 'did soundly beat the soldier, and cut him over the head'. When Evelyn went the following year to Bankside to witness the animal 'sports', he clearly did not like what he saw and was too disgusted to go there again. In his diary on 16 June 1670 he recorded that he went with some friends to the 'Bear Garden, where there was cock-fighting, dog fighting, bear and bull baiting' which he called 'butcherly sports, or rather barbarous cruelties'. The sight of the bulls tossing a dog into a lady's lap as she sat in one of the boxes made him most 'heartily weary of the rude and dirty pastime'. Bankside was also notorious for another type of pleasure and one that had a longer tradition – its many stews or brothels.

Prostitution on Bankside can be traced from the Roman settlement when slave girls and independent whores known as 'night-moths' frequented the area. The busy riverside opposite the City attracted cookshops and quayside inns, which were popular with the crews of ships. In 1162 Parliamentary Ordinances were issued regarding 'the government of the Stewholders in Southwark, under the direction of the Lord Bishop of Winchester'. It appeared there was an attempt to restore

Pepys wrote in 1663 of visiting a Mrs Palmers, a bawd, south of the river, '... thinking, because I had heard that she is a woman of that sort, that I might there have light upon some lady of pleasure (for which God forgive me) ...'

The outlaw borough of Bankside was the most notorious of the suburban red-light districts and attracted people from all classes. Along with its nearby alehouses, theatres and bear-baiting, Bankside could serve the needs and pleasures of both citizens and travellers.

The derivation of the term 'stew' probably comes from the word for a stove or heated room – a public bathhouse which sometimes served as a place of prostitution. However, the same word was used in the medieval period for a fish pond, and there were a number of fish ponds in the Pike Gardens along Bankside, hence the term 'stews bank', which was often applied to this region and might have had more than one meaning. There were three pike gardens along Bankside in the sixteenth century. These were the pike garden of Winchester House, the King's (or Queen's) Pike Garden, which lay a little to the west, and the Great Pike Garden near Maiden Lane. John Stow wrote that the stews, which were usually approached by boat across the river, had signs on their fronts, towards the Thames, 'not hanged out, but painted on the walls'. Some of the stews were bagnios or baths and Sir William Walworth, the Lord Mayor, was known to have owned several stew-houses. It seems that the term stew evolved to become increasingly synonymous with brothel despite its other earlier associations.

Historians have disagreed over the interpretation of 'stew' with some claiming that the term has been mistakenly taken to be a brothel (see Gillian Tindall *The House by the Thames*, 2007) while others have supported the view that the signs such as Boars Head, Cross Keys, Gunne, Castle, Crane, Cardinals Hat, Bell and the Swan indicated the presence of brothels. Richard Rex *("The sins of Madame Eglentyne", and other essays on Chaucer*, 1995) states that in 'fourteenth-century London the word "stews" already denoted brothels although the more vulgar "whorehouse" also dates from this period'. He adds that all the brothels in Southwark were owned by the Bishop of Winchester and 'permission to operate came only at a price and it was in the bishop's power to close or prevent operation of any brothel by declaring the operator in breach of one regulation or another'.

C. L. Kingsford argued in 1920 that the fish ponds, which were the original business enterprise on Bankside, gave their name to the red-light district:

> It will be observed how many of the holders of these pieces of ground were fishmongers. The explanation, no doubt, is that they had their origin in the ponds in the Pyke Garden. This suggests that the original meaning of the 'Stews' was simply the fish-ponds. When the district became notorious for houses of ill-fame, the transition of the name to its other meaning would have been easy. I am disposed to hazard the conjecture that Bankside was the name for the row of houses towards the east facing the river, and Stewes-side for the row of houses further west backing on the Stews or fish ponds of Pyke Garden.

The other area of confusion concerns the references to Bankside and 'Stewside'. Both names were interchangeable as the principal business along the bank changed from fish-mongering to brothel keeping.

As the stews and brothels were mainly on land owned by the Bishop of Winchester, many women who worked in the brothels of Bankside were known throughout London by the court term of Winchester Geese or Birds.

Prostitutes were said to have been denied burial in consecrated ground, although there is little evidence to support this. Shakespeare's familiarity with Bankside brothels is displayed through Doll Tearsheet (the saucy, knife-wielding prostitute who hangs out at the Boar's Head Tavern) and Mistress Quickly in the second part of *King Henry the Fourth* and in the misfortunes of the dim-witted Constable Elbow in *Measure for Measure*, who is the butt of constant jokes about his name and his malapropisms ('my wife who I detest' for protest). In *Henry VI* the Duke of Gloucester accuses the Bishop of Winchester of giving 'whores indulgence to sin'. He further berates the Bishop as a 'Winchester Goose', which is clearly intended as an insult. Winchester goose not only referred to a whore but also to a swelling in the groin, the result of venereal disease, and to one so affected. For example at the end of *Troilus and Cressida* 'some galled goose of Winchester' refers to an infected member of the audience, whether whore or client.

The Cross Bones burial ground on Redcross Way between London Bridge Station and Borough Station was the final resting place for some 15,000 people. The burial ground was excavated by archaeologists between 1991 and 1998 as a result of the extension to the Jubilee Line. Building work in the 1920s led to the exhumation of many bones, as did work in the 1990s. The report *The Cross Bones Burial Ground* (Museum of London Archaeological Service, 1999) and excavation were conducted by MoLAS on the medieval burial ground. It provided a final resting place for the poor of St Saviour's parish in Southwark. The parish supported several burial grounds including Deadman's Place (now Park Street), which was originally used for the interment of large numbers of plague victims.

John Stow (1525–1605) wrote in 1603 that the graveyard was used for 'single women' or 'Winchester Geese'. Stow, generally an excellent source, often relied on second-hand accounts and has been responsible for sowing one or two myths. Many graveyards became prey to the activities of the resurrection men – body-snatchers – and Cross Bones was no exception. These men would steal freshly buried bodies and sell them to surgeons who sought specimens for the anatomy classes at nearby Guy's Hospital. By the nineteenth century the area was overcrowded and disease-infested as well as a popular haunt for criminals. Not surprisingly, many paupers were interred in the burial ground. It was closed in 1853 because it was not only overcrowded but also a threat to public health. However the cholera victims and 'Geese' are not forgotten, as there is a small shrine erected by the local community and, for the last few years, the gate itself has been kept garlanded with flowers, ribbons and tributes.

Prostitutes were recorded as operating from private lodgings around St Thomas's Hospital and also the area of Paris Garden. When Ben Jonson (1572–1637) witnessed a wherry (a shallow rowing boat) being rowed up Fleet Ditch, he described it as 'The meat-boate of Beares college, *Paris-garden*'. One of the most infamous and luxurious brothels was located in the old manor house of Paris Garden and was frequented by King James I (r. 1603–25) and his court including James's favourite, the unpopular George Villiers, Duke of Buckingham.

Between 1630 and 1632 this most famous of London brothels was complete with fortified position, moat, drawbridge and portcullis. There were also garden-walks, for sauntering and 'doing a spell of embroidery', or 'fine work' such as flirtation. The summer house was proverbially infamous for intrigues.

The house was prominent enough to be indicated on Thomas Aldwell's 1627 survey of Paris Garden. Early in the reign of Henry VIII, William Baseley acquired the lease of the mansion house although it was then falling into ruins and the grounds were flooded. Baseley repaired the house and lived there himself for over twenty-four years. He made it into a public gaming place with bowling alleys, card games and dice. He obtained a royal licence to maintain it as such and the house thus began to acquire the reputation for licentiousness which culminated in the events of the early 1630s when it was run by 'a woman of ill repute', Elizabeth (Bess) Holland.

The term 'Holland's Leaguer' became associated with the brothel, which successfully withstood what amounted to a state of siege by the forces of law and order. When soldiers arrived to close the building down, 'Bess' Holland enticed them onto the drawbridge, which she then released, depositing them in the moat. To add insult to injury, the prostitutes proceeded to empty the contents of their chamber pots over the soldiers, who quickly began to retreat. Elizabeth Holland escaped the City authorities, in spite of two summons to appear before the Court of High Commission, and re-established her business elsewhere. The event spawned a demand for accounts of the onslaught in no less than three texts all titled *Holland's Leaguer* – a play by Shackerley Marmion, a ballad by Lawrence Price, and a pamphlet by Nicholas Goodman.

The comic stage play *Holland's Leaguer* by Shackerley Marmion premiered in 1631 and was first published in 1632. Marmion's comedy describes the activities of a group of men who visit the brothel which provides the location for the play. The brothel is portrayed as a place of flagrant sin out of reach of the authorities and the play questions the efforts of the local authority in licensing and controlling the liberties. The success of the play was clearly built on the scandal of the well-known Bankside brothel.

> You who desire news, list to my story,
> Some it will cause to muse, some will be sorry;
> From every quarter have the gallants resorted,
> To Holland's Leaguer, that fame hath reported.

Over one hundred years after the attempt to suppress brothels another attempt was made in 1650 when Puritans embarked upon reforming the manners of the multitude. Parliament passed an Act making adultery a felony punishable by death (although there were only a handful of cases carried out) and fornication was deemed to be a crime punishable by three months imprisonment. Linked to this was God's divine retribution – the pox – which was a punishment for all those sinners who resorted to the prostitute's abominable services. Special commissions were set up which would punish the convicted man with imprisonment and a fine. As for those 'great swarms of ... women [who] haunt the town in the taverns and playhouses', they would be taken to the prison where the executioner would strip them naked before the populace.

Even before the onset of Civil War Bankside was entering into a period of decline as a place of popular entertainment. By the 1620s the Rose theatre had been demolished and the Swan was in a state of decay. Bear- and bull-baiting continued after the Restoration. The famous medieval stews also declined, but prostitutes found other outlets, mainly continuing to ply their trade in the streets, alehouses and alleys.

Despite John Evelyn's disgust at the 'butcherly sports, [and] barbarous cruelties', bear-baiting, bull-baiting and cockfighting were very popular and part of the rich fabric of Bankside entertainments.

It is difficult to know when bear-baiting first appeared in England. Some sources suggest the reign of King John (r. 1199–1216) at Ashby-de-la-Zouch. William FitzStephen mentions such activity in London in 1183: '... huge bears, do combat to the death against hounds let loose upon them.' Bull-baiting with fighting dogs was more common from the reign of Henry II (r. 1154–89). We do know that the sport became very popular during the Tudor period. Southwark's association with the sport dates from as early as 1526, when the Earl of Northumberland is recorded as visiting Paris Garden to view the bear-baiting. Further references certainly establish the existence of the sport by the 1550s on Bankside. Thomas Burnaby, a merchant, bought a lease of the Bear Garden on the Bishop of Winchester's property in 1590 and let it to Richard Reve for a yearly rent of £120 under the description of 'All that Tenement ... on the Banke syde ... Together With the Beare garden and the Scaffoldes houses game and dogs and all other things thereunto'. John Stow, describing Bankside in 1598, wrote,

> There be the two Beare-gardens, the old and new places wherein be kept Beares, Bulles, and other beastes, to be bayted. As also Mastives in several kennels are there nourished to bait them. These Beares ... are ... baited in plottes of grounde, scaffolded about for the beholders to stand safe.

Many bears were bred and maintained in this country for the purpose of bear-baiting, although some would have been imported.

A bear-baiting 'arena' was erected on Bankside in the middle of the sixteenth century where the public were admitted by the payment of a penny at the gate for raised seats, and a third penny for 'quiet standing'. Great amounts of money changed hands in bets as well as for entrance to the rings. It also proved to be a lucrative business. The actor Edward Alleyn said that the profits were 'immense'.

In Agas's plan of London of 1560 the bear gardens are represented as plots of ground in the Clink Liberty with scaffolding for the spectators, with the names of 'Bowlle Baytyng' and the 'Beare Baytynge'. The buildings are circular, and appear to be imitations of the Roman amphitheatre. They are unroofed and stand in two adjoining fields, separated only by a small strip of land and a large pond. Inside they consisted of a lower tier of circular seats for the spectators, at the back of which a screen ran all round, in part open, so as to admit a view from outside. The performance was signalled by the display of little flags or streamers on the top. Nearby the dogs are tied up ready for the baiting to commence.

Robert Crowley (1517–88), poet, polemicist and Protestant clergyman, wrote of Paris Garden:

> What folly is this to keep with danger
> A great mastiff dog and foul ugly bear,
> And to this anent, to see them two fight
> With terrible tearings, a full ugly sight:
> And methinks these men are most fools of all
> Whose store of money is but very small.
> And yet every Sunday they will surely spend
> One penny or two, the bearward's living to mend.
>
> At Paris Garden, each Sunday, a man shall not fail
> To find two or three hundred for the bearward's vale:
> One half-penny apiece they use for to give,
> When some have not more in their purses, I believe.
> Well, at the last day their consciences will declare
> That the poor ought to have all that they may spare.
> If you, therefore, go to witness a bear-fight,
> Be sure God His curse will upon you light.

The last two lines turned out to be prophetic. In January 1583 a fatal accident occurred as if 'heaven-directed' at Paris Garden when the scaffolding, crowded with people, suddenly fell 'whereby to the number of eight persons men and women were slain, and many other sore hurt and bruised'. This was yet another cue for Puritans who saw it as a Divine retribution for pleasurable indulgences. Celebrated Presbyterian

John Field, in his treatise *A Godly Exhortation, by occasion of the late judgement of God, shewed at Parris-garden ...* (1583), pointed to the disaster as a manifestation of God's wrath, 'although some will say (and as it may be truly) that [the wood] was very old and rotten'. Field went on to emphasise that divine displeasure would not be appeased until such places, including theatres, had been closed down completely, and not just on Sundays. Lord Mayor Thomas Moulson, a leading Puritan, made religious capital out of the fact by sending a formal notice of the fatal event to Lord Burleigh, as a 'judgment of heaven for the violation of the Sabbath'. Similar moral warnings were also drawn from a disaster at a puppet show in 1599 and from the fires at the Globe Theatre in 1613. Sunday performances of bear-baiting were stopped early in the reign of James I. The Hope Theatre was used for bear- and bull-baiting on Mondays and for plays during the rest of the week.

Nonetheless the sport continued to be so popular that in 1591 an order was issued from the Privy Council forbidding plays to be acted on Thursdays, because that day had been long set apart for 'bear-baiting and such pastimes'. This was followed by a public notice from the Lord Mayor complaining that 'in some places the players do use to recite their plays to the great hurt and destruction of the game of bear-baiting and such like pastimes, which are maintained for her Majesty's pleasure'. Queen Elizabeth I had been entertained by Lord Leicester at Kenilworth with combats of dogs and bears. Robert Laneham, a junior court official, vividly described in a letter in 1575 the festivities at Kenilworth Castle:

> The bears were brought forth into the court, the dogs set to them, to argue the points, even face to face ... Very fierce, both the one and the other, and eager in argument. If the dog in pleading would pluck the bear by the throat, the bear, with traverse, would claw him again by the scalp ... thus with fending and fearing, with plucking and tugging, scratching and biting, by plain tooth and nail to (the one) side and other, such expense of blood and of leather was there between them as a month's licking ...

Queen Elizabeth did apparently visit Paris Garden on 26 May 1599, with the French ambassador where they saw a baiting of bulls and bears. She clearly endorsed and enjoyed the 'favourite holiday pastime of her London subjects'. The 'entertainments' in the bear garden were still under the patronage and countenance of royalty nearly a century later. In 1675 a warrant was signed by Lord Arlington ordering ten pounds to be paid to Mr James Davies, the 'master of his Majesty's bears, bulls, and dogs', for 'making ready the rooms at the Bear Garden, and baiting the bears before the Spanish ambassadors'.

Towards the end of Elizabeth's reign in 1596 Paul Hentzner (1558–1623), a German lawyer, set out on a three-year tour through Switzerland, France and England. In his *Travels in England during the reign of Queen Elizabeth* he commented on the theatres ('without the City') and made reference to 'another place' built in the form of a theatre which 'serves for the baiting of bulls and of bears; they are fastened behind, and then worried by great English bull-dogs'. He wrote of the dangers that the dogs faced and that 'fresh ones are immediately supplied in the places of those that are wounded or tired'. He also described what followed this entertainment:

> [There] often follows that of whipping a blinded bear, which is performed by five or six men, standing circularly with whips, which they exercise upon him without any mercy, as he cannot escape from them because of his chain; he defends himself with all his force and skill, throwing down all who come within his reach, and are not active enough to get out of it; on which occasions he frequently tears the whips out of their hands, and breaks them.' Hentzner noted that the English were 'constantly smoking tobacco. In the theatres, fruits, such as apples, pears, and nuts, according to the season, are carried about to be sold, as well as ale and wine.

Obviously the sports were incredibly cruel and bloodthirsty. A handbill claimed,

> Tomorrow being Thursday shall be seen at the Beargarden on the Bankside a great match played by the gamesters of Essex who hath challenged all comers

whatsoever to play five dogs at the single bear for £5 and also to weary a bull dead at the stake; and for your better content shall have pleasant sport with the horse and ape and whipping of the blind bear.

The noise of the bear gardens must have been deafening with the din of men betting on their favourites and the loud shouting of the respective partisans of dog and bear.

Bulls were, as a rule, baited to death, but the bears did not come cheap so the games were arranged for maximum blood-letting without allowing bears to actually die. Instead they were taunted and tortured by dogs or men with whips, lashing out to defend themselves. The nobility kept their 'bear-ward', who was paid, like a falconer or other retainer. Twenty shillings was the payment made in 1512 to the bear-ward of the 5th Earl of Northumberland. A travelling bear-ward depended on his patrons. When any bear-baiting was to take place it was publicly made known and the bear-ward would usually parade the bear, in advance of the baiting, through the streets preceded by a minstrel or two, carried by a monkey or baboon on horseback.

In the play *The Humorous Lovers* (1667) by William Cavendish, 1st Duke of Newcastle (1592–1676), the name of a famous bear is mentioned, 'Tom of Lincoln', and the bear-ward says, 'I'll set up my bills, that the gamesters of London, Horsleydown, Southwark may come in and bait him before the ladies, but first, boy, go fetch me a bagpipe; we will walk the streets in triumph, and give the people notice of our sport.'

The bears became celebrities with names such as 'Harry Hunks' the blind bear, and 'Sackerson' from Shakespeare, but they often broke loose terrifying the spectators. In Shakespeare's *Merry Wives of Windsor* Master Slender boasts of such an event in order to endear himself to Anne Page: 'I have seen Sackerson loose twenty times, and have taken him by the chain; but I warrant you, the women have so cried and shrieked at it, that it passed: but women indeed, cannot abide 'em; they are ill-favoured rough things.' Shakespeare referred to the bears frightening the 'fell-lurking curs' by the mere shaking of their chains and describes a 'hot o'erweening cur' running back and biting his owner who withheld him, yet when suffered to get within reach of the 'bear's fell paw clapped his tail between his legs and howled' (*Henry VI, Part 2*).

Samuel Pepys was a regular visitor to the bear-baiting arenas. He recorded on 14 August 1666, a few days before the Great Fire of London,

> After dinner, I went with my wife and Mercer to the BearGarden, where I have not been, I think, of many years, and saw some good sport of the bulls tossing the dogs—one into the very boxes; but it is a very rude and nasty pleasure. We had a great many Hectors in the same box with us (and one very fine went into the pit and played his dog for a wager, which was a strange sport for a gentleman), where they drank wine, and drank Mercer's health first, which I pledge with my hat off.

In May of the following year Pepys was there again, this time to see a prize fight which turned into a general fracas:

> … stopped at Bear-garden Stairs, there to see a prize fought. But the house so full there was no getting in there, so forced to go through an ale-house into the pit, where the bears are baited; and upon a stool did see them fight, which they did very furiously, a butcher and a waterman. The former had the better all along, till by-and-by the latter dropped his sword out of his hand, and the butcher, whether or not seeing his sword dropped I know not, but did give him a cut over the wrist, so as he was disabled to fight any longer. But Lord! to see in a minute how the whole stage was full of watermen to revenge the foul play, and the butchers to defend their fellow, though most blamed him: and there they all fell to it, knocking and cutting down many on each side. It was pleasant to see; but that I stood in the pit and feared that in the tumult I might get some hurt. At last the battle broke up, and so I away.

On 9 September 1667 he witnessed another fight at which there was the usual 'rabble':

... the yard was full of people, and those most of them seamen, striving by force to get in. I got into the common pit, and there, with my cloak about my face, I stood and saw the prize fought, till one of them, a shoemaker, was so cut in both his wrists, that he could not fight any longer; and then they broke off. His enemy was a butcher. The sport very good; and various humours to be seen among the rabble that is there.

As with the term 'stews', there may be a danger of generalising the term 'bear garden'. For example in 1620 a dispute arose between the Crown and the Bishop of Winchester as to the ownership of the ground in the neighbourhood of the Bear Gardens. Sir Howard Roberts and Walter H. Godfrey (*Survey of London*: volume 22, 1950) state that evidence clearly shows that the bear-baiting rings had been moved several times and that the 'Bear Gardens' had by that 'date become a generic term covering the sheds and kennels in which the bears, bulls and dogs were kept, as well as the actual rings and the adjoining houses, most of which were occupied by persons having some connection with the Bear Gardens'.

Bear- and bull-baiting continued in other places in London. Advertisements in the early eighteenth century appeared for the 'Bear Garden in Hockley-in-the-Hole, near Clerkenwell Green, [where] a variety of Bull-baiting and Bear-baiting' was to take place. Another advert promoted the sport at 'William Well's Bear-Garden in Tuttle Fields', Westminster, where, it said, '... there will be a green Bull baited, and twenty dogs to fight for a collar ... with other diversions of Bull and Bear-baiting.' However, the peak of Bankside bear- and bull-baiting had passed by the late seventeenth century.

In 1656 the Hope Theatre was demolished and replaced by the Davies Amphitheatre, the last bear-baiting ring built on Bankside, which stood between 1662 and 1682 and was visited by Pepys and Evelyn. The abolition of bear- and bull-baiting in England had to wait until 1835, although the practice had long stopped at Bankside. In August 2004 the Museum of London Archaeology Service (MoLAS) uncovered remains of the 'Davies' Bear Gardens', during an excavation at Union Works in Park Street, and also found evidence of a later glassworks on the site. Today a single red-brick house set among warehouses and offices down Bear Gardens, just a few paces from both the Globe and the Rose, marks the site of the last bear-baiting ring on Bankside. The house on Bear Gardens is now the Globe Education Centre.

7

The Clink & Other Prisons

In keeping with its role as the part of London across the river which the rest of London wanted out of sight and out of mind, Southwark had more prisons and places of detention per square acre than any other part of London. Although some of them are not strictly in the area we have delineated as 'Bankside', they were close by and we therefore give them a brief mention.

In the middle of the eighteenth century, three major institutions of confinement can be identified in London. There were the debtors' prisons, the gaols or jails, and the houses of correction usually known as 'bridewells'. In Southwark, debtors were confined particularly in the King's Bench and the Marshalsea. They were consigned to these places until such time as they were able to discharge their debts or Parliament let them off the hook by passing a debt declaring them bankrupt. The regime under which these prisoners lived seems curious to modern opinion because the inmates were maintained at the expense of their creditors. Debtors could live with their families, and there were some who, despite their apparent insolvency, lived like lords in luxury and with the best of everything. They enjoyed visits from friends and relations and even conducted businesses from the prison premises. They were free to leave the prison and work and earn wages or generate income, the idea of course being that they would eventually pay off what they owed. It was not unknown for some prisoners to sublet part of their accommodation within the prison. The entire system was corrupt. Prisons were let out to contractors whose main purpose was to make profits. They would provide almost any service and this was fully taken advantage of by those prisoners who, despite being debtors, had seemingly bottomless pockets. Many debtors were not the sort of people to allow mere technicalities about insolvency to get in the way of their enjoyment of life. It was another matter for the less well-off who could not find the resources to pay for the little privileges and perks that made life bearable. On occasions debtors and convicted prisoners were housed in the same quarters and that always spelt trouble because many of the debtors felt themselves a cut above the other inmates and were frequently peevish, querulous and, acting as barrack-room lawyers, would incite discontent and insubordination among the other inmates.

The Clink prison was located in Southwark, close to the City of London and to Westminster, but because the Thames formed something of an obstacle, Southwark managed to be remote at the same time. It was a 'liberty', which meant that it consisted of a group of manors, to the lords of which were granted certain privileges of the Crown and from which the sheriff's authority was excluded. One of these rights was that of 'sanctuary'. In concrete terms, this meant that any villain who resided peacefully in a place of such 'sanctuary' for a year and a day was then legally freed of the bondage associated with his status. The existence of this right of sanctuary in relation to Southwark is first recorded in 1181. It was also a place to which criminals and ne'er-do-wells resorted safe in the knowledge that, being in a sanctuary, they were more or less immune from pursuit by the authorities. One lord of the manor in Southwark was the Bishop of Winchester and the area under his jurisdiction was known as the 'Liberty of the Clink'. He, of course, had his palace in the locality. It is said, although without supporting evidence, that one or two bishops were not above sampling the pleasures offered by the prostitutes, who were often referred to as 'Winchester Geese'.

The bawdy reputation of Bankside was well known, and since the area attracted many people of what would then have been called a 'lewd' character, the Bishop operated a prison. In it the worst miscreants or at least those who were caught were placed to cool their heels and ruminate on the error of their ways. This prison became known as 'The Clink' (the word seems to have been mentioned for the first time in 1503). 'Clink' went on, of course, to be one of many generic slang names applied to prisons. Whatever the origin of the word, it evokes images of keys noisily turning in sturdy locks, jangling on a gaoler's belt and body irons being rattled by helpless, despairing prisoners in soiled rags lying surrounded by their own bodily excretions. There was no shortage of potential inmates given that fugitives from the law also had the right to claim sanctuary in the Liberty and many of them did not behave decorously when they arrived and took up residence there. Some of these were people wanted for misdemeanours in the City and the existence of this criminal sanctuary virtually on their doorstep was a constant source of irritation to the City authorities because there was absolutely nothing they could do to intervene in what was going on almost on their doorstep. On the other hand, the advantage of having the Liberty in Southwark was that it got some of the worst undesirables away from the City. The Bishop was too busy to involve himself in the confinement and punishment of those that fell foul of the law in his fiefdom. The running of the prison was franchised out as an operation intended to produce a profit for the franchisee. The latter would also administer physical punishments such as placing offenders in the pillory or the stocks, humiliating wrongdoers by carting them publicly around the streets or administering public whippings. What kinds of offenders were likely to experience the Bishop's hospitality? Right up there at the forefront were the brothel keepers, the pimps, the prostitutes and their punters. The pursuit of sex for cash is necessarily fraught with all manner of possible confusions, misunderstandings and disagreements, all of which may have violent outcomes and bring those involved to the attention of the authorities.

It is possible that some kind of prison was opened at Bankside as early as 1161 but we do know that whatever form it took and whatever kind of inmates it housed, it was attacked during the Peasants' Revolt in 1381 and again in 1450 during Cade's Rebellion. On both occasions the rebels took a great delight in releasing the inmates.

We can be pretty sure that experience of incarceration in the Clink is likely to have made inmates rue the mixture of stupidity with certain amounts of bad luck that caused them to be put there in the first place. The cells were underground, and given the ill-drained nature of Bankside at the time, they would have been damp and dank at best and possibly even under water when tides were particularly high on the river. Some air and light would have penetrated through iron gratings, and where these abutted on the street, it might have been possible for inmates to beg for food or alms from passers-by. A few groats might manage to make life better for a prisoner since the warders were willing to sell just about anything except liberty.

The Clink may have started out as an episcopal or ecclesiastical prison but it is probably best known as a place for incarcerating debtors. It also held religious dissidents in Tudor times. These included John Rogers, the first martyr of the persecution of Protestants in the reign of Queen Mary, and John Hooper, Bishop of Gloucester. They both died in 1555. Persecutions continued in the reign of Elizabeth, although now it was Catholics who were on the receiving end. Among these were prominent Jesuits such as William Weston and John Gerard, although they were imprisoned rather than executed. Other Catholic recusants were housed within its dismal walls over the following years. The Clink seems to have decayed and gradually gone out of use other than as a place for housing debtors but it was hated so much that the Gordon Rioters burned it down to the ground in 1780 and it was not thought worth rebuilding.

Strictly speaking, Horsemonger Lane Gaol was just outside the area. This was completed in 1798 at the suggestion of John Howard, the respected prison reformer. Roughly three quarters of the prison housed convicts and the rest of the residents were debtors. Hangings took place on the roof of the gaol and attracted large crowds. One who witnessed a hanging was Charles Dickens and he was appalled by what he saw:

I do not believe that any such community can prosper where such a scene of horror as was enacted this morning outside Horsemonger Lane gaol is permitted at the very doors of good citizens, and is passed by unbeknown or forgotten.

Among the inmates between 1813 and 1815 was Leigh Hunt (1784–1859), the poet and essayist. He had fallen foul of the laws on libel because he had called the Prince Regent 'a fat Adonis of forty'. Fat, yes. Adonis? The prison was demolished in 1879. The site was under what is now the Newington Recreation Ground near Harper Road.

The King's Bench prison was certainly in existence during the Peasants' Revolt. In 1554 it numbered among its inmates John Bradford, who had been condemned to death in St Saviour's and who was shortly after burned at the stake at Smithfield as a heretic. Many other victims of religious persecution were housed in the King's Bench over the following period when religious bigotry and intolerance were at their height. The prison was as bad as any, and in 1624 it was claimed that eighty prisoners died of starvation.

During the Commonwealth, with an eye to political correctness, the prison was renamed the 'Upper Bench' but with the Restoration of the Monarchy it reverted to its original name. In 1670 one Richard Baxter was placed in the prison as a result of his stand against the Act of Uniformity, which established new regulations for the Church of England after the Monarchy had been restored. He does not seem to have found his sojourn too onerous. He was accompanied by his wife and as she explained in his autobiography: 'We kept house as contentedly as at home, though in a narrower room, and I had the sight of more of my friends in a day than I had at home in half a year.' It was not unknown for debtors allocated to this prison to be allowed to live in their own private accommodation nearby – for a financial consideration, of course. A particularly unusual prisoner in the King's Bench was the King of Corsica, who spent several years there after 1752, attempting to work off his debts.

In 1758 the King's Bench moved from the east side of Borough High Street to a new and much larger site only a short distance away in St

George's Fields. Once again those inmates with money could pay to make their lives more tolerable. Some of the warders had arrangements with local brothel keepers and inmates of the prison could enjoy cut-price services once they had greased the warders' greasy palms. Among its early prisoners was Tobias Smollett, who in 1760 was found guilty of libel. While he was in the King's Bench he wrote his novel *Sir Lancelot Greaves*. A more controversial inmate was John Wilkes (1727–97) whose scathing attacks on corrupt and incompetent politicians made him the darling of the London mob. William Combe (1741–1823) wrote *Dr Syntax's Three Tours* while trying to work off his debts. He did not succeed. Benjamin Robert Haydon, an appalling painter but trenchant art critic who was not afraid to attack the big names in the world of art, not surprisingly made many enemies in high places and spent many periods whiling away his time in the King's Bench while he had a cash-flow problem. Dickens gave the King's Bench a mention in *David Copperfield* because Mr Micawber was confined there.

The King's Bench was largely destroyed in the Gordon Riots and was replaced by a building in which the contrast between the luxurious accommodation available for those able to pay for it and the conditions which were forced on the poorer prisoners was even more stark than normal. Many of the well-off debtors who were consigned to the King's Bench bought days out at 4s 2d for a day and a reduction to 3s 10d for a second day immediately following. Some paid more to reside close by in what was called the Liberty of the King's Bench Prison. There is even a story, possibly apocryphal, that an ostensible inmate was living in the East Indies! A notable inmate to escape from the King's Bench was Lord Cochrane (1749–1831). Possessing every bit as much flair for naval tactics and leadership of men as Horatio, Lord Nelson, but having the capability of rubbing all the most powerful people up the wrong way, Cochrane's greatness is only now being fully recognised. Enemies had conspired to frame him for involvement in a swindle for which he was wrongfully convicted and imprisoned. It is typical of the man that he made a rope and swarmed down an external wall but managed to survive and get away after the rope broke about twenty feet above the ground. In 1842 the name was changed to the Queen's Bench and it took over large numbers of debtors previously housed in the Fleet and Marshalsea prisons. It later became a military prison and was finally demolished in 1880. The original King's Bench was between Borough High Street and Tennis Street.

Close by in the Borough was the Marshalsea prison. The original site was between the present Newcomen Street and Mermaid Court on the east side of the High Street. This building dated from the fourteenth century and was long used as a state prison, second only in importance to the Tower of London. When rebels arrived in Southwark bent on attacking London, it seemed de rigueur to attack one or more of the prisons in the district and the Marshalsea was no exception, being attacked by Wat Tyler's rebels in 1381 and again by Jack Cade's followers in 1450. This prison was notorious for its awful conditions and in 1504 there was a riot and mass breakout. Those involved were ruthlessly hunted down and many of them hanged. In 1557 the Marshalsea housed Gratwick, a Protestant heretic who was condemned to death and burned in St George's Fields. When Elizabeth succeeded Mary on the throne, one of her first actions was to incarcerate Bonner, the last Catholic Bishop of London, in the Marshalsea, where he died several years later. In 1601 one Christopher Brooke took up residence for the unusual crime of giving a young lady by the name of Anne More in matrimony to the poet John Donne without the knowledge and therefore the consent of her father.

Conditions in the Marshalsea were atrocious. In 1728 the blame for this state of affairs was placed on the frugality and cruelty of the keeper, William Acton, who used the post to supplement his other income as a butcher and so systematically kept his expenses to an absolute minimum. Many prisoners died of starvation and neglect. Eventually Acton was brought to court and given a short prison sentence, but little was done to ensure that a similar situation did not occur again. In 1738 an anonymous pamphlet called *Hell in Epitome* described the Marshalsea:

An old pile most dreadful to the view,

Dismal as wormwood and repenting rue.

Thither the graduates in sin resort

And take degrees becoming Satan's court,

There are instructed in the Paths of Vice,

There sell good Linen, there they purchase lice.

John Wesley (1703–91) was so horrified by the conditions he found on a visit in 1753 that he declared, 'Oh shame to man that there should be such a place, such a picture of hell upon earth!'

As was the case with some other prisons, the site of the Marshalsea was moved a couple of times to locations nearby. The final reincarnation of the Marshalsea was opened in 1811. Charles Dickens's father was briefly imprisoned for debt in 1824 and this experience was incorporated by the novelist into *The Pickwick Papers* and *Little Dorrit*. The Marshalsea was closed in 1842 by which time it contained just three prisoners. In Angel Place off the High Street a piece of wall from the Marshalsea can still be seen.

The White Lion was the name given to the Surrey County Gaol, which seems to have been established in a hostelry of this name in the sixteenth century. It was one of the many prisons of the time that were in effect let out to private enterprise to manage for the purposes of making profits. This motive often meant hard commons for the inmates. It is known to have housed prisoners at the time of the major religious bigotry of the sixteenth and seventeenth centuries. It was almost certainly a most ramshackle building and it required a major rebuilding, which started in 1721. After that it is known to have housed convicted criminals, Jacobite rebels and those Gordon Rioters of 1780 who were so crazed with drink that they could not resist arrest. By that time its days were numbered and it became a soap factory when its functions were taken over by Horsemonger Lane Gaol.

8

Places of Worship

There were three churches that served and two that still serve the Bankside area. St Olave's once stood on Tooley Street and Christ Church still operates to the west on Blackfrairs Road. Southwark Cathedral, formerly St Mary Overie and St Saviour, is, along with Lambeth Palace, one of the most important medieval buildings in South London. Nearby were St Thomas's on the north side of St Thomas Street and also a chapel dedicated to St Thomas Becket that once stood in the middle of old London Bridge from where pilgrims en route to Canterbury threw their badges and shells into the river. Typical of the dissenting tradition of many who lived in Southwark, there were a diverse range of Nonconformist chapels.

Southwark Cathedral, or the Cathedral and Collegiate Church of St Saviour and St Mary Overie, has been a place of Christian worship for over 1,000 years. From the Dissolution in 1540 until 1905 it was known as the parish church of St Saviour and after 1905 it became Southwark Cathedral. It is London's second oldest church, after Westminster Abbey. Southwark Cathedral is located on the historic site of a Roman villa which was here before any Christian place of worship. Evidence of the Roman past can be seen in the south choir aisle of the Cathedral where a Roman mosaic, discovered in 1833, is set in the floor. Roman statuary and inscriptions were also discovered in the crypt in 1977. Evidence of a Roman and Saxon past is abundant around London Bridge and the Borough. Nearby Stoney Street was probably the continuation of the Roman Watling Street as marks of the ancient causeway have been discovered on the northern side. The Saxons gave the name of 'Street' to the Roman roads and in this case they gave it the addition of Stoin or Stoney from the pavement of which it was composed.

St Swithun, Bishop of Winchester between 852 and 867, is believed to have set up a college of priests on the site of the present cathedral (Saxon foundations were found in 1999). However, the first conclusive proof of a church comes in the Domesday Book of 1086. A monasterium is recorded as being present during the reign of Edward the Confessor (1042–66) with its own wharf for the unloading of goods from the river. This says something about the strategic position of the church located as it is between London Bridge, the only river crossing in London, and St Mary Overie Dock to the west, which still stands. Over the centuries the tower, which dominated the landscape and is featured in a number of early views, gradually became less visible with the growth of railway viaducts, warehouses and buildings.

In 1106 the priory church of St Marie was founded by two knights, William Pont de l'Arche and William Dauncey as a house for canons of the Augustine order. Part of their duties was to give relief to the sick and needy. To do this they built a hospital and dedicated it to St Thomas of Canterbury. As with many medieval religious foundations, the early history of the church is obscure. By the 1120s it was transformed from a secular foundation to a religious house of canons, following a more formalised rule, notably under the influence of William Giffard, then Bishop of Winchester. A series of fires over the next two centuries caused much damage to the church. In 1212 a fire destroyed much of the building including the hospital dedicated to St Thomas Becket in the south of the church. This subsequently led to further rebuilding, which was in the new pointed-arch style from France and the choir and aisles form the earliest surviving Gothic building in London. In addition to the fire the riverside location of the church made the building vulnerable to the encroachments of the Thames. There was further disaster in the

1390s when another fire damaged the south transept and parts of the choir.

The main structure of the church was built between 1220 and 1420 and it was during the fourteenth century that the church became known as St Mary Overie (or Overy – over the river). The derivation of the name St Mary Overy is disputed. A curious, but discredited, legend connects the building of the original London Bridge with the church of St Mary Overy. John Stow chronicled the story that was told by the last prior of the church, Bartholomew Linsted. The story concerns a ferryman who, before there was a bridge across the river, ferried people 'betwixt Southwark and Church Yard Alley'. The man died and left the business to his daughter, Mary. With the profits of the ferry trade she built a religious House of Sisters on the east part of St Mary Overy's church. Mary's miserly father, John, apparently faked his death in order that his household might forego a day's victuals. No sooner had the old man been decently laid out, than those about him fell to feasting and making merry, rejoicing at the death of the old miser. He could take this no longer and rose up in his sheet with a candle in each hand. However one the guests thought it was a ghost and quickly seized a broken oar and struck him so hard it killed the old man. An interesting story which probably says more about the power and durability of myth than actual history.

The House of Sisters bore the name of Mary Overs or Overee. The surname of her father, John the ferryman, was probably an Anglo-Saxon version of his profession, a person who took people 'over the ree' or river, thus it became Overee. Some writers have suggested that the religious house was originally founded in honour of the popular Saxon Saint Audrey, or Etheldreda, of Ely. Another probable derivation of the name is from 'over the rie' – 'over the water'. Londoners north of the Thames invariably designated the whole of the southern suburbs as 'over the water' and the phrase may be as old as the time of the building of St Mary's 'over the rhe.'

The tower of the church, which rises above the crossing at the centre of the church, was completed in 1520 and the magnificent altar screen was installed at the same time. The Reformation, which took place in the following decade, would usher in changes that affected religious houses throughout the country. These changes included the dissolution of monastic houses and abbeys, the creation of new dioceses, the forbidding of various Catholic practices (such as elaborate crosses and crucifixes) and the Catholic Mass, which was replaced by Holy Communion. The Parliament of 1539 and 1540 ruled that the parishes of St Mary Magdalene and St Margaret should be united with the church of the dissolved monastery of St Mary Overie, henceforth to be called St Saviour's church. Soon after the amalgamation, St Margaret's church was divided into three portions for use respectively as a Sessions' Court, a Court of Admiralty, and a prison. It stood on the ground where the old Southwark Town Hall was built.

The Canons surrendered St Mary Overie and its buildings at the Dissolution with little resistance. The closing of the priory also saw the closure of the hospital. In 1552 the Lord Mayor of London persuaded Kind Edward VI (r. 1547–53) to re-found St Thomas's Hospital. With regard to the remaining monastic houses, they were given to Sir Anthony Browne, Master of the King's Horse, who built himself a mansion to the north-east of the church and sublet the buildings to tradesmen.

During the religious persecution of Protestants under Queen Mary (r. 1553–58), Stephen Gardiner, Bishop of Winchester, set up his consistory court in the retrochoir. The retrochoir is thirteenth-century early English in design and the oldest complete part of the Cathedral, started in 1215. It is also thought by many to be the most beautiful part of the cathedral, although it has a mixed history. It was here that Gardiner sentenced seven men to death for heresy, including John Hooper, Bishop of Gloucester, and John Rogers of London. There is a statue of Rogers in the altar screen. When Gardiner died in 1555, his bowels were buried beneath the High Altar. It was also from this time that the retrochoir was left to fall into disrepair. During Elizabeth's reign it was screened off and, as John Stow records, it was let to a baker. By 1576 parish registers show that the lessee of the retrochoir was called upon to repair a number of broken windows and remove nuisances and, in the following December, a further entry states that fourteen members of the vestry went into part of the choir to see whether their orders had been attended to. They found the place turned into a stable with hogs, a dung heap and other filth and were forced to take legal proceedings to keep the tenant to his contract. However, the vestrymen themselves were not indifferent to creature comforts as in April 1569 they ate a calf's head pie in the vestry in celebration of Easter. However, the retrochoir became part of the church once again in 1623.

Despite attempts during the brief reign of Queen Mary I to restore the Catholic faith, the Protestant path set out under Henry VIII continued after the accession of Queen Elizabeth I in 1558. In September 1559 an order was issued for the sale of certain 'Popish ornaments' (e.g. altar cloths, candlesticks, small bells, vestments, etc.) at St Saviour's, to meet the expenses of repairing the church. Two years later in May 1561 it was ordered that 'all the church books in Latin be defaced and cut according to the injunctions of the Bishop'.

During the reign of Elizabeth (1558–1603) the Puritans, those who wished to purify the church from any Catholic association, grew in influence. The vestrymen at St Saviour's clearly disliked what was happing on their doorstep with the 'immoral' theatres of Bankside. Nonetheless they managed to work out a favourable compromise by accepting a contribution from the takings of the performances at the theatres. The money went towards parish charities.

Similar deeds of benevolence came when Queen Elizabeth encouraged her subjects to found charitable grammar schools such as the one at Southwark:

Thomas Cure, William Browker, Christopher Campbell, and other discrete and more sad inhabitants of St Saviour's, had, at their own great costs and pains, devised, erected, and set up a grammar-school, wherein the children of the poor, as well as the rich inhabitants, were freely brought up ... it shall be one grammar-school for Education of the Children of the Parishioners and Inhabitants of St Saviour, to be called 'A Free Grammar-school of the Parishioners of St Saviour in Southwark,' to have one master and one under-master.

It was in the reign of King James I (1603–25) that the parishioners, or more specifically the vestrymen, tired of paying rent for the church to the Crown, banded together and bought the church from James in 1614 for £800. They renovated it, made repairs to the fabric and also acquired the right to appoint their own clergy. In addition they were helped by financial donations from wealthy parishioners.

During the period of Civil War and Commonwealth (1642–60) St Saviour's was in the hands of Presbyterians and one of the ministers, John Crodacott, held his post until shortly after the Restoration in 1660, when he was ejected for not accepting the new Prayer Book. As a hardline Puritan he had tried to suppress the reinstitution of Christmas as a holiday, which had led to 'tumults ... in the streets'. However, St Saviour's was spared damage during the Civil War and its new tower was completed by 1689 with the four pinnacles we see today.

We are indebted for the seventeenth century views from Bankside of the City to the drawings of Bohemian artist Wenceslaus Hollar (1607–77). Some of his famous 'Views of London' were produced in the 1660s and are reputed to have been drawn from the tower of St Saviour's. Although he is buried in St Margaret's, Westminster, there is a memorial to him in the south transept of Southwark Cathedral.

During the eighteenth century St Saviour's had two chaplains who were popular preachers, Thomas Jones and Henry Sacheverell (1674–1724). Sacheverell, who was elected chaplain of St Saviour's in 1705, claimed some notoriety by two sermons he gave in 1709 which attacked the Whig government for their toleration of religious dissenters. He was charged with seditious libel, tried, convicted, and sentenced to a three-year suspension from preaching. The trial created a furore, and the light sentence made Sacheverell the victor in the eyes of the public.

By the 1820s not only was the church of St Saviour's in bad repair, it was also seriously threatened by the reconstruction of the old London Bridge. The new approach road to the bridge was within 60 feet of the east end of the church and fifteen feet above the churchyard level. Those who paid the church rate in the Borough were not necessarily church-goers and therefore resented paying for its upkeep. The debate over the future of the church was at stake with opinion divided between those who felt it was of architectural importance and those that believed 'St Saviour's Folly' was a 'damp old monastery' that should be demolished and replaced by a parish church more suited to the needs of the local populace.

The pro-restoration lobby won the day and thanks to the energies of the architect George Gwilt (1746–1807) the eastern portion of the choir, aisles and retrochoir were restored. The Bishop's Chapel (east of the retrochoir) and the Chapel of St Mary Magdalene (east of the South Transept) were both demolished. The nave was also in a poor condition and in 1831 the roof was removed for safety reasons. It remained open to the elements for seven years. In 1838 a rather makeshift nave was constructed which caused the great Victorian architect A. W. Pugin (1812–52) to describe it as being 'as vile a preaching place as ever disgraced the 19th century'. No sooner was this accomplished than the London, Chatham & Dover Railway Company built a great viaduct right next to the restored church.

In 1851 two Jewish synagogues existed in the Borough. One of these dated from the mid-eighteenth century, possibly to serve the needs of Jewish inmates of the debtors' prison, and was known as Nathan Henry's Synagogue. This closed when Henry died in 1853. It was situated behind his house in Marker Street. The other synagogue, founded by secessionists in 1823, was situated in Prospect Place, St George's Road. The 1851 census showed that between 300 and 400 Jews lived in Southwark.

The area became increasingly overcrowded and one of the poorest boroughs in London. This made it increasingly difficult for the cathedral at Winchester to support a church in South London. The Thames had marked the northern boundary of the Kingdom of Wessex, of which Winchester was the capital. The diocese of Winchester stretched from the Thames to the Channel Islands until 1877. After a short experiment that involved transferring authority to Rochester, an Act of Parliament formed the Diocese of Southwark in 1904. The following year the Cathedral came into being as the Cathedral and Collegiate Church of St Saviour and St Mary Overie with Edward Talbot, the Bishop of Rochester, enthroned as the first Bishop of Southwark. The diocese of Southwark covers an area from the Thames to Gatwick Airport and from Thamesmead to Thames Ditton and includes a population of over 2.5 million.

Southwark Cathedral houses many memorials and tombs. Not surprisingly, given its close proximity to many of the playhouses that were located in Bankside, several prominent actors and writers are memorialised in the church. One of the more recent and tragic events commemorated by a memorial tablet in the nave is to the *Marchioness* disaster in 1989 in which fifty-one people lost their lives when the *Marchioness* collided with a pleasure craft, the *Bowbelle*, on the River Thames. Adjacent to the memorial tablet are a few surviving wooden roof bosses from the original fifteenth-century building.

The south aisle of the nave has a memorial to Shakespeare designed by Henry McCarthy in 1911. It shows Shakespeare resting across a Bankside landscape with images in the background of St Saviour's church, Winchester Palace, and the Globe and Rose theatre. Above this recumbent alabaster figure is a stained-glass window designed by Christopher Webb, which replaced the one that was destroyed during the Second World War. It was unveiled on the anniversary of Shakespeare's death in April 1954 and depicts characters from some of Shakespeare's plays including Bottom and Puck (*Midsummer Night's Dream*), Malvolio and Olivia (*Twelfth Night*), Romeo and Juliet, King Lear, Othello, Hamlet and Lady Macbeth. Shakespeare's brother Edmund was buried in St Saviour's in 1607. Although the location of his grave is unknown, an inscribed stone in the paving of the choir commemorates Edmund.

To the right of the Shakespeare memorial is a commemoration tablet to Sam Wanamaker CBE (1919–93), American artist, director and producer, and possibly best known as the inspiration behind the rebuilding of Shakespeare's Globe Theatre, which helped to revive an interest in Bankside. Sadly he died before the Globe was completed.

An unusual brass epitaph in the south choir aisle erected during the period of the Commonwealth is to a ten-year-old girl, Susanna Barford, who died in 1652. The inscription describes her as 'The Non-such of the world for Piety and Vertue in soe tender years'. Below these words there is an epitaph in rhyming couplets the last part of which reads,

This world to her was but a tragic play,
She came and sawt,
Dislk'd and passed away.

Also in the south choir aisle are memorials to Sir Frederick Wigan (1827–1907), a prominent hop merchant and benefactor, Bishop Talbot, the first bishop of Southwark Cathedral in 1905, and Abraham Newland (1730–1807), chief cashier to the Bank of England from 1782 to 1807. Newland presided over the issue of the first pound note. The expression 'an Abraham Newland' came to mean a bank note, because without his signature no Bank of England note was genuine. William Emerson, who died in 1575 at the age of ninety-two, has a monument with the succinct epitaph 'he lived and died an honest man'. His son, Thomas, founded one of the parish charities and gave his name to Emerson Street, slightly east of the Globe Theatre.

The Humble monument in the north choir aisle reflects the influence of Flemish refugees who worked as sculptors on Bankside. They sculptured the monument which shows Alderman Richard Humble (d. 1616) and his two wives, Margaret and Isobel, knelt in prayer. Another monument is to John Trehearne (porter to King James I), who is shown with his wife. Trehearne was one of the 'Bargainers' – those who helped to buy the church from King James I. A plaque to the right of this monument is to Thomas Cure, who founded Cure's College, a set of almshouses to the north of the church.

The memorials in the Chancel and Sanctuary reflect the connection of the area with the theatre. Here is Edmond Shakespeare (d. 1607), the brother of William and an actor, John Fletcher (1579–1625), a dramatist who wrote sixteen plays and collaborated with William Shakespeare, and Philip Massinger (1583–1640), who collaborated on fifty-five plays.

In the centre of the cathedral (the Crossing) is the Harvard Chapel. John Harvard (1607–38) was the son of a butcher whose shop stood north-east of the cathedral. Harvard was baptised in what was then St Saviour's in 1607. In 1636, a year after graduating from Emmanuel College, Cambridge, he left to start a Puritan colony in the New World. He arrived in Boston along with his personal library of over 300 books. He left his money (£779) to the college of Newtown which became Harvard University. For music lovers there is also a plaque dedicated to song writer Oscar Hammerstein (1895–1960) in the Harvard Chapel.

A window in the north transept celebrates the Diamond Jubilee of Queen Victoria in 1897. A lesser-known but interesting individual was Southwark-born Lionel Lockyer (c. 1600–72), a seventeenth-century quack doctor who was famous in his time for his miracle pills, which he claimed included sunbeams as ingredients. Part of the epitaph on his tomb reads,

> Here Lockyer: lies interr'd enough: his name
> Speakes one hath few competitors in fame:
> … is virtues & his PILLS are so well known …
> That envy can't confine them under stone.
> But they'll survive his dust and not expire
> Till all things else at th'universall fire.
> This verse is lost, his PILL Embalmes him safe
> To future times without an Epitaph.

A series of stained-glass windows along the north aisle depicts a number of famous literary people associated with Southwark. Above the old Norman entrance in the cloisters, one of the windows shows the pilgrims in Geoffrey Chaucer's *The Canterbury Tales* leaving the Tabard Inn for their journey to Canterbury. Other windows depict a contemporary of Chaucer, John Gower, with his wife Agnes Groundolf; John Bunyan (1628–88), author of *The Pilgrim's Progress*, preached at a Baptist Chapel in Duke Street; Dr Henry Sacheverell, a chaplain of St Saviour's and provocative preacher; Samuel Johnson (1709–84), whose influence seems to touch many parts of London, was a frequent visitor to Southwark and became friends with the Thrale family, who owned a brewery west of Southwark Bridge; and Oliver Goldsmith (1730–74), author of *The Vicar of Wakefield*, who spent a brief spell as a doctor on Bankside.

The cathedral came under critical spotlight on 16 November 1996 for hosting the twentieth anniversary service for the Lesbian and Gay Christian Movement. In 2001 Nelson Mandela opened a new northern cloister, with facilities such as a refectory, shop, conference centre, education centre and museum supported by a £4.5 million lottery grant through the Millennium Commission. The glass-covered 'street' that links the cathedral to the new buildings is known as Lancelot's Link. From a viewing platform within this 'link', one can see the gravelled surface of the Roman road that ran from the bridgehead across the Cathedral site to meet the riverbank opposite the Houses of Parliament and the Saxon foundations of the early church. To the east of the medieval remains are the brick arches of a seventeenth-century pottery kiln.

Any visit to the cathedral, especially on a Saturday during the summer, will usually find it thronged with people sitting in and around the cathedral grounds or moving between there and Borough Market or beyond to the other attractions on Bankside. And yet Southwark Cathedral is still an overlooked London landmark. Maybe with the ever-increasing tourism that Bankside and the Borough attract, the profile of Southwark Cathedral might finally be acknowledged for the important historic building it is.

The present-day Christ Church is an Anglican parish church in Blackfriars Road. The first church on this site was built in 1670, paid for by a legacy from John Marshall, a local businessman and a member of a Southwark family of 'whitebakers'. It was in 1682 that the parish of Christ Church was created in the manor of Paris Garden. Shakespeare mentioned the parish in his play *Henry VIII* as being a disreputable place. Marshall's will of 1627 provided and directed that a new church should be built and a rector be appointed and paid for in that manor.

At the time of the foundation there was no bridge at Blackfriars and no direct major connection between the area to the south or to the City. In 1694 an Act of Parliament enabled the parishioners to levy rates for the maintenance of their minister, and empowered the trustees to build a steeple and furnish it with bells.

However, problems emerged when the marshy ground on which the church was situated threatened the foundations – so much so that the building quickly deteriorated. In 1721 it was stated to be in 'a very decaying condition, the churchyard, by reason of the great increase of the inhabitants, had become incapable to receive their dead, [and] the graves both within and without the church were filled with water as soon as dug'. Eighteen years later in 1739 an Act of Parliament empowered the trustees to demolish the church and rebuild it in an improved enclosure. Two years later the new Christ Church was completed in the Italian Romanesque style with a clock tower rising in three stages from the ground, surmounted by an octagonal lantern and cupola.

The development of Christ Church was accompanied by the draining of the surrounding marshy land that in turn attracted an expanding population looking for work along the increasingly industrial Bankside. By 1774 development between Blackfriars Bridge and Borough High Street had been so rapid that St Saviour's parish attempted to ease congestion along the crowded alleyways by making a direct thoroughfare between London Bridge and Blackfriars Bridge. This would join Duke Street and what is now the western part of Charlotte Street, thus creating Union Street.

This second church survived for 200 years until German bombs destroyed it in 1941. A cross of concrete in the grass at the rear now marks where its last remnant fell in flames from the destruction. The current building, which was consecrated on 17 December 1959, was paid for and owned by Marshall's Charity. John Marshall is commemorated in the porch of the church by his coat of arms and the attached church hall is also named after him.

The outward appearance of the present church hides a much more interesting interior, notably the stained-glass windows which were installed in 1959 and 1984–85 and whose images reflect the changes in the locality. The 1959 windows depict the historical changes since Christ Church was founded in 1670 whilst the 1984–85 windows at ground-floor level were installed in 1984 to celebrate the twenty-fifth anniversary of the opening of the building, illustrating local companies and organisations.

The windows include depictions of the construction on the South Bank and a river providing a channel of trade for skins, wood pulp, food and other resources for local factories and workshops, and the lost occupations of men who once plied the river between ocean-going cargo boats and Thames wharves.

Local employers such as Lloyds Bank and supermarkets are shown, something unusual in church stained-glass windows, particularly the image of a Sainsbury's shopping trolley! The change and continuity of riverside industry is portrayed in a window showing the emergence of consortia and giant enterprises, notably sea containers from the 1980s.

One window reflects the Kirkaldy Experimental Works. After the Tay Bridge disaster in 1879 this machine tested the material with which it was renewed. In 1984 the Experimental Works, a unique Victorian building, became a museum of engineering and much more, a flexible space for innovative enterprise.

Christ Church states that the 'hope for a strong, just and democratic economy should be an aspiration of the churches'. One window with the heading of 'Unity is Strength' displays the association of the church with trade unions in which it offers facilities to twelve Trade Union branches. This is further reflected in the Wapping Memorial Sculpture in the Hall, which records the struggle of print workers against the decision by Rupert Murdoch to move his newspapers to Docklands. It is accompanied by a poem written by a previous rector, Peter Challen. Other windows celebrate the many industries associated with Bankside: printing, a dominant industry in the environs of Blackfriars Bridge for two hundred years (the *Financial Times* building still stands at Number One Southwark Bridge); the building industry, which has a long history in the area; engineering – notably in relation to the railways and the small industries operating under the railway arches; power regeneration – Bankside Power Station was a vital source of power for London; and baking – J. Sainsbury had their bakery in Stamford Street, west of the church. Finally a window named 'Mother and Children of a Bygone Age' represents the 'local residential community and the unacknowledged domestic economy'.

Christ Church is a relatively new church erected on the site of two previous ones. It not only serves the local community but also reflects the many changes experienced by the community of Bankside over the years.

St Olave's church once stood near London Bridge, on the north side of Tooley Street. St Olave is the anglicised version of St Olaf, patron saint of Norway and once the saviour of London from the Danes, as well as the patron saint of seafarers. There were at least six churches dedicated to 'St Olave' – five within the City and the one at Southwark – all dating from the eleventh century. The first mention of a church standing on this site is in 1096 in relation to its priest 'Peter de St Olavo' who was party to a land transaction involving Bermondsey Priory. In 1327 a papal mandate directed the Bishop of Winchester to relax sixty days of enjoined penance to all who contributed within three years to the repair of St Olave's. The repairs were necessitated by its proximity to the river as the constant lapping of the tide against the walls had not only damaged the church but had also carried away bodies from the graveyard. It seems this was a regular hazard over the years. In 1617 the church was repaired and beautified yet again at the cost of the parishioners.

In 1640 with the calling of the Long Parliament, which set the country on the road to Civil War, conflicts of religious opinion developed. The churchwardens at St Olave's removed the altar rails, which were seen as symbolising Popish ceremony, dividing the minister from the congregation. For this action they were prosecuted. In 1641 the churchwardens petitioned the House of Lords against what they viewed as an illegal prosecution. They argued that many hundreds of the parishioners had refused to come to the sacrament while the rails remained and that they had taken them quietly away and disposed of them for the benefit of the parish. Another 'unnecessary ceremony', which had been attacked from the reign of Queen Elizabeth by Puritans, was the way in which the sacrament was administered. Another petition from the curate of St Olave's complained of the violent conduct of certain parishioners who, after five hundred persons had received the sacrament on their knees, insisted that the curate should administer it to them while they sat. If he dare refuse they threatened to drag him about the church by the ears.

The church was subject to more repairs in 1697 when a gallery was installed to accommodate the boys of the parochial free school. In 1720 the church had an organ and also 'a very good parsonage house' situated in the churchyard, on which 'much cost had been bestowed'.

In 1736 St Olave's was famous for being 'the last church in London remarkable for possessing 4 aisles and 3 rows of pillars'. However, time and tide as well as the digging of graves caught up with St Olave's by 1737 as the church was in a ruinous condition. A report in January 1736 stated that as a result of digging graves too near the foundations of a pillar, the whole of the north side of the church fell down. However, an Act of Parliament allowed for the levying of rates in order that the church could be rebuilt. The succeeding church, designed by Henry Flitcroft, was built between 1737 and 1739 of Portland stone and completed in 1740. It consisted of a small chancel, a nave with aisles and a vestibule and a north-western tower designed in the classical style. The aisles were separated from the nave by Ionic columns and were fitted with galleries. The church also contained a wooden sword-rest dated 1674 and bearing the City arms and the Southwark mark. This sword rest is now displayed on the north wall of the North Transept of Southwark Cathedral.

In 1817 it was reported that the tithes for the upkeep of St Olave's were not sufficient to maintain the rector and the rectory house, both of which were in need of repair and inconveniently situated. Almost one hundred years after the building of the church it was damaged by fire on the night of 19 August 1843. Only the tower and the bare walls remained, while the only wooden structure to escape the fire was the pulpit. Nonetheless it was speedily rebuilt in 1844 to the same design. During this period it was very much a docklands church but as the industrial expansion of the area led to population decline, the parish went into decline too.

In 1926 the church was declared redundant and the nave was demolished, leaving a forlorn tower, removed in 1928. At the same time it was decided to establish a new district and parish in the north-eastern portion of the old parish of Mitcham, to which the dedication of St Olave was transferred. St Olave's of Tooley Street was replaced by St Olaf House, which was designed with an Art Deco façade by H. S. Goodhart-Rendel for the Hays Wharf Company in 1928–32 as offices and warehousing.

On the north side of St Thomas Street stood the parish church of St Thomas's, originally erected for the use of the hospital. The church may have originated as a chapel of the medieval hospital, but it is not known when it was first built on the present site. Nonetheless there was certainly a medieval church here. The church was named after two different saints. At the Reformation it was renamed St Thomas the Apostle following the abolition of the St Thomas Becket cult in 1538.

Although additions were made to the church in the early seventeenth century, including the bell tower, the governors of the hospital argued in 1697 that the building was in such a state of decay that people were afraid to go inside.

The present church was constructed between 1699 and 1702 at a cost of £3,718, provided by the coal duty, which included compensation to the owners of two small houses to the east of the old church which were also pulled down. The church was built by architect Thomas Cartwright (1635–1703), who was employed by Sir Robert Clayton, president of the St Thomas's Hospital. The building was in the form of a rectangular building of red brick with rusticated stone angles, standing on two parallel brick vaults.

In 1821 the church acquired a herb garret and an operating theatre in the roof space of the building. What might seem strange makes sense when it is realised that the wards of the South Wing of St Thomas's Hospital were built around St Thomas's church. Placing the theatre in the herb garret (which was used by the hospital's apothecary to store and cure herbs used in healing) of the church provided a separation from the ward and gave a separate entrance for students. Being located in the roof also allowed the theatre to benefit from the large skylight above, and it provided an ideal area for demonstrating surgical skills. A description of the students packing the theatre to witness an operation has been left by a St Thomas's surgeon, John Flint South:

> The first two rows ... were occupied by the other dressers, and behind a second partition stood the pupils, packed like herrings in a barrel, but not so quiet, as those behind them were continually pressing on those before and were continually struggling to relieve themselves of it, and had not infrequently to be got out exhausted. There was also a continual calling out of 'Heads, Heads' to those about the table whose heads interfered with the sightseers. The theatre, which dealt mainly with amputation, was closed down before antiseptic surgery was invented.

By 1898 the parish had a small population which did not exceed 500, so the following year it was united with St Saviour's. The 'Old Operating Theatre', including the herb garret, is now a museum and makes for an excellent visit.

Another notable and historic church, which is slightly beyond the boundary of Bankside but is worth a brief mention, is St George the Martyr opposite Borough Underground Station. It is one of the ancient parishes of Southwark and probably the first church in London to be dedicated to St George.

The earliest record of the church is for the year 1122 but little is known about the original Norman church. We know it was rebuilt at the end of the fourteenth century and appears on some early maps and can be seen in Hogarth's picture of Southwark Fair in 1733. It was just after this date that the church was demolished and rebuilt, the present structure being consecrated in 1736. The church has a Georgian appearance and a spectacular new ceiling was added in 1897. St George's has particular associations with Charles Dickens, who lived nearby in Lant Street. Between 1855 and 1857 he wrote *Little Dorrit* and set several scenes in and around St George's church. There is a small representation of Little Dorrit in the east window of the church. During the Second World War the church suffered blast damage and a major restoration was carried out at the beginning of the 1950s.

The Civil War of the 1640s brought not only conflict and destruction but also the proliferation of radical ideas as a result of the lifting of censorship. During the years that followed many diverse religious and political ideas were expressed and published in pamphlets. London was a particular centre for such ideas and Southwark witnessed its share of radical groups. Prior to the outbreak of war a congregation in Southwark was recorded as being one of seven separatist churches discovered in London. King Charles I (r. 1625–49) intervened to recommend that the Lords take severe action against this particular congregation, especially in view of some of the seditious opinions held by them.

The area adjacent to the north of St Saviour's, Montague Close, became a refuge for both Presbyterians and radical Independents with congregations setting up in the Close. Along Bankside, Anabaptists (who rejected conventional Christian practices such as wearing wedding rings, taking oaths, and adhered to the idea that Baptism is to be administered to believers only) and Fifth Monarchists, a millenarian group who believed that the second coming of Christ was imminent, were to be found living near St Mary Overie Dock.

The Restoration of monarchy under King Charles II (r. 1660–85) subdued much of the radical fervour of the previous decades. As a reminder of this a painted Royal Arms, which hangs in the retrochoir of Southwark Cathedral, was inscribed with the warning 'meddle not with those who are given to change'. However, after the upheavals of the 1640s and 1650s, the Church of England would no longer hold a monopoly on religious opinion. Southwark, the outlaw borough, had a long history as a centre for non-conformity and continued to attract dissidents and dissenters.

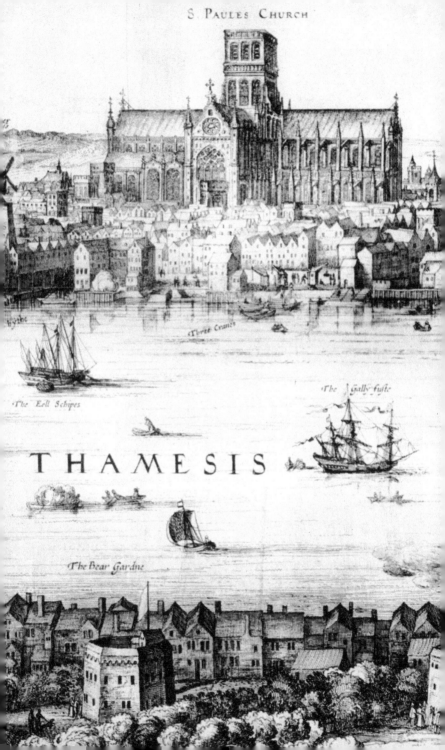

S. PAVLES CHVRCH

hythe

Three Cranes

The Eell Schipes

The Gally fuste

THAMESIS

The Bear Gardne

2. A plaque marks the site of the
Anchor Brewery in Park Street.

3. The Anchor on Bankside.

Above: 4. Bankside Lofts in Hopton Street and luxury apartments of NEO Bankside.

Previous page: 1. Claes Visscher's *Panorama of London* of 1616, with St Paul's Cathedral
towering above the huddle of buildings leading down to the river.

5. Seafood stall at Borough Market.

6. One of a number of old cannon bollards around Bankside.

7. Corporation of London buildings off Great Guilford Street.

Top of page: 8. John Norden's view of London Bridge *c*. 1593.

Left: 10. The memorial to Lionel Lockyer, seventeenth century quack doctor in Southwark Cathedral.

Above: 9. Cannon Street
Railway Bridge.

Right: 11. The memorial
to John Gower in
Southwark Cathedral.

12. A gruesome reminder of past times. A gibbet hanging outside the Clink Prison Museum.

13. The replica of the *Golden Hind* in St Mary Overie Dock, Pickfords Wharf.

14. The famous George Inn, Borough High Street.

15. A stone in Park Street which marks the site of the original Globe Theatre in Southwark.

16. The modern Globe Theatre.

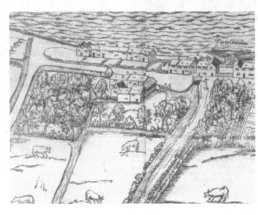

17. Ralph Agas, Map of London, *c.* 1560, showing Paris Garden and the moated manor house with gardens.

18. The tall tower of Guy's Hospital.

19. London, Chatham & Dover Railway coat of arms.

20. Hopton's Almshouses built in 1752 on Hopton Street.

Top of page: 21. An illustration of King's Bench prison.

Above: 22. Remains of the wall of Marshalsea prison. Charles Dickens, whose father was imprisoned at Marshalsea for debt in 1824, used his father's experience in his novel Little Dorrit.

Right: 23. The Clink Prison Museum on Bankside.

24. Millennium Bridge – the newest bridge to span the Thames connects Tate Modern with St Paul's Cathedral.

25. No. 49 Bankside, 'The House by the Thames', which dates from 1710.

26. The Old Operating Theatre on St Thomas Street.

Above left: 27.
The Shakespeare
memorial in
Southwark
Cathedral.

Above right: 28.
The rose window
in the remains of
Winchester Palace.

Right: 29.
Southwark
Cathedral.

Above left: 30. Portrait of Chaucer, *c.* 1412.

Above right: 31. A selection of Canterbury Pilgrims from an early edition of Chaucer's *Canterbury Tales* which first appeared in 1387.

Below: 32. Plaque commemorating the site of the Tabard Inn.

Top of page: 33. Southwark Bridge opened in 1921.

Above: 34. Tate Modern, previously Bankside Power Station.

Right: 35. Shard London Bridge, March 2010, on its way to becoming the tallest building in Europe.

36. The houses in Southwark, close to the south end of London Bridge.

37. Ferryman's seat at the corner of Bankside and Bear Gardens.

38. Medieval wooden roof bosses. The one at the top is the Devil devouring Judas Iscariot.

39. An execution at Horsemonger Lane Gaol in the nineteenth century.

Above: 40. The site of Horsemonger Lane Gaol today.

Next page: 41. The church of St Mary Overy, Southwark, and London Bridge. Note the spiked heads of executed felons in the right foreground.

St. Dunston in the east

St. Helley

St. Andrew

Nonconformist chapels and houses of worship sprang up around Bankside. In 1672 five independent and Presbyterian chapels were located in Southwark, as well as Quaker and Anabaptist meeting houses. Many Flemish people, among whom were Anabaptists, settled in Southwark after fleeing from Catholic persecution in Flanders. The Independent congregation received a licence in Winchester Yard in 1672. In Globe Alley there was a large meeting of Presbyterians in 1669 and in 1676, to which one of the most influential Nonconformists leaders, Richard Baxter (1615–91), ministered. An academy for dissenting ministers was established at Globe Alley, Maid Lane by Joshua Oldfield (1656–1729), a Presbyterian minister. Benjamin Keach (1640–1704), a Particular Baptist preacher, was pastor of a Baptist church in Tooley Street for thirty-six years. Keach wrote forty-three works of scripture, one of which, *The Child's Instructor*, saw him fined and pilloried in 1664.

In 1687 a Baptist meeting house was built in Gravel Lane, which used to extend northwards near the present Sumner Street. In the eighteenth century Zoar Street, which is marked on the 1745 edition of Rocque's map, was cut through beside the chapel. The name Zoar has an interesting association as it means a place of refuge or sanctuary. The chapel was, from the beginning, used as a school and it is the earliest Nonconformist school in London for which any detailed information is available. Reading material was limited to the Bible before 1722 but thereafter hornbooks and spelling books were bought for the juniors. Early in the nineteenth century Zoar Street was rebuilt but later demolished during the Second World War by enemy action.

In 1778 the Catholic Relief Act brought a limited freedom to Catholic priests, who could now move without fear of imprisonment, run their own schools and acquire property. The Act sparked the massive Gordon Riots two years later when Lord George Gordon, on 2 June 1780, gathered a large crowd in St George's Fields, Southwark, to march on Westminster. The riots became violent, turning into a week of burning, plundering and killing in which many Roman Catholic chapels and houses were destroyed. In 1786 there was only one Roman Catholic chapel in the whole of South London, located at Bermondsey. It was here that Father Thomas Walsh, a Douai priest, for £20 a year hired a room in Bandyleg Walk. John Strype in his *Survey of London* (1720) located the unusually named street as near Queen Street, which 'runs Westwards from Redcross Street to Pepper Street, receives Whitecross Street, and Worcester Street, and crossed by Bandy Leg Walk; It is a clean, and open Street, with good built Houses: at the upper end of the Street next to Pepper Street is a pretty Bowling Alley.' Within two years, the numbers attending the little chapel had increased so rapidly that a new building became essential.

9

Disasters & Accidents

Bankside has had a troubled history and has rarely been out of the news. Three of the four elements – fire, air and water – have all at times had a disastrous impact on the district.

The Romans were sophisticated but barbarous. It was almost certainly the Romans who invented organised firefighting. London and its offspring at the southern end of the bridge were largely composed of timber buildings with thatched roofs which presented an appalling fire risk, especially when cooking was done on open fires and candles provided illumination.

The Romans called their firefighters 'vigiles'. Archaeologists have unearthed evidence that they were needed. Excavations in Southwark have revealed what are now compacted areas of ash and burnt fragments that could only have come from one or more large and generalised fires.

William the Conqueror was a heavyweight, a man of great administrative ability and ruthless efficiency. It was somehow typical of the man that he introduced a couvre-feu or curfew in London. This required all citizens to extinguish their domestic fires and candles at nightfall. So many fires started in the home when sparks from the fire or a dropped candle ignited the dry straw that was scattered on the floor. William's measure was unpopular and was abolished in 1100 by his son, Henry II, a lesser man.

Several centuries followed in which fire prevention and effective firefighting resources were largely neglected. In 1212 (or 1213), what started as a small domestic fire on London Bridge became a major conflagration hungrily consuming much of the wooden bridge and its buildings and spreading into the equally vulnerable buildings in the City on one side and Southwark on the other. Much of Borough High Street was destroyed as was the church of St Mary Overie on the site of which Southwark Cathedral now stands. A total of 3,000 people lost their lives on this occasion. There was little that anyone could do except stand and watch.

Unfortunately some of those viewing the excitement from the bridge found themselves trapped because both ends of the bridge caught fire. Many of them fell or jumped into the river and were swept away to their deaths by the strong currents.

In 1613 the Globe at Bankside caught fire when sparks from a cannon fired during a performance set the thatched roof alight. Primitive fire engines are first recorded in use in 1633 when they proved rather ineffective at dealing with another fire on London Bridge. This fire left a significant gap in the buildings on the bridge and, as luck would have it, they had not been rebuilt by the time of the Great Fire in 1666. The fire encroached onto the northern end of the bridge where it petered out because it could not cross this gap. Had that gap not been there, the fire would have consumed the bridge and then equally greedily would have gone to gorge itself on the buildings of Bankside and the Borough. As it was, Samuel Pepys, who had retreated to Bankside to watch the conflagration, wrote in his diary that showers of sparks were flying across the Thames and landing near him. It was a miracle that Bankside did not burn down.

The word 'traumatic' is considerably overused today where hyperbole has become the norm in the media. However, there is no question that London was traumatised by the Great Fire. One outcome of this was the idea of insurance against fire. Subscribers would pay to receive assistance from a force of firefighters provided by their insurance company in the event that fire broke out on their premises. They would then receive compensation for the damage done by the fire, on a scale estimated by 'experts' working for the insurance company. Although there might appear to be some possible flaws in such an arrangement, the idea caught on and soon a number of insurance companies were providing men in distinctive uniform to attend fires at those premises which had fully paid-up insurance policies lodged with them. The premises that were insured would be identified by a distinctive metal mark on their façades – this came to be known as a 'firemark', although the fact that they were probably belching fire and smoke might also have helped to draw the attention of the firefighters to them. Gradually the phrase 'fire brigades' came to be applied to the forces employed by the companies.

In May 1676 fire broke out in the basement of an oil shop in Borough High Street. An explosion occurred and the fire spread into adjoining premises. Charles II, who seems to have had a great (obsessive?) interest in fires, was quickly on the scene to direct the firefighting operation. A pumping engine played an honourable role in the battle to contain the flames as it successfully sucked hundreds of gallons of water from the Thames and directed them onto the fires. In direct contrast to their reluctance to do so in the Great Fire ten years earlier, the authorities ruthlessly pulled down buildings which lay in the path of the advancing fire and this helped to minimise the effects of what could have been a far worse fire. As it was, about 500 buildings were destroyed. These included some historic taverns and, perhaps needless to say, some brothels, including the Tabard, perhaps the most historic of all Southwark's old inns.

London developed in the seventeenth and especially the eighteenth century as a major centre of industry and commerce. The consequent rapid growth of wealth invested, for example, in docks, warehouses, industrial premises and other factors of production and in raw materials and goods stored awaiting processing or distribution or actually in transit meant that fires could pose a major threat to the realisation of profits. Now not just wealthier citizens wanted protection for their homes and contents but industrialists and others in the world of commerce also became interested in insurance against fire damage. Insurance was becoming big business and in 1791 the Phoenix, the Royal and the Sun insurance companies created a joint fire brigade called the 'Fire Watch', which was based at five stations including one in Southwark. This part of the south bank of the river had innumerable warehouses, often packed to the gunwales with items in transit and many of which were highly flammable. It is worth commenting that the drive to establish these early brigades was concern to save property. The need to save lives was not mentioned. The 'Fire Watch' was transformed into the London Fire Engine Establishment in 1830 with more insurance companies taking part. This started operating in 1833 under the command of James Braidwood, who had held a similar position in Edinburgh where the municipal authority operated a fire service. Braidwood was a natural leader who enthused those for whom he was responsible, and he developed a scientific approach to training. He also believed in systematic fire prevention and worked tirelessly to raise awareness of the issue with those who might have need of his services. He designed a new and more practical uniform for his people and London firemen came to be known as 'Jim Bradys'. Soon the LFEE had two stations in Southwark. One was in Tooley Street and the other in Southwark Bridge Road.

From the 1830s, steam-powered pumps were beginning to replace manual machines and were far more effective although, perhaps curiously, Braidwood did not have a particularly high opinion of their usefulness. He feared that the powerful jets of water they could direct at buildings on fire might cause stresses in the masonry which would cause them to collapse.

Braidwood was immensely respected, and under his stewardship, the LFEE became increasingly efficient. It was in the course of duty that Braidwood met his nemesis. On the late afternoon of 22 June 1861, what at first was a very minor fire was discovered in a bale of cotton in a six-storey warehouse in Tooley Street. This fire spread with alarming speed, engulfing large quantities not only of cotton but of other highly flammable substances such as hemp, tallow, flour, brandy, various kinds of oil and also sugar. Fire engines and firefighters rushed to the scene of what, it quickly became clear, was certainly going to become a major incident. By the time that Braidwood arrived to take command the fire was generating enormous heat and sparks were being borne on the wind. As ill-luck would have it, the sparks did not have to go far because the warehouses were densely packed with only the narrowest of alleys running from the riverfront to Tooley Street between them.

By eight o'clock about 1,000 yards of these buildings along the river were ablaze. The river itself was on fire as a highly combustible mix of rum and tallow spread across the water. The magnificent if awful spectacle drew huge crowds whose presence made it difficult for firefighters and their appliances to reach the scene. Significantly, in the light of Braidwood's apparent aversion to steam-pumps, the manual pumps of the LFEE were proving rather ineffective at trying to spray adjacent buildings to keep them cool. It was left to steam-pumps operated by the rival Hodges Brigade to reach the upper stories but even they could do little to stem the spread of the fire. At about seven in the evening, Braidwood was directing operations and was in a narrow, smoke-filled alley when the gable end of a high building collapsed without warning and he and his assistant were buried under tons of rubble and burning wood. It took three days to recover the bodies and as long as four weeks to extinguish the fires completely. Scarcely an undamaged building was left on the riverfront between London Bridge and Tower Bridge. The cost of the losses was put at over £2 million. Braidwood's death was widely mourned and his funeral procession was a mile and a half long. It was the grandest funeral in London since that of the Duke of Wellington, nine years earlier.

Braidwood's successor was Eyre Massey Shaw, an Irishman with a strange little goatee beard who was London's fire supremo for the next thirty years. He gained an even more illustrious reputation that that enjoyed by Braidwood. In 1866 the Metropolitan Fire Brigade was created and the efficiency and extent of the brigade's services was enormously enhanced over the next decades. In 1878 a headquarters building for the whole Metropolitan Fire Brigade was opened in

Southwark and the site included a rather grand residence for the head of the fire service and his family. Keeping up local historical tradition, it was called 'Winchester House' and was located in Southwark Bridge Road. In 1919 the Hop and Malt Exchange in Southwark Street suffered a major fire.

London received some damage from aerial bombing by Zeppelins in the First World War when three people died. A total of 670 people died in London from aerial bombing in this war. Although the case for Zeppelins as weapons was by no means conclusive, it was clear that warfare was now taking to the skies. This horrible new dimension to war meant that people in Britain now felt so much more vulnerable because the 'moat' of the North Sea and the Channel no longer afforded its traditionally high level of protection. Technology moved on apace. People across the world were horrified with the revelation of the huge number of civilian casualties that occurred when the town of Guernica was bombed in 1937 during the Spanish Civil War. It was evident that warfare from the air had arrived and that London was likely to be singled out for bombing in the event of what seemed to be the imminent war with Germany. Civilians were likely to find themselves, if not exactly in the front line, at least very much at the centre of things. Southwark with its large concentration of warehouses containing highly flammable substances and goods had already experienced serious fires which spread with frightening rapidity. There were also concentrations of slum housing, much of it in multi-occupancy and where there were already a disproportionate number of fires. A drive started to recruit and train volunteers for the Auxiliary Fire Service and plans began to be drawn up to put the LFB on a war footing. It was evident that firefighting during and after aerial bombardment would require unprecedented amounts of water, and so a series of large new water mains was built to serve the parts of London thought to be most at risk. Southwark was not served by any of them. However, 'Dams' were established. These were emergency water supplies often, as in the case of one in Great Suffolk Street in Southwark, open to the elements and unfortunately an irresistible draw to the children of the locality, especially in hot weather. Sadly there were fatalities as a result. On 17 August 1940, the first incendiary bombs fell on the area for which the LFB was responsible. When Germany lost the Battle of Britain, it was clear that the Luftwaffe was going to concentrate on bombing London off the map. On 7 September the Blitz began.

Southwark was hit hard, especially with incendiaries. Such was the heat generated by large burning buildings that the firefighters had their work cut out simply trying to cool down adjacent buildings and prevent them from catching fire. This happened, for example, in Borough High Street on the second night of the Blitz. No one could have foreseen at the time that the bombing would go on relentlessly and continuously for more than fifty more nights. The Southwark fire station was bombed and, on 10 May 1941, no fewer than seventeen firefighters were killed by a land mine in Blackfriars Road. Many other buildings and substantial numbers of people who lived or worked in the locality were victims of air raids. The last recorded raid by enemy aircraft on London was on 19 April 1944. By that time raids by conventional craft had become no more than sporadic but a new horror made its appearance in June 1944. This was the V1 Flying Bomb. The noise of these approaching was bad enough but worse followed when the sound suddenly cut out and a brief, eerie and emotion-laden silence followed only to be broken by a massive explosion. It is not to underestimate their physical effects to say that the V1s or 'Doodle-bugs' were also psychological weapons. In 1944 more than fifty people were killed when a V1 landed in Union Street. Possibly even worse, because its silent approach gave no warning of its imminent arrival and its destructive effect, was the V2 rocket, the first of which fell on Chiswick in September 1944. Unlike the V1 bomb whose destructive effect was comparatively confined, just one V2 rocket produced a much larger explosion which was capable of destroying large swathes of buildings. One fell on New Cross killing 268 people and one on Smithfield killed 233. The last V2 fell on 27 March 1945. A total of 327 firefighters were killed in the war and over 3,000 seriously injured. The firefighters of Southwark played a valorous role throughout these years.

The following list identifies the major fires in the Southwark area since the 1830s. On 14 November 1841 two firefighters were killed at an incident in Blackfriars Road. On 19 August 1843 at Toppings Wharf a serious fire occurred in riverside warehouses and also engulfed a church. Already mentioned has been the fire at Cotton's Wharf, Tooley Street, in which James Braidwood was killed. Two firefighters were killed on 26 February 1911 in a fire at a paper and rag warehouse in Bankside. On 9 August 1971 at Wilson's Wharf, Battlebridge Lane off Tooley Street a big fire in a riverside warehouse required the attendance of fifty pumps.

Currently there are operational fire stations in Wolseley Street, SE1 and Southwark Bridge Road. The London Fire Brigade Museum is situated in Winchester House, Southwark Bridge Road.

The river Thames has taken more than its fair share of victims down the centuries. One minute they were alive, next minute gone and the river just simply kept rolling along as if nothing had happened. The late 1980s were a good time for those now-forgotten creatures, the yuppies, intent as they were on hedonism and conspicuous consumption. According to the 'filter-down' theory of economic growth, they deserved their high incomes because they were 'wealth creators' and some of the wealth they created, so we were assured, would in an unspecified and mysterious way ooze down to the rest of us less-talented mortals. We are still waiting. However, this was the age of the yuppie and the yuppies were determined to enjoy it. One of the expensive pleasures to which they had become addicted was the hiring of rivercraft for all-night discos, parties and booze-ups, particularly on warm summer nights. Unfortunately there had been a number of traffic accidents on the river when such craft had collided with other vessels. Until 1989, none of these had been serious incidents although it did seem as if some of the vessels involved were undermanned and their crews not well trained in keeping watch and in observing the rules of navigation.

Just after one in the morning of 20 August 1989 the 90-ton pleasure steamer *Marchioness* left Charing Cross Pier for a cruise down the river. She had 130 passengers on board and they were celebrating the twenty-sixth birthday of the organiser of the trip. It was a lovely balmy summer's night and the revelry soon got under way. They had booked the *Marchioness* for a five-hour cruise. The vessel was old – in fact a veteran of the Dunkirk evacuation, and although she had been modified for the role she was undertaking, she had a blind spot. This was the physical difficulty for crew members to maintain an adequate watch aft and to communicate, if necessary, with the vessel's bridge. The vessel was travelling at about 3 miles per hour and approaching an acknowledged tricky part of the river. This was where Blackfriars Road, Blackfriars Railway, Southwark Bridges and Cannon Street Railway Bridge had to be negotiated in quick succession.

Another vessel was making its way downstream. This was an altogether more mundane craft than the *Marchioness*. It was a 1,450-ton dredger called *Bowbelle*, which had set sail from further upstream and was proceeding at approximately 6 miles per hour. This ugly, if functional ship, was twenty-five years old and was no less than 80 yards long. It needed to be heavily constructed in order to perform its work. Just as the *Marchioness* had a poor lookout aft, so *Bowbelle* had a poor field of vision ahead. It was a night of fine visibility but *Bowbelle* was not displaying the navigational lights at her masthead because the masts needed to be lowered in order to pass under the various bridges as she moved downstream.

The party on board the *Marchioness* was hotting up as the ship moved slowly downstream, everyone blissfully unaware of the awful fate that was about to strike. The *Marchioness* passed under the central arch of Southwark Bridge and then intended to thread the central arch of Cannon Street Railway Bridge. Meanwhile the *Bowbelle*, moving at about twice the speed of the other vessel, had passed under the central arches of both Blackfriars Bridges and was also intending to sail under the central arch of Southwark Bridge. A few seconds after a quarter to two, between Southwark and Cannon Street Bridges, the *Bowbelle* hit the *Marchioness* twice with sufficient force to destroy the latter's stern and to roll her over. It took less than half a minute for the smaller vessel to sink. The tragic accident accounted for fifty-nine of those on board the *Marchioness* being killed.

There is nothing new, except in terms of the scale and the possible implications for today's future generations, in human beings causing environmental damage. Humans have, with apparent insouciant abandon, polluted the air and the waters and poisoned the soil while at the same time consigning innumerable species of fauna and flora to permanent oblivion. In these activities they have also frequently threatened their own health and well-being.

With its expanding population and growing industry London hungered for fuel. Wood and charcoal in the quantities that were needed were running out by the late medieval period. The capital then hungrily consumed vast amounts of coal over many centuries, and as it became ever bigger, it did so on a scale that wholly justifies that modern form of expression, 'a disaster waiting to happen'. Most of this fuel was what was then called 'sea-coal' because it was brought by sea down the East Coast from pits in Northumberland and Durham. The trade is remembered in the name Seacoal Lane in EC4. It is likely that sturdy little collier ships sailed up the Thames past London Bridge and into the lower part of the River Fleet where they discharged their cargo. By the end of the sixteenth century, it is likely that about 50,000 tonnes of coal were being landed in London annually. In 1667 a great fog beset London and was the cause of many road traffic accidents.

Concerns about air pollution in London were being expressed as early as the second half of the thirteenth century. They would have seemed particularly cogent given that foul smells or miasmas were thought to be harmful to health. In the case of sulphurous emanations, it was true. London, of course, could boast an impressive portfolio consisting entirely of noxious odours, that given off by burning coal being only one of them. London had a myriad of businesses using coal and Southwark was a particular centre of industrial activity. Lime-burners, brewers, soap-boilers, dyers and smiths were among those who were especially blamed for creating the pollution.

Before effective chimneys were designed, coal could not really be used for domestic purposes and its use was almost exclusively industrial. However, as the timber shortage worsened and effective domestic flues were built, so the use of coal steadily increased. In the eighteenth and the nineteenth centuries, London was notorious for its choking atmosphere, exacerbated in certain kinds of weather. Londoners may to some extent have become inured to it but new residents and visitors alike were struck by the acrid smell in the smoke-laden air which also caused coughing and stinging in the eyes. It is an inescapable fact that the availability and use of coal was a critical factor in enabling the growth of London. It was a necessary evil yet contemporary observers commented that smoke given off by coal-burning not only affected people but also buildings. The stonework of Old St Paul's Cathedral, for example, was badly damaged by smoke pollution. John Evelyn, whose diaries reveal much about life in seventeenth-century London, described the City as being cloaked in 'such a cloud of sea-coal, as if there be a resemblance of hell upon earth, it is in this volcano in a foggy day: this pestilent smoak, which corrodes the very yron, and spoils all the moveables, leaving a soot on all things that it lights: and so fatally seizing on the lungs of the inhabitants, that cough and consumption spare no man'. The problem of the unburned carbon particles intensified over the following centuries and reached its peak with appalling results after the Second World War. No wonder that London was often referred to, possibly with some affection, as 'The Smoke', much as Edinburgh was nicknamed 'Auld Reekie' because it had its own version of this toxic fog. Charles Dickens referred to smoke as 'London's ivy'. When we think of the London of Jack the Ripper or Sherlock Holmes, in our mind's eye we immediately create an image of the hours of darkness, damp cobbled streets with the clip-clop of horses and hansom cabs and a misty aura around each gas street lamp. At least the fog masked the stark drabness of many of the capital's streets. In *Bleak House* (1852–53) Dickens treats us to a description of fog on the river around the Pool of London, just below London Bridge:

> ... fog everywhere, fog up the river ... fog down the river, where it rolls defiled
> among the tiers of shipping and the waterside pollutions of a great (and dirty)

city. Fog creeping into the cabooses of collier-brigs; fog lying out on the yards, and fog hovering in the rigging of great ships, fog dripping on the gun-whales of barges and small boats.

By any kind of modern criterion, the continuously built-up area of medieval and early modern London was small and densely populated until modern forms of transport accelerated the existing long-term tendency to the creation of suburbs and the absorption into the 'Great Wen' of large numbers of peripheral villages. Urbanisation affects local climate conditions. A substantial built-up area creates what is known as an 'urban heat island'. This is not just the result of the burning of fuel but also arises from the fact that the materials from which urban buildings are constructed tend to absorb and retain heat. It means that London, because of the size of its population relative to other towns in Britain, the extent of the burning of industrial and domestic fuel and also because of other geographical and geological factors, developed a micro-climate which made it particularly susceptible to air pollution caused by the burning of fossil fuels.

Fogs and the River Thames had a long association. Before the eighteenth century, these fogs were probably natural but in the nineteenth century they were changing in frequency, density and colour and people were voicing the opinion that this was due to the amount of unburned coal particles in the air above the capital. The fogs for which London became so notorious probably peaked between about 1840 and 1890 and were definitely in decline after that time. There had been days when a pall of darkness lay over London and it never really got light. The sun was obscured although there was little or no fog and as such was therefore quite different from what came to be known as 'high fog' which was most frequent in the mornings. This was gloom combined with lesser or greater quantities of fog. Some of the fogs were impenetrable enough for people, completely disorientated, to walk or fall into the Thames and this happened on a number of occasions in the Bankside area in the 1860s and 1870. They drowned. Mortality always increased after a period of frequent fogs.

The worst fogs were those that settled and stayed for several days when, with little or no wind movement, pollutants in the air built up into serious and what could be lethal concentrations. The most famous of these was 'The Great Smog' of 1952 which was followed by some 4,000 deaths that were thought to be attributable to a period of sustained aerial pollution. The word 'smog' for this mixture seems to have been coined in 1905. Early December 1952 had witnessed temperate winter days with a little weak sunshine and light breezes. Then the winds dropped, the air grew damp and the skies grey. An anticyclone was poised above the City of London and the Bankside and Borough areas of Southwark.

Fog settled over the Metropolis on Thursday and people shrugged their shoulders thinking that they were in for yet another 'pea-souper', so called because they were more or less the colour and consistency of pea soup. No one, however, could remember seeing fog as thick as that which greeted them on Friday morning. And it simply got worse. Those out in it had smarting eyes and noses assailed by an acrid, choking smell. To blow the nose after a few minutes out in this miasmic murk was to find the handkerchief liberally peppered with a black residue of a somewhat sooty consistency. Bare skin and clothes soon bore an unwelcome sooty patina. People coughed and expectorated and before long the medical services were reporting a dramatic increase in patients with respiratory problems. The smog was triggering or exacerbating the existing symptoms of emphysema, asthma, bronchitis and heart disease. By the evening the anticyclone was motionless. The uncongenial dampness and dirt which seemed to find its way into every interstice of body and clothing meant that only those with little alternative were out on the streets. To cheer themselves up, when they got home, they banked up their fires. This only made a bad situation worse.

Saturday dawned and the only change was that the smog had become even more tangible and impenetrable overnight. Those who had to go out crashed into street furniture and other walkers. Some fell down steps and stairways or found themselves in the middle of the road in imminent danger of being run down by the few vehicles that were moving, albeit slowly. Trains at least had rails even if drivers could not see the signals. Buses groped their hesitant way along unrecognisable streets, sometimes preceded by the conductor trying to make some sense of his surroundings. The health services were besieged and people were dying. Emergency ambulances could move only at a snail's pace if at all. On Sunday it was every bit as bad. On Monday there were signs of improvement and on Tuesday the Great Smog itself was over even if its effects were not. It took many years and several more smogs, admittedly not so severe, for steps to be taken that should prevent any repetition.

In late November 1703, London was shaken by a tempest of terrifying power. Tiles, chimneys and brickbats rained down on anyone foolish enough to venture out. Church steeples plummeted to the ground. Two hundred Londoners were injured by falling debris while others had escapes which were nothing less than miraculous. On the Thames where it passed Bankside, ships and barges were torn from their moorings and many were smashed to smithereens on the starlings of London Bridge. More than sixty wherries belonging to watermen were sunk. Two watermen were drowned. A man and two children were killed when a house collapsed in a Southwark street. The church of St Saviour's sustained serious damage.

From the middle of the fourteenth century, the bubonic plague frequently ravaged England. Its best-known and most virulent visitation was that known retrospectively as the 'Black Death'. It carved its terrifying swathe right across the country in 1348–50. Bubonic plague is an infectious disease caused by the bacterium *Pasturella pestis* which is spread from the black house rat, *Rattus rattus*, to man by a flea. This chronic outbreak arrived at what is now Weymouth with rats that lived aboard ships. The damp, warmish overcrowded hovels of English peasants and town-dwellers attracted the rats – they in turn attracted the fleas. The characteristic sign of infection was the appearance of a 'bubo', which was a hard enlargement of a gland, often in the groin. Skin blotches appeared at about the same time. Buboes were agonising and some people committed suicide in order to avoid the pain and hasten death. Death would usually come on the third or fourth day and was a great relief. A variation was pneumonic plague. This could affect people not necessarily bitten by fleas. It was spread by droplet infection and inhaled. While some people survived bubonic plague, the pneumonic version was invariably fatal. Its most obvious symptom was the spitting of copious quantities of blood.

Southwark was already an unhealthy district, low-lying and with many stagnant or brackish swamps. The housing was squalid, overcrowded and unsanitary. The conditions encouraged pestilence and people died in such large numbers that pits were dug and the nameless corpses simply thrown in. Dogs, cats, pigs, horses and other creatures living in close proximity to man also died in untold numbers. Plague returned to England on several further occasions, and London as a cosmopolitan seaport was an obvious point of ingress for the disease. Southwark had many ships along its quays and mariners looking for fun in what would now be termed the 'entertainment quarter' of Bankside. The latter district attracted Londoners bent on pleasure as well as many visitors to the Metropolis. No wonder Southwark was probably more badly affected by the plague than any other particular district.

By the mid-seventeenth century, the mistaken feeling had grown that in the event of another major visitation of plague, Southwark would have some degree of immunity because the Thames would act like a moat. This belief was rather naïve. When the serious outbreak occurred in 1665, it once more spread with terrifying rapidity and mass burial pits had to be dug once more. Large numbers of fires were lit around the pits in the belief that sulphurous and nitrous particles in the coal had a purifying effect. When these fires were clearly achieving very little, people resorted to age-old 'preventatives' such as garlic, vinegar and various herbs. Quack doctors produced any manner of antidotes. They may not have worked but they gave hope and the quacks themselves became rich as a result.

10

Hospitals & Bankside Buildings

A number of notable buildings on Bankside, such as the Globe, Tate Modern and Southwark Cathedral have been discussed in other chapters. This chapter will look at a selection of well-known and lesser-known buildings on and around Bankside. There are a number of listed buildings in the area including Southwark Cathedral, the remains of Winchester Palace, the Hop Exchange, the former St Thomas's church on St Thomas Street, and Guy's Hospital main building. In addition there are listed monuments and memorials that stand independently in public spaces such as the War Memorial on Borough High Street and the statue of Thomas Guy in the entrance courtyard to Guy's Hospital. There are also numerous listed street artefacts, notably the cannon bollards in the cathedral area and a red K2 telephone kiosk in St Thomas Street.

We have already noted how Southwark was once a residential area for a number of ecclesiastical houses and mansions before it established a reputation for its brothels and bear-baiting. It was the home to the Bishops of Winchester and Rochester, the Abbots of Hyde, Beaulieu, Battle and Waverley and the Priors of Christ Church, Lewes and St Swithun's, and on Tooley Street was the residence of the Warenne Earls of Surrey.

Within a short walking distance along Bankside are two medieval buildings. To the west of the medieval priory, which became Southwark

Cathedral, are the remains of Winchester Palace. Winchester Palace was the London residence of the Bishops of Winchester from the twelfth century until the Civil War of the 1640s. Southwark was the largest town in the old diocese of Winchester (Winchester being the old Saxon capital), and the Bishop, who was very powerful, needed to be in London on royal or administrative state business. In fact most of the holders of the Diocese of Winchester from the beginning of the fourteenth century until the mid-sixteenth century held high offices of state. Eight of them were Chancellors and their London residence became a place of importance. The land became known as the Bishop of Winchester's (or later the Clink) Liberty.

Winchester Palace was built by Walter Giffard, Bishop of Winchester, on land held by the Prior of Bermondsey, which was leased for a payment of eight pounds a year. In the sixteenth century John Stow mentions the palace as being 'a very fair house, well repaired, with a large wharf and landing-place, called the Bishop of Winchester's Stairs'. It was, in fact, a stately palace, with gardens, fountains, fish ponds, and an extensive park, long known as Southwark Park, which reached back in the direction of Lambeth, and which is still kept in remembrance by Park Street. It is unlikely that any twelfth-century work now remains, but portions of the fourteenth-century Great Hall can be seen on the south side of Clink Street. As early as 1174 an agreement was made between the Bishop and the Prior and canons of St Mary Overie Priory, which allowed the canons to use the quay or dock on the river between the priory and Winchester House. The Bishop was allowed free access to his residence by road from London Bridge.

In 1238 Simon de Montfort stayed there. The Great Chamber was the scene of a ceremonial presentation in 1341 when the Great Seal was presented to the new Chancellor, Sir Robert Pawing, by King Edward III in the presence of Queen Isabella and the magnates of the realm. The enlargement of the hall, and the building of the great rose window in the east end, dates from the middle of the fourteenth century. Henry Yevele, a master craftsman, began work on the rebuilding of Westminster Hall in 1394, and it is possible that he was also responsible for the design of the Great Hall of Winchester Palace.

Winchester Palace consisted of the Great Hall, a range of domestic buildings to the west and a range of buildings on the east side of the courtyard. Further east were the privy garden, tennis court and bowling alley bounded by St Saviour's Dock. The Great Hall, approximately 80 feet long, 36 feet wide and 42 feet high, was the most prominent feature of the palace.

By the early sixteenth century Winchester House began to fall into disrepair. In 1528 Richard Fox, the then Bishop, wrote to the Lord Treasurer asking to be excused the non-payment of a debt because he had 'been at great charge in repairing his ruinous houses in Southwark'. In 1554 insurgents under Sir Thomas Wyatt entered Southwark in an attempted rebellion against the government of Queen Mary I (r. 1553–58). Wyatt issued a proclamation that no soldier of his should take anything without paying for it but some of the rebels attacked the Bishop of Winchester's house, destroying many of his goods, and all his books.

Notable visitors to the palace included Queen Elizabeth I, who dined there in 1577, and the Swedish envoy, John, Duke of Finland, who came to solicit the hand of Queen Elizabeth for his elder brother, Eric, the son and heir of the King of Sweden. One of the last big ceremonial events to take place was the marriage feast of Lord Hay and Lucy, the daughter of the 9th Earl of Northumberland in 1617. Lancelot Andrewes (1555–1626), who oversaw the translation of the King James Version of the Bible, was the last bishop to use Winchester House.

The small and obscure prison of the Bishops of Winchester, the Clink, became a synonym for all prisons. In 1632 it was described as lying under the mansion house of the bishop. It was probably below high-water level and lay between the river on the north and the common sewer on the west and can, at best, be described as uncomfortably damp. It was used for victims of sixteenth-century religious persecutions. In 1555 John Rogers and William Hooper were sent there and later burned at the stake at Smithfield for heresy. It is likely that the Clink fell into disuse after the sale of Winchester House and its grounds in 1649. In 1720 English historian John Strype (1643–1737) described the prison as 'of late years [and] of little or no account'.

At the outbreak of Civil War in 1642 the House of Lords agreed that the house should be turned into a prison for Royalists and Thomas Davenish was appointed keeper. We are given some idea of the properties around the palace when in 1649 the trustees for the sale of episcopal lands sold the whole property to Thomas Walker of Camberwell for over £4,000. The land included 'wharfes and wharfage at St Mary Overie Dock ... buildings, gardens and yards ... and the kitchen Garden Wall of the said manor house and the tenements lands and garden and all the Cottages or tenements anciently called the Pond Garden alias Pikeyard and now commonly called the Clink Garden ... together with a gatehouse leading from Stewes Bank towards the Burrough of Southwark'.

At the Restoration in 1660 the Bishop of Winchester regained possession of Winchester House and the Liberty, but the process of disintegration had gone too far. Consequently in 1662 the Bishop obtained a private Act of Parliament to enable him 'to lease out the tenements now built upon the site of his mansion house in ... Southwark'. The palace was mostly destroyed by fire in 1814, which made part of the Great Hall and the west gable end with its rose window more visible.

In 1941 German incendiary bombs fell on the flour warehouse at the south-west corner of the junction of Clink Street and Stoney Street and completely gutted it. The wall of the fourteenth-century Great Hall and the rose window, which was first restored in 1972, are all that remain above ground today. Winchester Square, once the courtyard of Winchester House, is now effectively a service area to Palace House, overlooking the dock. It is a Scheduled Ancient Monument managed by English Heritage.

At the eastern end of Southwark Street stands the Hop Exchange, which was built about 1865 and designed by R. H. Moore. This is a large and magnificent range of buildings, several floors high. An essential ingredient in the making of beer was the hop imported from the Continent until around 1400 and then grown in England from the sixteenth century. The major hop-growing counties were Kent, Sussex, Hampshire, Hereford and Worcestershire. The hops that were harvested from farms in Kent were brought by railway to London Bridge Station, or by boat up the River Thames and stored in the many warehouses in the Borough area, which was the centre of London's brewing industry from the seventeenth century.

Hop picking was done by hand until the 1930s and was a traditional summer holiday occupation for many Londoners. Hops were subject to excise duty from 1710 to 1862 and were marketed through special exchanges and warehouses, the most impressive of which was the Hop Exchange on Southwark Street, with its large dealing floor and three galleries of offices below. The Hop Exchange provided a single market centre for dealers in hops and a glass roof allowed business on the trading floor of the Great Hall to be conducted under natural light. A fire in 1920 led to the top two floors being removed, and the Hop Exchange was then converted into offices.

The Hop Cellars, which were reputed to be part of the notorious Clink prison, were situated beneath the Hop Exchange, covering an underground area of nearly one acre. It was acknowledged to be one of the finest and largest private cellars in the country. The J. Lyons Company, which also provided the 'Joe Lyons' Corner Houses and teashops, moved from earlier premises in Regent Street to the Hop Exchange in 1903. The Hop Cellars provided storage for all of the company's wines, spirits, ports and sherries, which were shipped in casks and bottled by the Hop Cellars' staff. Although Lyons used the cellars from 1903 until 1972, they did not own the Hop Exchange until 1944 when they bought the entire freehold of the building. By the 1960s the upkeep was becoming too great and it was decided to restore the front of the building to its original height and form, together with the Exchange Hall, and to replace the offices with new ones. The Lyons business eventually outgrew their premises and moved to Greenford in 1972.

151

The building has been faithfully restored and stands as a unique surviving example of a premises that was once so important in the commercial life of London in the nineteenth century. In 2004 Southwark Council nominated the building for inclusion in the blue plaque scheme, but it was turned down. The Hop Exchange building is now used as a venue for receptions, dinners, exhibitions and fashion shows.

For centuries almshouses have provided charitable housing for older people. They are generally maintained by a charity or the trustees of a bequest. The area of Bankside has had, and still has, a number of almshouses.

The Hopton's Almshouses on Hopton Street were built in 1752 with the assistance of trustees appointed under the will of Charles Hopton. Charles Hopton was born around 1654 and admitted in his infancy to the freedom of the Fishmongers' Company. Charles lived in Golden Square, Westminster, in 1697, and from 1711 until his death in 1731 he lived on the north side of Petty France in the parish of St Margaret, Westminster. Despite his contribution to the building of the almshouses, he does not seem to have lived in Southwark. However, in 1706 he became a copyholder of land near the Pudding Mill, the site of a watermill, which stood near the river bank on Bankside.

There is no record of Hopton marrying and when he died he left much of his property variously to his cousin Thomas Jordan, friends and charities, and the remainder of his property to his sister, Elizabeth. After her death in 1793 the property was then left to trustees for the establishment of almshouses in Christ Church. At the first committee meeting, held on 10 July 1752, twenty-six 'poor decayed men' of the parish were chosen to occupy the houses. Almsmen were allowed to marry but the original rules prevented children of the almsmen becoming chargeable to Christ Church parish. The almsmen, which included gardeners, watermen and fishermen, were each also to receive a 'chaldron' (around 28 cwt.) of coals and a payment of not less than £6 a year.

Today the complex includes two garden squares with centre lawns and roses, edged with shrubs. Outside the gates is a drinking fountain and cattle trough. The almshouses were rebuilt and modernised in 1988 and are owned by the Anchor Trust. They are still used for housing and are made available for men and their wives from the Southwark area.

In Deadman's Place (now Thrale Street) there were almshouses for sixteen poor persons. They were founded in 1584 by Thomas Cure, and called Cure's College. Thomas Cure was saddler to Edward VI, Queen Mary, and Queen Elizabeth I, and was also Member of Parliament for the borough of Southwark. Another group of almshouses was built close by in Soap Yard (near to Park Street) and endowed by the retired actor Edward Alleyn. Alleyn directed in his will (1626) that his executors should, within two years of his death, erect ten almshouses for five poor men and five poor women. The almshouses were built on part of an enclosure called the Soap Yard belonging to the College of the Poor. The College of the Poor was founded in 1584, and was largely endowed. These almshouses provided a home for sixteen poor persons, one of whom was to act as warden, and prayers were to be read daily. In 1717 Edward Edwards left a gift in his will that included land to be used for a charity school and almshouses, as well as an endowment for Christmas Day distribution of beef and beer. The land was bought in 1752 on what is now Burrell Street where forty almshouses were built and later rebuilt in 1895. Another benefactor was John Walter, who left money for the building of the Draper's almshouses, which were relocated in 1819 to Glasshill Street.

In 1762 the Quakers, or Society of Friends, took a lease on some land on the west side of Redcross Way. They already owned a burial ground in this area but the new lease was for the building of a Meeting House. The Meeting House was enlarged in 1799 and continued in use until 1860, when the whole site was sold to the Metropolitan Board of Works as a result of the formation of Southwark Street. However, part of the land was bought and laid out as a garden in 1887 by Julie, Countess of Ducie, and others at the suggestion of Octavia Hill.

Many of the back streets of Bankside were overcrowded and packed with factories and slum dwellings. The social reformer and co-founder of the National Trust Octavia Hill (1838–1912) established Redcross

Garden in 1887 as an 'open air sitting room for the tired inhabitants of Southwark'. She went on to build six neighbouring model dwelling cottages in order to improve housing for the working poor, alongside a community hall. Redcross Garden was laid out on the site of a derelict paper factory and a hop warehouse. The Redcross Cottages were designed by Elijah Hoole. Octavia advocated small-scale high-quality homes, which provided an alternative to the cramped, impersonal tenements that had been built across the road. The cottages are now owned and managed by Octavia Housing and Care, a housing association.

Also in Redcross Way are the Cromwell Buildings, a five-storey balconied tenement block built by the Improved Industrial Dwellings Corporation. They are notable as the oldest model development remaining in the area, built in 1864 as one of the earliest housing improvement projects in the Borough.

Attempts to improve the lot of working-class families were developed on Blackfriars Road, which had, by 1870, along with the surrounding area been overwhelmingly urban for more than fifty years. The population was at its peak and the population density was increasing as housing gave way to new railways from London Bridge to Charing Cross and Canon Street. With growing urbanisation the quality of housing fell and the area had one of the worse records for unsanitary conditions and mortality rates. George Peabody was an American businessman who had established a business in London in 1837. Over a period of four years Peabody gave £350,000, 'To ameliorate the condition of the poor ... and to promote their comfort and happiness' by the erection of model tenements. In London a number of these tenements, known as Peabody Buildings, still serve their original purpose of housing working-class families. Peabody Square, Blackfriars Road, was not the first example of purpose-built model dwellings built on a partly philanthropic basis, but it was certainly the largest.

Anyone visiting the Globe Theatre might spot a nearby tall, white house with a plaque above the door. 49 Bankside is tucked between the Globe Theatre and Tate Modern and is variously known as 'Wren's

House', Cardinal's Wharf, or, thanks to Gillian Tindall's book, *The House by the Thames* (2007). The plaque above the door describes the house as the place where Wren lived but this is something of a misnomer, as Wren never actually lived there. The association with Christopher Wren and the house is based on the notion that he stayed at 49 Bankside to chart the progress of St Paul's on the other side of the river. However, it was in fact from another house a few yards further west that he watched his great dome develop. There is also another (incorrect) claim that in 1502 Catherine, Infanta of Castile and Aragon and later first queen of Henry VIII, took shelter there on her first landing in London.

Tindall's book charts the history of the house, which was built in 1710 (making Wren's stay during the construction of St Paul's highly unlikely), the people that lived in it and the immediate neighbourhood. Its residents have been, in the main, hard-working families, notably those using their success as coal and iron merchants to climb up the social scale. The site on which the house stands has history within its foundations. It was built 'in the footprint of an Elizabethan house' and also an inn called the Cardinal's Hat, dating from around 1570, whose vaulted Tudor cellars survive as the present house's dark and cavernous basement. The Cardinal's Hat appears to have started life in the 1570s as a brothel.

By the early eighteenth century the neighbourhood was on the up, and the old timber-framed houses of Bankside were gradually being replaced by sturdy brick ones. Tindall has not been able to identify the first owner of the brick and timber house that now stands on the site, but she has established a thorough record of the owners and occupants from about 1750 to the present. Edward Sells was the first known occupant, taking possession some time around the middle of the eighteenth century, as London was undergoing a dramatic change. He was a waterman, ferrying people across the Thames from the City to the south bank. Sells entered the coal business, living and working at the house on Bankside, and the family did well for generations, buying and selling shiploads of coal and buying a number of houses along the river.

The arrival of the railways in the 1860s made Bankside a dirtier and less desirable place to live, and the Sells family sold up to a scrap iron merchant called Moss Isaacs. The 'cycle started all over again', with his descendants in turn moving to more prosperous places. By 1939 the house was occupied by film director, Robert Stevenson (who had a prolific career as a director, making a number of Disney films later in his life). An 'eccentric' civil servant called Sir William Montagu-Pollock was the next person to own the house and then the Swedish writer Axel Munthe. In the Second World War the house was lucky to escape serious bomb damage.

It was Munthe's son Malcolm who lived there in 1945, described by Tindall as a fantasist and a dreamer. He was responsible for putting up the Wren plaque and also let it to a family until the 1970s, after which the house fell into disrepair and was used as a squat. During the 1980s Malcolm's son Guy – known as an 'escort' of Princess Margaret, took an interest in the house and restored it. Today the house continues as it started in 1710 as a privately owned dwelling and is not open to the public.

The workhouse for the area of St George the Martyr was on the north side of Mint Street in Southwark, originally dating from 1729 although a new building on the same site was erected in 1782. By 1869 it had been taken over by St Saviour's Poor Law Union. It was a cramped premises housing males at the west end and females at the east. The building was subject to a critical review by the medical journal *The Lancet*, which revealed a catalogue of appalling conditions. This led to the passing of the Metropolitan Poor Act in 1867, which introduced major changes in the provision of care for London's sick poor and also resulted in the creation of the Metropolitan Asylums Board. The Mint Street site continued in use until 1920 but all the buildings have since been demolished.

Various schools that have been set up over the centuries add to the wealth of interesting buildings that populate the area. In 1559 the wardens of St Saviour's church obtained Letters Patent granting a lease for sixty years of the rectory on condition that they erect a grammar school for the parish within two years. Two years later the vestry paid £40 to Mathew Smyth for the purchase of St Saviour's Grammar School. This was part of the house known as the Green Dragon, which gave its name to Green Dragon Court. It had previously been known as Cobham's Inn and had belonged to Joan, Lady Cobham, who at her death in 1370 had left legacies to St Thomas's Hospital and to St Mary Overie Priory. In 1676 the building in Green Dragon Court was destroyed in the Great Fire of Southwark but a new building was constructed on the same site. The enlargement of Borough Market in 1839 meant that the school site was required, so another building was constructed in Sumner Street in 1839. In 1896 St Saviour's Grammar School agreed to amalgamation with St Olave's. The Sumner Street building was used for a church day school for St Peter's parish.

In 1560 Henry Leeke, a Southwark brewer, left a will, part of which granted £8 a year towards the founding and maintenance of a new free school. The following year the churchwardens of St Olave's were ordered to receive Leeke's legacy and 'prepare' a schoolmaster by Michaelmas Day. It was in 1571 that St Olave's Grammar School was established in Tooley Street and the charter stipulated that the school be called 'The Free Grammar School of Queen Elizabeth of the Parishioners of the Parish of Saint Olave in the County of Surrey'. The school survived the Great Fire of Southwark, although a major renovation and extension was undertaken in 1676. In 1829 the school had to move because the site was needed for the approach to the new London Bridge. Although a new building was erected in Bermondsey Street in 1834 this building did not last long due to the rapid expansion of the railways. Another building was erected on the same site in 1894.

In St Saviour's parish a charity school stood at the corner of Redcross Street and Union Street, on a site which had been a burial ground – supposedly the 'Single Women's Burying Ground'. In 1674 twenty children were educated here through the benefaction of Mrs Elizabeth Newcomen, who is commemorated by a memorial in Southwark Cathedral. A school for boys and girls was established in Zoar Street in

1687 supported by voluntary contributions. It was established for forty children, raised to fifty, and in 1781 to 200.

The Surrey Institution, although built in 1778 as the Rotunda, was an organisation devoted to scientific education and research founded by private subscription in 1807. The name was determined by the use of a property on Blackfriars Road, then part of the county of Surrey. The building had been the final home of the Leverian Museum, housing the collection of Sir Ashton Lever, but had fallen into disrepair. It was renovated to include a large lecture hall capable of accommodating 500 people and a galleried library which opened on 1 May 1808. However, the institution only had a short life and was dissolved in 1823. Thereafter it was used for a variety of entertainment ventures until 1855.

Schools, before the late nineteenth century, had relied largely on charity and were consequently under resourced. The Elementary Education Act of 1870 was the first to provide education for the population of England and Wales. It created elected school boards, which had power to build and run schools where there were insufficient voluntary school places; they could also compel attendance. The School Board for London (SBL – better known as the London School Board) was an institution of local government and the first directly elected body covering the whole of London. Between 1870 and 1904, the SBL was the single largest educational provider in London. In north Southwark around seven schools were built providing places for five thousand children.

The Victorians also recognised that protecting the riverbank along Bankside from flooding was a concern and a safe wall was essential for both businesses and property. The very busy stretch between Blackfrairs Bridge and London Bridge was often congested with traffic. In 1862 a Parliamentary Commission examined plans for the embanking of the River Thames on the Surrey side.

Realising the need to protect against flooding, the enquiry asked Samuel Pegg, who lived at Bankside and was one of the Board of Guardians, about the best plan for embanking the Bankside part of the river, and for forming a roadway – 'all to be done with the least interference to property'. In 1845 the Clink Commission had raised Bankside from Bank End (the end nearest to London Bridge) to the end of Holland Street near Falcon Dock. Pegg said that the embankment was not raised high enough because of the 'great opposition from the various wharfingers'. He acknowledged that there had been flooding which had gone over the present embankment costing the Clink Commission about £3,600; the wharfingers had to pay their own expenses. The flooding had caused much distress and, Pegg added, 'it had brought a great many extra paupers into the workhouse from the overflowing of Bankside and the low lying districts of St Saviour' parish'. The roadway along Bankside, which was too narrow, was very busy with local traffic, and stoppages were frequent. Pegg noted that 'if we could get the wharfingers to raise their premises it would be a benefit, and it would prevent the water coming in that district' particularly the area around 'Falcon Dock near Pellatt's Gllass House'. An indication of the activity along the Bankside front can was reflected in the names of businesses such as Mr Brooks Wharf, Mr Kilvington's Wharf, Lancaster & Co. Wharf, Bradley's Foundry, Mr Browning's Timber Yard, Mr Astell's Timber Yard and Honduras Wharf.

The Commission also revealed the problems of living along the riverfront at Bankside, which was fraught with dampness and the problems associated with this. Arising out of the evidence regarding the embankment and the widening of the narrow road along Bankside it was stated that 'it is a general complaint at Bankside that the premises and cellars become damp by percolation' because the 'wharf wall is leaky'. Pegg commented, 'I wanted my brother to live in one of the houses on Bankside and his argument was that it was so very damp that the family would have a doctor in the house three parts of the year.'

Another witness who was called to give an expert opinion was J. Howe, surveyor to St Saviour's District Board of Works. He was asked to comment upon the condition of the premises on Bankside: 'I am sure they are damp … but I think that a great deal of that damp arises from the bottom.' He said that a great deal of the water 'percolates through the gravel from the bottom and not from the wall … The walls are not deep enough to prevent the water getting under the foundations and saturating the cellars of the houses. When the water flowed over the river bank, those cellars were filled up to the top.'

Such were the joys of living along the riverfront in Victorian Bankside.

St Thomas's Hospital was named after Thomas Becket, which suggests it may have been founded after 1173 when Becket was canonised. It was originally run by a mixed order of Augustinian monks and nuns, dedicated to Thomas Becket, and provided shelter and treatment for the poor, sick, and homeless. In the early thirteenth century the priory was destroyed by fire and the hospital was rebuilt on a new site on the east side of Borough High Street. At the time of the Black Death in the 1340s the hospital suffered like almost every English religious house. The mortality amongst the brethren had left no one fit to rule the place.

In the fifteenth century, Sir Richard ('Dick') Whittington (c. 1354–1423), Lord Mayor and MP, endowed a laying-in ward for the hospital for unmarried mothers. It was in the grounds of the hospital that the first complete translation of the Bible into English was made. In 1533, Thomas Cromwell and Sir Thomas More suggested that the Scriptures should be translated into 'the vulgar tongue'. Miles Coverdale made the translation and James Nicholson printed the Bible from premises in St Thomas's.

During the 1530s when religious houses were under threat of dissolution and reasons were being sought to justify closing them down, a complaint was made by certain parishioners of St Thomas's Hospital in 1536. It was against the master and brethren of the hospital, accusing them of maintaining improper characters within the precincts, refusing charitable relief to those in sickness, and even to those willing to pay. With regard to the services in the church they complained that the usual three or four sermons in Lent had not been given, they had often scant two masses in a day, and they had been forced sometimes to seek a priest about the Borough to sing high mass. The institution fell victim to the Reformation and was dissolved in 1539. Its members at this time consisted of a master and six brethren, and three lay sisters who made forty beds for poor infirm people. The hospital was reopened in 1551 and rededicated to Thomas the Apostle as Becket had been decanonised. It was reopened through the efforts of the City of London, who obtained the grant of the site and a charter from Edward VI (r. 1547–53) and has remained open ever since.

In December 1664 John Evelyn recorded how part of St Thomas's was used as a military hospital: 'We delivered the Privy Council letters to the Governors of St Thomas's Hospital, in Southwark, that a moiety [part] of the house should be reserved for such sick and wounded as should from time to time be sent from the Fleet during the war.' A great deal of damage was done to the property in 1676 as a result of the fire of Southwark. By the end of the seventeenth century the hospital and church were largely rebuilt through the generosity of merchant banker Sir Robert Clayton (1629–1707). Clayton, who was president of the hospital and a former Lord Mayor of the City of London, employed Thomas Cartwright (Master Mason to Christopher Wren) as architect.

In the final months of the hospital Florence Nightingale (1820–1910) became involved with St Thomas's, setting up on this site her famous nursing school. It was partly on her advice that the hospital agreed to move to a new site. The hospital left Southwark in 1862 when the site was compulsorily purchased to make way for construction of the Charing Cross Railway viaduct from London Bridge Station. The hospital is now located at Westminster Bridge Road. Many parts of the old hospital survive on the north side of St Thomas Street including the old parish church (1704), the Old Operating Theatre (now a museum), and the row of Georgian houses near Joiner Street.

Sir Thomas Guy (1644–1724), a governor of St Thomas's, founded Guy's Hospital in 1721 as a place to treat 'incurables' discharged from St Thomas's. The original buildings comprised a courtyard facing St Thomas Street, and included a hall on the east side and on the west side the Chapel, Matron's House and Surgeon's House. Guy was born in Southwark as the son of a wharf owner and coal-dealer. In 1668 he began his own bookstore in Lombard Street selling Bibles imported from the Netherlands. Guy gained a reputation as a miser, largely because a rival bookseller, John Dunton, accused him of paying low wages and refusing to help the charities. Guy was in fact a stock speculator who had invested in government securities and bought shares in the South Sea Company. In 1720 he sold his stock at a huge profit in what was known as the South Sea Bubble and amassed a large fortune.

When Thomas Guy died in 1724 he left the residue of his estate to trustees who were instructed 'to finish and fit up the two new squares of building in Southwark ... some time since begun, and intended for an Hospital for reception of ... four hundred poor persons or upwards, labouring under any distempers, infirmities, or disorders, thought capable of relief by physick or surgery'. Guy also suggested that lunatics not exceeding twenty in number might be admitted to the hospital. Thomas Guy laid the first stone and lived just long enough to see the beginnings of his hospital, which was opened a year after his death in 1725 with one hundred beds and a staff of fifty-one. Guy was reburied in the new hospital chapel in 1780. Despite substantial bomb damage during the Second World War, the original eighteenth-century chapel remains intact, including the tomb and statue of Thomas Guy.

When prison reformer John Howard (1726–90) visited the hospital in 1780, bugs were a particular problem. Nonetheless he praised the ventilation, sanitation, iron bedsteads and the new vapour baths. Extensions to the hospital were made over the years and more ground on the north-west side of the hospital was acquired from St Thomas's in 1756. The Maze Pond estate, south of the hospital, was bought in 1806 and further land was acquired in 1816 and 1833. On a less medical note but nonetheless a historical one, staff at Guy's founded the Guy's Hospital Football Club in 1843. A number of clubs have claimed to be the first and therefore the oldest football club but Guy's claim to this distinguished record is credited in the *Guinness Book of Records*.

Many eminent physicians and personalities are associated with the institution, such as the prominent pathologist Thomas Hodgkin (1798–1866), who discovered Hodgkin's Disease as well as bringing the stethoscope from Paris to the UK. He was a contemporary of Thomas

Addison (1793–1860) and Richard Bright (1789–1858), both of whom served at Guy's. Addison, who joined Guy's in 1817, is regarded as one of the 'great men' of the hospital. He was promoted to assistant physician on 14 January 1824 and in 1837 he became a full physician at Guy's. Addison was a brilliant lecturer who attracted a large number of medical students to his lectures. Richard Bright was an early pioneer in the research of kidney disease. He first joined Guy's in 1813 before returning to Edinburgh to be granted his medical doctorate. He came back to Guy's during the 1820s to teach, practise and research medicine.

More sensationally, physician William Gull (1816–90), who treated the Prince of Wales for typhoid in 1871, was the first to use the term 'anorexia nervosa' and was also a suspect for Jack the Ripper. He was a Governor of Guy's and served as one of the Physicians-in-Ordinary to Queen Victoria. In 1842 Gull was appointed to teach at Guy's Hospital, and the Treasurer gave him a small house in King Street. The following year he was appointed Medical Superintendent of the wards for lunatics, and it was largely due to his influence that these cases shortly ceased to be treated at the hospital, and the wards were converted from this use. In 1871, as Physician-in-Ordinary to the Prince of Wales, Gull treated the Prince during an attack of typhoid fever. The earliest known allegation that links the Whitechapel murders with a prominent London physician was in two articles published by a number of US newspapers between 1895 and 1897. However, it was in the 1970s with the expanding Ripperology industry and the naming of almost any known figure around East London during the 1880s that William Gull's name was offered as a likely candidate to be Jack the Ripper. None of these theories have been established as historical truth.

The poet John Keats (1795–1821) was a medical student at Guy's from 1814, but one year later, he abandoned the profession of medicine for poetry. A blue plaque in St Thomas Street records his time at Guy's.

Other famous physicians who worked at Guy's include Sir Alexander Fleming (1881–1955), best known for his discovery of penicillin;

Sir Frederick Gowland Hopkins (1861–1947 Cambridge), who was awarded the Nobel Prize in 1929 for the discovery of vitamins; John Hilton (1804–78), who was president of the Royal College of Surgeons and surgeon-extraordinary to Queen Victoria, he was considered to be the greatest anatomist of his time; Philip Henry Pye-Smith (1839–1914), a physician and medical scientist whose interest was physiology, specialising in skin diseases; Iain West (1944–2001), a forensic pathologist who was involved in examining numerous deaths, including those of Robert Maxwell, TV presenter Jill Dando and the British police officer Yvonne Fletcher, who was shot from the Libyan embassy in 1984.

In 1974, the hospital added the thirty-four-storey Guy's Tower (143 metres high – 469 feet), making it the tallest hospital building in the world. Following the merger of Guy's and St Thomas' Hospitals into one Trust, Accident and Emergency Services were consolidated at St Thomas' in 1990 (the omission of the possessive 's' from St Thomas's is fairly recent. The hospital trust claims that is grammatically correct, as there are two men called St Thomas linked to the hospital's history: Thomas Becket and Thomas the Apostle). Today over 8,000 staff work in Guy's Hospital and St Thomas' Hospital. They are two of the oldest teaching hospitals. One of the services that the trust provides is dental care (in 1799 Guy's became the first London hospital to appoint a dental surgeon) looking after over 120,000 patients a year.

On the outskirts of the Borough on old Kent Street was a hospital for lepers. John Stow writes of it as the Loke or Lazar-house for leprous persons. No precise date is known for its foundation but it was probably of twelfth-century origin, like so many similar establishments outside English towns. Reference to it is made in the time of Edward II (r. 1307–27) when it had evidently been for some time endowed. From 1315 to 1328 protection was granted for the master and brethren of the hospital, and their men and lands, but by 1328 it was stated that the brethren had no sufficient livelihood unless they were 'succoured by the faithful'. This was one of the four leper hospitals built outside

London, for the injunctions against lepers entering the city were very stringent. Although leprosy was almost extinct in England by the beginning of the seventeenth century, the memory of the lepers who used to wander in the neighbouring fields was preserved in their name of Lock Fields until they were built over in the nineteenth century. An Act of Parliament in 1565 directed that Kent Street should be paved with hard stone as far as the Lock Hospital.

11

Inns & Taverns

Bankside, the Borough and Southwark have had many inns and taverns which have played a significant historical role in this most historic of districts. Stow (1525–1605), in his great *Survey of London*, wrote: 'From thence (the Marshalsea) towards London Bridge, on the same side be many fair inns for receipt of travellers, by these signs: the *Spurre, Christopher, Bull, Queen's Head, Tabard, George, Hart, King's Head.*' Although many of them are now forgotten, others have become immortalised through their mention in literature even if the buildings themselves are long gone. This area has had its ups and downs. It is now very much on the up and while many of its famous hostelries have vanished without trace, others are remembered in street names. Again, because the area is being regenerated and its riverside location has such pulling power, new drinking places are appearing appropriate to the very different conditions of the twenty-first century. Those who use them are generally well heeled and have leisure and pleasure in mind. Historically, the drinking places of Bankside were notorious as the resorts of those seeking pleasure often of a fairly debauched sort. They would, however, have been much more workaday places than today's glitzy bars and bistros and have very little else in common with them.

Close to the foot of London Bridge and prominent for that reason was a pub called The Bear-at-the-Bridge-Foot. This apparently opened for business in 1319, although that date cannot be advanced with certainty. In a poem printed in 1691 it is described as The Bear, 'which we soon understood was the first house in Southwark built after the flood'. Perhaps we should stick with 1319 because there is a record that in that year that one Thomas Drinkwater erected an inn at the bridge-foot. It was then leased and the lessee agreed to buy all his wines from Drinkwater, who, in return, would provide such things as drinking vessels, curtains and cloths. It features in the diaries of Samuel Pepys as one of his many watering holes. He used it as his base when he made visits to Southwark Fair. Pepys, not to put too fine a point on it, was quite extraordinarily randy. If he espied almost any female of childbearing age, he wanted to grope her and frequently did. At the Bear he met the beautiful young Frances Stuart. He was transported with lust but was aware that he needed to tread carefully because she was a mistress of Charles II. If that was not bad enough, the Dukes of York and Richmond were patiently waiting in the wings, eager to take Frances on once Charles had had his fill of her. For once, Pepys's lust went unrequited. Pepys also mentions a Frances Browne, who was the wife of the landlord and who in February 1667 committed suicide by throwing herself in the Thames. An entry in his diary for 14 September 1665 can be taken as typical:

> I away back again to the Beare at the Bridge foot, being full of wind and out of order, and there called for a biscuit and a piece of cheese and gill of sacke, being forced to walk over the Bridge ... and the plague being all thereabouts.

A piece of doggerel concerning the Bear dates from the 1650s:

> Farewell Bridge Foot and Bear there-by
> And those bald pates that stand so high.
> We wish it from our very souls
> That other heads were on those poles.

In the middle of the seventeenth century the Bear had a landlord called Colonel Cornelius Cooke who was an officer in Cromwell's New Model

Army. Charles II, often called 'The Merry Monarch', was effusively welcomed at the Restoration. This had little to do with whether he would be any great shakes as a Head of State. The reason that he was welcomed back was because of his libertarian views and practices. These were counterpoised by the pervasive, pious and self-righteous practices of the Puritans who, for a decade or more, had been able to dictate and to a significant extent enforce what they decided was morally correct behaviour. Ordinary folk had had enough of po-faced Puritanism and, perhaps understandably, they launched into something approaching an orgy of hedonistic self-indulgence. At one time there were archery butts in the grounds of the Bear and these grounds contained the landing stage for boats which plied to and from Greenwich and Gravesend. In 1633 an order was issued requiring the backdoors to all taverns to be closed. This is because fugitives used them as escape routes from the long arm of the law. But the Bear was exempt because it housed the landing place of the river craft. One of the places where pleasures were to be had was the Bear and one of the pleasure-seekers was William Wycherley (c. 1640–1716), the dramatist. To start things swinging, the well-to-do patrons drank canary, a sweet wine. It is said that some of the ladies used to remove their drawers, whereupon their swains used to drink the canary filtered through their loved ones' undergarments. Charles Dickens makes several references to the pub in *Oliver Twist*. The Bear was sacrificed on the altar of that modern bane of public houses – it was demolished for road widening around 1761.

Along what is now Borough High Street was the Boar's Head. This stood opposite the house in which John Harvard lived and was the property of Sir John Fastolfe. The first record of it is dated 1459. It went into terminal decline in 1720 and whatever was left of it was pulled down in 1830.

The White Hart was first mentioned in 1406, although it was older than that. It achieved fame by being the place Jack Cade made his base during the insurrection in 1450 named after him. He was at the head of an army of Kentishmen and men of Kent numbering between 20,000 and 45,000. They had fifteen complaints about oppression, injustice and misgovernment. It shows how far we need to go to ensure that those with power do not abuse it because many of these complaints have a resonance today. The insurgents were concerned about corruption in high places which meant that taxes were higher than they needed to be and were unjust and extortive, that those with money could obtain justice more easily and that people in power surrounded themselves with parasitical favourites. The rebellion was a failure and Cade was hunted down and killed. Shakespeare has a rebel clearly based on Cade in *Henry VI, Part 2*. He makes a speech which immortalises the inn where he had his temporary headquarters when he said, 'Hath my sword therefore broke through London gates, that you should leave at the White Hart in Southwark?' Cade was demonised by Shakespeare and other writers. Those in positions of power rarely like rebels. Shakespeare, a man of words, was well able to provide the kind of historical 'spin' which would be approved of by the rich and influential people who flocked to see his works.

> In the Borough there still remain some half dozen old inns, which have preserved their external features unchanged, and which have escaped alike the rage for public improvement and the encroachments of private speculation. Great, rambling, queer old places they are, with galleries, and passages, and staircases, wide enough and antiquated enough to furnish material for a hundred ghost stories.

This is from *The Pickwick Papers* by Charles Dickens and shows him applying his perceptive eye to the remaining inns of the High Street. His much-loved character Sam Weller arrives at a bustling White Hart just in time to prevent the elderly Rachael from marrying the rascal Jingle. The White Hart was demolished in 1889 by which time it was occupied by a railway company. For 'White Hart', some historians would substitute the 'George'.

It is to Dickens that we are indebted for this delightful and graphic description almost certainly of one or other of these inns:

The yard presented none of that bustle and activity which are the visual characteristics of a large coach inn. Three or four lumbering wagons, each with a pile of goods beneath its ample canopy, about the height of the second-floor of an ordinary house, were stowed away beneath a lofty roof which extended over one end of the yard ... A double tier of bedroom galleries, with old clumsy balustrades, ran round two sides of the straggling area, and a double row of bells to correspond, sheltered from the weather by a little sloping roof, hung over the door leading to the bar and the coffeeroom. Two or three gigs or chaise-carts were wheeled up under different little sheds or penthouses; only the occasional heavy tred of a carthorse, or rattling of a chain at the further end of the yard, announced to anybody who cared about the matter that the stable lay in that direction. When we add that a few boys in smock-frocks were lying asleep on heavy packages, woolpacks and other articles on heaps of straw, we have described as fully as need be the general appearance of the yard of the 'White Hart Inn', High Street, Borough.

Unquestionably the doyen of the district's pubs now is The George in Borough High Street. In fact it is the only survivor of the ancient inns of the Borough. It was originally called The George and Dragon, and the first reference to it comes in 1554 when it was the property of a Mr Colet who was MP for Southwark. In 1634 the landlord was reported for the heinous crime of selling drink during the time of divine service. John Taylor, 'The Water Poet', mentioned the wagoners who came from all over Surrey and Sussex and lodged at The George. The inn burned down in the Great Southwark Fire of 1676 and rebuilding took place quickly afterwards. Perhaps the greatest days of The George were when the coaching system developed from the seventeenth into the nineteenth centuries. It was the starting point and terminus for many regular stagecoach services and also for stage wagons which likewise ran to regular scheduled timetables. The longer-distance coaches mostly operated to towns on the south coast but there were also shorter routes such as that which Dr Johnson used when he went to visit his friends the Thrales at Streatham. Guy's Hospital secured the freehold in the 1840s which in turn was sold to the Great Northern Railway Company in 1873. They used it as a goods depot for road vehicles and a booking office. At that time, The George had the layout typical of old coaching inns with a central yard surrounded by three wings. Two of these were demolished in 1889 to leave the one seen today, which, again typical of its ilk, has open galleries giving access to the bedrooms. The George is mentioned by Dickens in *Little Dorrit*. Maggy refers to Little Dorrit's brother, Tip, who, she says, goes into the inn to write begging letters to Clennam. On display in the bar is a life insurance policy deposited by Charles Dickens, who left it as a pledge when he borrowed from the landlord. He never redeemed the pledge. The George is owned by the National Trust, a recognition of its historical importance.

If it still existed, the Tabard would probably give The George a run for its money in the fame stakes. It is not known when this hostelry opened its doors for the first time but there is a suggestion that it may have been as early as 1304. The Abbot of Hyde in Hampshire had a town house in the Borough and attached to it was an inn for travellers. It is likely that the Abbots of Hyde were cronies of the Bishops of Winchester, who had such a dominant presence in this neighbourhood.

The fame of the Tabard lies in its being chosen by Chaucer as the place where his immortal pilgrims mustered before setting out for Canterbury. The tomb and memory of Thomas Becket (1118–70) was the object of their reverence. Becket was an able and ambitious man who became a priest but, as with many others of that profession, showed more interest in secular matters. He met with considerable success as a soldier, a diplomat and in matters of state. However, it all changed when he was appointed Archbishop of Canterbury in 1162. It was as if he suddenly discovered God and he became a zealous upholder of the interests of the Church, not least against royal attempts to encroach on its power. These actions brought him into sharp conflict with Henry II. When the latter muttered a casual comment that he wished he could be rid of this turbulent priest, four knights within earshot took him at his word and promptly went to Canterbury and murdered Becket in the cathedral. Now, martyrs were great money-spinners for the Church and Becket was quickly canonised and a shrine made to his memory. Believers were then encouraged to make their way to this shrine, say their prayers there and part with good money in order to demonstrate the strength of their convictions. While the pilgrims rolled up in their thousands, the coffers of the Church were filling up with gratifying speed. It helped that no fewer than 400 miracles were ascribed to the revered remains of Becket.

Many pilgrims came from London and places north and tended to gather in Southwark. It made sense to travel as members of a party, not only to deter robbers along the route but to make a social event of it – after all, a pilgrimage could be fun as well a devotional gesture.

We do not know to what extent Chaucer was bringing together characters he had actually observed because some authorities claim that he was referring to an actual pilgrimage that took place in April 1388.

Chaucer is best known for his *Canterbury Tales* and especially for the Prologue. In writing about a group of pilgrims making their way to Canterbury, he reveals great insights into human nature. His pilgrims are a real cross-section of society, ranging from the nobleman to the ploughman. These are some of English literature's immortals. There is a brawny monk who loves nothing more than hunting, a learned, devout but poor parson, a louche pardoner selling surcease from sin at a price, a portly physician who waxed rich from tending those afflicted by pestilence, the buxom wife of Bath and many others. In fact one of Chaucer's most memorable characters is not a pilgrim at all but the host of the Tabard. He is reputed to be based on a landlord of this inn called Henry or 'Harry' Bailey.

The Tabard lived off its literary associations for a couple of centuries. For a brief time it changed its name to the Talbot, although there is some dispute that this ever happened. While the Tabard had heraldic and chivalrous associations, the Talbot was a large hunting dog which has now become extinct. It could be that Talbot was substituted for Tabard out of ignorance because it sounded similar. At the Dissolution of the Monasteries in the late 1530s, the Tabard was sold. A few years later a description was given of the interior of the inn:

On the ground-floor, looking on to the street, was a room called the 'darke parlour', a hall, and a general reception-room called 'the parlour'. On the first floor, above the parlour and the hall, were 'the middle chamber', 'the corner chamber' and 'Maister Hussye's chamber'. These had garrets above them. Other rooms were called 'the Entry Chamber' and 'the Newe Chamber', 'the Flower de Luce' and 'Mr Russell's chamber'.

The Tabard closed in 1875 and was demolished amidst a wave of protest that a building with such literary associations should be lost. However, it is likely that the original inn was demolished and rebuilt on the same site in 1628. This building was razed to the ground in the Southwark Fire of 1676. It was rebuilt again on the same site and apparently along the lines of its predecessors with the external galleries so characteristic of ancient inns. The building finally knocked down in 1873 or 1875 was, therefore, a bit like the hammer with five new heads and three new handles which was still the same hammer.

The Catherine Wheel stood close to the present Borough Tube Station and did a brisk trade in the seventeenth and eighteenth centuries as a staging point for regular wagon services and a place of refreshment for the wagoners. It was demolished about 1780.

In Lambeth Road there once stood the Dog and Duck. This was a place of ill-repute. It was a resort of low life and was adjacent to an area of open ground with several ponds. The patrons used to extract great pleasure from watching small hounds hunting out and killing ducks. This place became so notorious as a meeting place for criminals that the magistrates closed it down. The grounds contained a spring, the water of which was famed for its purgative qualities.

At the junction of Bankside and Bankend and at the southern end of Cannon Street Railway Bridge stands The Anchor. It is the proud boast of this pub that Shakespeare used it in between performances at the Globe Theatre just round the corner. Another playwright who quaffed a pot or two here was Christopher Marlowe (1564–93). Marlowe was a hardened toper, a brawler and generally something of a wide boy but he gained acclamation for his literary achievements. This building suffered severe fires in 1750 and 1876, being rebuilt on each occasion, but ironically is perhaps best known as the place from which in 1666 a horrified Samuel Pepys watched the Great Fire wreaking its destruction through the City on the opposite side of the river. Even at that distance, the heat of the conflagration could be felt and he was showered with sparks. He was in despair, hearing the roar of the fire, the crack of burning wood and masonry and the sound of buildings collapsing. Dr Johnson knew The Anchor well. He was very friendly with the Thrale family, who at that time owned the nearby brewery, and they allowed him a room there in which he could work away at the compiling of his dictionary. He was a naturally gregarious man and took time out from his labours to socialise in the pub and there he enjoyed the company of, among others, Oliver Goldsmith and David Garrick. For many years The Anchor was a basic pub catering for the dockers, carters and others who worked nearby, but its star has risen along with that of the immediate locality, and it is now something of a honeypot in what is a revived and gentrified district.

In the middle of the seventeenth century there was something of a crisis caused by a severe shortage of small change. Halfpennies and farthings in particular were in short supply. Small traders in particular needed these denominations and they took matters into their own hands by issuing tokens, particularly of those values. Those tokens issued by reputable business people circulate in their localities and were regarded as being as good as a coin of the realm. The government meanwhile thought it sensible to turn a blind eye. A number of publicans issued such tokens and they usually showed a fairly crude representation of the inn concerned and the name of the publican on the obverse side. The reverse was likely to show the name of the street and usually the initials of the issuer and perhaps his wife. One such inn was The Bear at the Bridge Foot. Two tokens exist and both show a bear with a chain on the obverse.

12

Literary & Theatrical Bankside

Southwark has a unique historic and literary heritage. It has associations with some of the greatest of literary figures, notably Chaucer, Shakespeare and Dickens. The area of Borough and Bankside with its trade, commerce and great medieval inns provided many literary settings. Its independence from the City made it a haven for 'undesirable' elements including playwrights and actors. It became the home of the Shakespearean Stage as well as the starting point for the pilgrims on their journey in Chaucer's *Canterbury Tales*. In addition it was also the inspiration for a number of Dickens's novels.

One has only to walk around the streets of Southwark to find in their names literary references. We encounter Chaucer Drive, Chaucer House, Geoffrey Chaucer School (renamed the Globe Academy) and the Chaucer ward area covering Bankside. There is the Charles Dickens Primary School, Charles Dickens public house, Copperfield Street, Quilp Street and Little Dorrit Court. St George the Martyr Church is also known as Little Dorrit's church because, in the novel, she was christened and married here.

Geoffrey Chaucer (*c.* 1343–1400) was born in London, although the exact date and location of his birth are not known. His famous work, *The Canterbury Tales*, is a collection of stories written in Middle English between 1387 and 1400. It is the story of a group of twenty-nine rumbustious pilgrims who come from all layers of society and tell stories to each other while they travel together on a journey from Southwark to the shrine of Saint Thomas Becket at Canterbury Cathedral. In 1170 Thomas Becket, Archbishop of Canterbury, was murdered and pilgrimages took place shortly after, encouraged by the Augustinian orders at both Southwark and Canterbury, as a retracing of Becket's last journey. An additional incentive for the pilgrimage was that the spirit of Becket was said to have performed miracles by healing the sick and giving sight to the blind.

When Chaucer started to write *The Canterbury Tales* over 200 years after the death of Becket, he was writing at a time when the pilgrimage had reached its height. Many pilgrimages had become associated with leisure rather than being a form of penance. In the sixteenth century the shrine of Thomas Becket was destroyed under Henry VIII and pilgrimages to Canterbury effectively came to an end.

In the Prologue to *The Canterbury Tales* the Tabard Inn (which stood next door to the present-day George Inn) is the place where the pilgrims assemble to embark upon their journey:

> In Southwark, at the Tabard, as I lay
> Ready to start upon my pilgrimage
> To Canterbury, full of devout homage,
> There came at nightfall to that hostelry
> Some nine and twenty in a company
> Of sundry persons who had chanced to fall
> In fellowship, and pilgrims were they all
> That toward Canterbury town would ride.
> The rooms and stables spacious were and wide,
> And well we there were eased, and of the best.
>
> ... In Southwark, at this noble hostelry
> Known as the Tabard Inn, hard by the Bell.
> But now the time is come wherein to tell
> How all we bore ourselves that very night

When at the hostelry we did alight.

And afterward the story I engage

To tell you of our common pilgrimage.

London pilgrims who lived on the north side of the Thames had to cross London Bridge and make their way through Southwark if their destination was Canterbury, and the Tabard, which was not far from London Bridge, was a logical starting place for the journey. It is believed that the Tabard was originally intended as an ecclesiastical hostel designed for those who would make the pilgrimage to the shrine of St Thomas.

The Tabard was a good-size timber building, probably two-storey, with a balcony running round a big courtyard. The kitchens, eating rooms and bedrooms would occupy three sides; the horses' stalls would be in the fourth. The innkeeper would keep horses to hire to travellers who did not ride their own mounts.

From Chaucer we learn much about the host and landlord of the Tabard, Henry 'Harry' Bailey, who is described as large, deep-eyed, bold of speech, shrewd, manly, and well informed. Harry had a big-armed 'blabbing shrew' for his wife, no wonder then that he was ready to go on the pilgrimage to Canterbury, while his wife stayed at the Tabard.

In the Prologue we can imagine Harry Bailey standing in the open doorway of the inn hearing the tramping of hoofs coming from the street that led from London Bridge knowing that pilgrims were making their way to the Tabard. It was early spring when Harry welcomed his travellers. At this time of the year the roads would have been more passable than they had been in the winter. A particular date is given in a later verse, 28 April, which corresponds to our 7 May. The inn must have been a busy scene bustling with serving men running about and stable boys rubbing down the horses and putting them into the stalls. The pilgrims would have taken their supper, although it was hardly more than the middle of the afternoon, but most people dined at ten in the morning. Kitchen boys would have served the various dishes. After their meal the pilgrims were happy and good-natured and ready to start their journey early next morning.

During the supper Harry Bailey announced 'a pastime' to amuse the group on their pilgrimage. The plan was that each would tell 'two stories going and two more on the homeward ride'. The one who told their story best was to be given a sumptuous dinner by the other members of the party when they returned (a great ploy to get them back to the inn), and Harry was to be the judge of the stories. Harry proposed to go with them as their guide and at his own expense. His genial warmth is his most outstanding characteristic and Chaucer comments that the Host is the fairest burgess in the whole of Cheapside and is fit to serve as a marshal in a lord's house.

The pilgrims agreed to the proposal and for several days and nights they discharged their promise. However, the full tales were never completed. Only 24 of a possible 120 are in the book and the incomplete book finishes before they even get to Canterbury! Nonetheless the tales that were told depict human frailty and folly as well as its nobility. Here you find pomposity, humility, vice, comedy, tragedy, love and lust.

The only figures in *The Canterbury Tales* that may be paired with historical personages are Chaucer himself and Harry Bailey, who is associated with 'Henri Bayliff, ostlyer (hotelier)' recorded by the Southwark Subsidy Rolls in 1380–81. He had also represented the borough in the parliament held at Westminster in 1376. The cook, Roger Hodge, also called Hodge of Ware, was actually based on a real London cook known to Chaucer as Roger Ware. (Hodge was a nickname for Roger). Chaucer clearly intended his London readers to recognise this poor cook with his ulcerated knee. Harry Bailey mocks the cook for being notorious for his soggy pasties, his reheated pies, his unwholesome parsley garnishes and his fly-filled shop.

People travelling from the south often stopped to refresh themselves before entering the City. At nightfall the huge doors of the City gates were shut at the sound of the curfew bells so that late arrivals and early starters were obliged to spend the night south of the river. Pilgrims who left London for Canterbury often spent the night in Southwark in order that they could begin their journey before the City gates opened for the day. Chaucer makes the point that his pilgrims 'made forward early for to rise'.

To cut off ones head, and to laie it in a platter,
which the iugglers call the decollation of Iohn Baptiſt.

The forme of ẙ planks, &c.

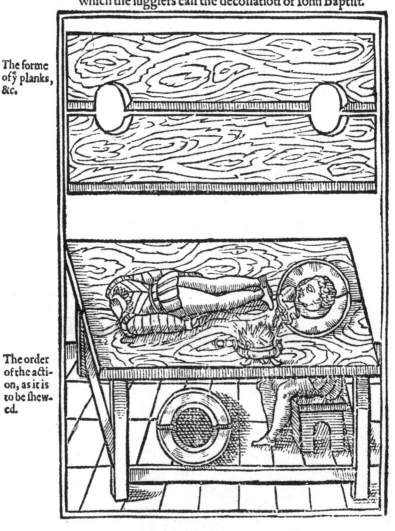

The order of the acti- on, as it is to be ſhew- ed.

42. Among the many entertainers operating on Bankside were conjurors.

Above: 43. The Albion
Flour Mills at Bankside.

Left: 44. Christ Church
as it looked in 1817.

Opposite page bottom:
46. An illustration of the
London & Greenwich
Railway, 1836.

HOLLANDS
LEAGVER:
OR,
AN HISTORICAL
DISCOVRSE OF THE
Life and Actions of Dona Britanica Hollandia the Arch-Mistris of
the wicked women of
EVTOPIA.

Wherein is detected the notorious
Sinne of Panderisme, and the Execrable
Life of the luxurious Impudent.

LONDON,
Printed by A.M. for Richard Barnes.
1632.

Vnto this Island and great Plutoes Court,
none are deny'd that willingly resort,
Charon or'e Phlegeton will set on shoare,
and Cerberus will guard you to the doore:
Where dainty Deuils drest in humane shape,
vpon your sense soone will make a rape.
They that come freely to this house of sinne,
in Hell so freely may haue entrance in.

Above: 45. The pamphlet *News from Holland's Leaguer* – named after a famous
Bankside stew.

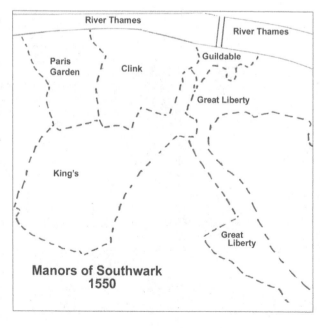

Above: 47. *Southwark Fair*, by William Hogarth, 1743.

Left: 48. The Manors of Southwark by the sixteenth century.

49. Fish Pond Houses. These houses in Shakespeare's time stood adjacent to the Royal Fish Ponds on Bankside.

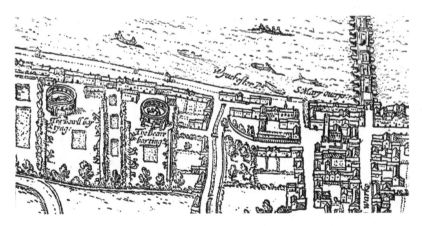

50. Bankside as depicted on the plan of London included in Georg Braun and Franz Hogenberg's *Civitatis Orbis Terrarum* (1572). The bull- and bear-baiting arenas are shown; the first playhouse in the district was built later. That was the Rose, erected in 1587 by Philip Henslowe and John Cholmley.

51. Bear-baiting. Londoners flocked to Southwark for such 'entertainments'.

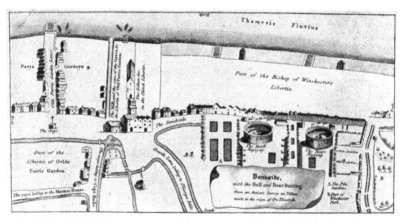

52. Bankside. A very early plan of the site on which the Elizabeth playhouses were subsequently built.

Above: 53. The engraved portrait of William Shakespeare on the title-page of the First Folio of 1623, by Martin Droeshout.

Right: 54. The Globe Theatre on Bankside, home of Shakespeare's company.

56. Warrant of James I dated at Greenwich on 17 May 1603, ordering the issue of Letters Patent authorizing the king's servants, including William Shakespeare, Richard Burbage, John Hemming and Henry Condell, to play 'comedies, tragedies, histories, enterludes, pastoralls & stage plaies... within their now usuall house called the Globe'.

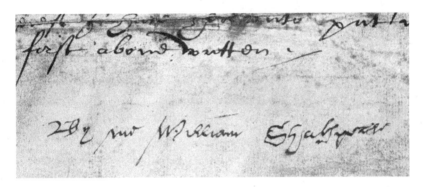

57. William Shakespeare's signature on a page of his will.

Right: 58. Richard Burbage (1568–1619), the leading man in Shakespeare's company, the Chamberlain's Men formed in 1594. Richard and his brother erected the Globe playhouse on Bankside in 1599.

Opposite page: 55. The Bankside area of Southwark, shown on Wenceslaus Hollar's *Long View of London* of 1647.

Mʀ. WILLIAM
SHAKESPEARES
COMEDIES,
HISTORIES, &
TRAGEDIES.

Published according to the True Originall Copies.

LONDON
Printed by Iſaac Iaggard, and Ed. Blount. 1623.

Left: 59. The title page of the First Folio edition of Shakespeare's plays.

Below: 60. The Swan theatre, redrawn from Visscher's view of 1616.

tectum

porticus

sedilia

orchestra

mimorum
ædes

ingressus

proscænium

planities siue arena.

quintum si diversis et permictuea, bestiarum comestah
omi destinatum, in quo multi ursi tauri, et stupenda
magnitudinis canes, distinctis caueis & septis aluntur; qui
ad

61. The interior of the Swan Theatre on Bankside, built in 1595.

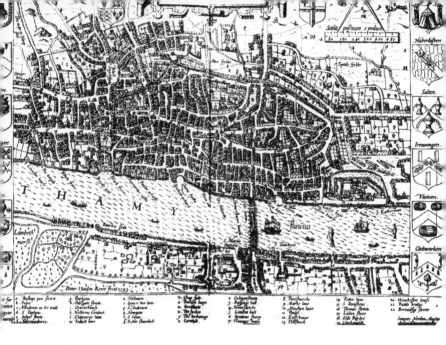

Peter Vanden Keere fecit 1593.

The vpright man   The counterfet Cranke.
Nicolas Blunt   Nicolas Geninges.

These two pictures, liuely set out,
One bodie and soule, God send him more grace:
This monsterous dissembler, a Cranke all about,
Uncomly coueting, of each to imbrace,
Money or wares, as he made his race,
And sometyme a Mariner, and a seruingman:
Or els an artificer, as he would faine that,
Such shyftes he vsed, being well tryed,
Abandoning labour, till he was espied,
Conding punishment, for his dissimulation,
He surely receiued with much exclamation.

Above: 62. John Norden's plan of London of 1593, showing the city.

Left: 63. Rogues and vagabonds.

Opulentus mercator Londinensis in Anglia.   Nobilis puellæ ornatus apud Londinenses.   Vulgarium feminarum in Anglia vestitus gentilis.   Plebeij adolescentis in Anglia habitus.

Above: 64. Costumes of the Elizabethan period.

Right: 65. An apothecary's shop. Bankside was 'full of apothecaries' shops'.

Following page spread: 66. This section of Anthonis van den Wyngaerde's pen-and-ink drawing of *c.*1544 shows Southwark with the frontage of two-storey houses in its High Street broken by the Earl of Suffolk's house Southwark Place.

67. Card games were a popular form of recreation in the many inns on Bankside.

Left: 68. Winchester Palace after Wenceslaus Hollar, 1660.

Below: 69. A convivial marriage festival at Horsleydown, east of Southwark, on the south side of the Thames.

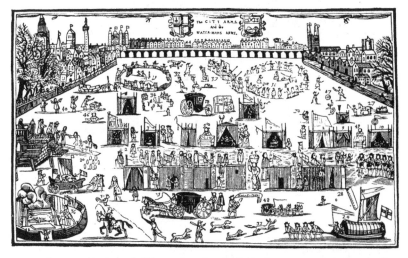

70. In very cold winters the Thames above London Bridge froze over, sometimes so deeply that a frost fair could be held on the ice.

71. St Saviour's church, Southwark. William Shakespeare was a parishioner for a time and in 1911 a memorial was erected to him, with a reclining effigy in alabaster. His brother Edmund was buried here in 1607.

Next page, left: 72. This section of Hollar's view of London from Bankside of 1647 shows a part of Southwark in the foreground, with London Bridge and the City. The buildings along the river came right down to the waterside, with occasional quays.

Next page, right: 73. Hollar's view has the crowded roofs of Southwark in the foreground, with the gables of the buildings facing the High Street that were to be destroyed in the fire of 1676. St Olave's church, dedicated to the king of Norway, who died in 1030, was rebuilt in 1740 and demolished in 1928.

2. Gray Church   S. Dunston in the East   3. Alhallows barking

Lyon kay   Billings gate

IDGE

The Tower.

Tower Wharfe

S. Olafe

Above & below: 74. & 75 The Great Fire, which began in the early hours of 2 September 1666 and continued to burn for four days. The first is from the viewpoint is to the south of St Mary Overy's church in Southwark. The second shows the western edges of Southwark.

Opposite page images: 76, 77, 78 & 79. Street sellers also sold useful household items such as fine lace and pots and pans, and second-hand clothes, while the chimney-sweep and his boy went around the streets to attract business.

The choice of Southwark as a starting point rather than another London landmark and also the choice of an innkeeper to act as a form of governance may seem strange. Southwark functioned as a dumping ground for all types of outcasts such as migrants, prostitutes and criminals as well as marginal trades such as tanning, brewing, lime-burning and innkeeping. 'Foreign brewers' (the first common beer brewers were believed to be assembling there by 1336) congregated in Southwark where they could ply their trade freely outside the jurisdiction of the Brewers' Company, much to the annoyance of the monopolistic City brewers. Southwark was an independent parliamentary borough (although it lacked a charter of incorporation) as well as a separate urban entity just across the Thames. It recognised no single authority but was divided between five jurisdictions each with its own courts. The Crown exercised authority through sheriffs, coroners and justices who also controlled the courts and prisons of the Marshalsea and King's Bench. The relationship between the City and Southwark was marked by dissensions, controversies, problems and differences. So it is in fact not surprising that Chaucer does not establish any form of governance until his pilgrims have left the City and this is then done in a public house.

Another pub, the Bell, is named in the Prologue: 'In Southwark, at this noble hostelry Known as the Tabard Inn, hard by the Bell.' It is difficult to know precisely which *Bell* this is as Southwark provided an embarrassment of riches. Rendle and Norman, *The Inns of Old Southwark* (1888), list half a dozen or more with this name, thus it becomes a problem to single out the particular Bell to which Chaucer referred. They also mention a Bell alehouse in 1723 in Montague Close (at the north-west corner of what was St Mary Overie). John Taylor, the Water Poet, in his *Travels and Circular Perambulation among the taverns of England* (1636), names nine Bells, among them the 'Bell at Saint Thomas in Southwarke'. This would presumably be an inn connected with the Hospital of St Thomas a Watering, on the eastern side of Borough High Street, about halfway between the end of London Bridge and the Tabard Inn. In 1732 there was also a Bell in Clink Street.

There are several references to Southwark in *The Canterbury Tales*. The discussion between the Host and the Miller, which precedes the tale, is fascinating. The Miller appears to be a lover of drink, paying tribute to the 'ale of Southwark'. He is so drunk he can barely sit on his horse, though he may be exaggerating the effect of the drink for comic reasons. He apologises for the roughness of the tales to follow: 'I'm quite drunk, I know it by my sound: / And therefore, if I slander or mis-say, / Blame it on ale of Southwark, so I pray.'

In 2003 Southwark Council erected a blue heritage plaque to commemorate the site of the Tabard Inn. It was unveiled by medieval enthusiast and former Monty Python star Terry Jones, who noted in his speech that *The Canterbury Tales* is not only hugely significant culturally (it was the first long-form poem to be written in English, rather than Latin), but also historically.

In the north aisle of Southwark Cathedral a window above the old Norman entrance to the cloisters depicts pilgrims leaving the Tabard Inn for Canterbury. Charles Eamer Kempe (1837–1907), the designer, was said to be unhappy about portraying a public house in stained glass. The rector, Canon Thompson, replied that as Christ had been born in an inn he could see no problem.

A contemporary and friend of Chaucer who had Bankside connections was the poet John Gower (*c.* 1327–1408). Gower, born in Kent, was a lawyer and a poet who flourished at the courts of King Richard II and Henry IV. Chaucer dedicated his *Troilus and Criseyde* to 'moral Gower'.

Southwark, free from the restrictions of the City, suited Gower as it provided a lively vantage point from which to view the vibrant life of a diverse society. His observations can be seen in his satires ('estates') where he comments on the characteristics of various classes and social groups, such as merchants, traders, and gossipy neighbours. The same themes attracted him over and over: the perplexity of human corruption and the idea that people always behave badly. He criticised not only the lower classes (particularly the agricultural labourers of the Peasants' Revolt) but also Church officials and rich merchants.

Gower's wealth enabled him to be a great benefactor to St Mary Overie church. He lived late in life as a layman at the priory of St Mary Overie and married Agnes Groundolf in January 1397. She is thought to have been his nurse and his second wife. Gower is buried in Southwark Cathedral in a tomb of his own design (there is a window above the monument which commemorates John and his wife Agnes). His effigy's head rests on three of his great books: *Speculum Meditantis*, *Vox Clamantis*, and *Confessio Amantis*. After his death Gower was praised, along with Chaucer, as a founder of the English poetic tradition and his magnificent tomb inspired William Shakespeare, who included Gower as a character in three of his plays. In Charles Dickens's *The Uncommercial Traveller*, a collection of literary sketches and reminiscences, the author admits to a profound ignorance of London churches 'saving that I know the church of Old Gower's tomb (he lies in effigy with his head upon his books) to be the church of St Saviour's, Southwark ...'

It was no accident that the growth of theatres in the sixteenth century took place in areas beyond the jurisdiction of the City. William Shakespeare moved to London around 1586 and lived there until 1613. This was at the height of the playhouse boom at Bankside, and the area was to have a great influence on him and his works. He was inevitably drawn towards Southwark where he wrote many of his greatest works, including *Hamlet*, *Othello*, *Macbeth*, *King Lear* and *The Tempest*. Bankside's reputation for 'stews' and prostitutes influenced Shakespeare when he recreated the brothel madam Mistress Quickly, who appears in three of the History plays. In *Measure for Measure* the plot revolves around ridding the city of its pimps and whorehouses under the order of the Puritan ruler, who is then seized with lust and tries to blackmail a novice nun into having sex with him.

It is believed that Shakespeare lived at a site now partially covered by Blackfriars Bridge. It is also likely that he worshipped in St Saviour's, now Southwark Cathedral, where he was also present for his brother's funeral. He frequented local inns, often in the company of Edward Alleyn and Ben Jonson, and may have visited The George Inn.

Shakespeare's connection with the theatres of Bankside was made clear by Ben Jonson, who wrote,

Sweet Swan of Avon, what a sight it were
To see thee in our waters yet appear,
And make those flights upon the banks of Thames
That so did take Eliza and our James.

It was at the Globe Theatre that Shakespeare was part proprietor and was also here that some of his plays were first produced, and he himself performed in them. The Globe was built in 1599 using timber from an earlier playhouse, the Theatre, which had been built in Shoreditch in 1576. The lease on the land that the Theatre in Shoreditch stood on ran out and James Burbage, who had built the Theatre, realised that he would need to find a new home for his company.

In 1598 Burbage's sons, Richard and Cuthbert, rented a new plot of land in Bankside, and hired a carpenter, Peter Street, to take the Theatre apart, timber by timber. They took the timbers by cart down the river and carried them under cover of darkness across London Bridge to Bankside to build a new playhouse. The Burbages shared their building costs with five members of the Lord Chamberlain's Men, including Shakespeare. The Bankside playhouse was named the Globe, referring to spherical models of the earth and explained in a painted sign showing Hercules, the legendary strongman, holding a globe on his shoulders.

On 29 June 1613, during a performance of *Henry the Eighth*, a theatrical cannon, set off during the performance, misfired, igniting the wooden beams and thatching, and sent the Globe up in flames. Sir Henry Wotton gave an eye-witness account of the fire in a letter dated 2 July 1613:

... I will entertain you at the present with what happened this week at the Banks side. The King's players had a new play called All is True, representing some principal pieces of the reign of Henry the Eighth, which set forth with many extraordinary circumstances of pomp and majesty even to the matting of the stage

205

... Now King Henry making a Masque at the Cardinal Wolsey's house, and certain cannons being shot off at his entry, some of the paper or other stuff, wherewith one of them was stopped, did light on the thatch, where being thought at first but idle smoke, and their eyes more attentive to the show, it kindled inwardly, and ran round like a train, consuming within less than an hour the whole house to the very ground. This was the fatal period of that virtuous fabric, wherein yet nothing did perish but wood and straw, and a few forsaken cloaks; only one man had his breeches set on fire, that would perhaps have broyled him, if he had not by the benefit of a provident wit, put it out with a bottle of ale.

John Taylor (1578–1653) commemorated the event in the following lines:

As gold is better that in fire's tried,
So is the Bankside Globe, that late was burn'd;
For where before it had a thatched hide,
Now to a stately theatre 'tis turn'd;
Which is an emblem that great things are won
By those that dare through greatest dangers run.

It appears that no one was hurt and the Globe was rebuilt the following year. With the outbreak of Civil War in 1642 the Globe, as with other theatres, fell victim to Puritan zeal and was pulled down two years later. Landowner Sir Matthew Brend demolished the Globe Theatre and built tenement houses on the site. The *History and Antiquities of St Saviour's* (1795) states that 'the passage which led to the Globe Tavern, of which the playhouse formed a part, was, till within these few years, known by the name of Globe Alley, and upon its site now stands a large storehouse for porter'. At the Restoration in 1660 many theatres were reopened but the Globe was not rebuilt – until 1997.

The Bankside that Shakespeare experienced would have seen crowded tenements being built, houses divided up into apartments and gardens that were rapidly disappearing beneath building extensions. The streets and alleys were teeming with life and the area was also home to industries such as tanneries and glassworks. The growth in population attracted theatres to the area and Southwark became the home of the Globe, the Rose and the Swan. They were surrounded by a plethora of more than 300 inns and alehouses as well as other types of entertainment, that included bowling, bear-baiting and brothels. Such a rich and diverse array of pleasures and characters provided Shakespeare with much material and inspiration for his plays.

The Rose, built in 1587, was the first Elizabethan theatre on Bankside and home to many of Shakespeare's and Christopher Marlowe's first productions. The site chosen was near the Thames, on land recently reclaimed from the river. A tenement with two gardens, known as the Little Rose, was leased in 1585 to two South London businessmen, Philip Henslowe and John Cholmley, who signed an agreement to build a playhouse in Bankside and run it together for eight years. Cholmley appears to have died some time before the eight-year partnership was up. Henslowe lived in Clink Street and had several property interests in the area as well as holding minor positions at court. He is said to have been a generous man, and in 1587 the carpenter John Griggs built the theatre for him. The new building was made of timber, with a lath and plaster exterior and thatch roof. In May 1591 the Admiral's Men, a troupe of Elizabethan actors, arrived at the Rose and remained the playhouse's mainstay company.

Henslowe and his son-in-law Edward Alleyn, the well-known actor, became partners in several theatrical ventures. They bought the nearby Bear Garden and later established both the Hope and the Fortune playhouses. We know from certain details contained in Henslowe's account book about the extent of the expenditure on the theatre, the plays subsequently staged there, the audiences, and props and costumes. For example the plays included Marlowe's *Doctor Faustus*, *Jew of Malta* and *Tamburlaine* and Shakespeare's *Henry VI, Part 1* and *Titus Andronicus*. From the evidence in the diary we also learn that there was a greater level of social mixing among the spectators. 'Lewd disposed persons' such as harlots, cutpurses, cozeners and pilferers also frequented theatres. When the Corporation expelled actors from the City in 1574 they responded by establishing playhouses outside the jurisdiction of the City. The poet John Taylor noted that three or four thousand people were being carried over the river every day to the plays on the Bankside. Audiences were active and participated vocally, particularly if a play did not catch their interest. Boredom diverted itself into a variety of activities ranging from card playing to swearing, spitting, munching apples and cracking nuts.

The success of the Rose encouraged other theatres to be built on Bankside which swiftly overtook the Rose. Performances at the Rose began to be reduced in the face of this new competition, as people turned to comedies and tragedies rather than the great history plays for which the Rose was renowned. The Rose appears to have fallen out of use by 1603 and had been abandoned as a theatre by 1606.

Our knowledge of the form and location of the theatres relies for detail upon early maps and panoramas of London which show that many of the theatres were located in the Bankside area. For centuries after, only Rose Alley remained to indicate that this historic building had stood nearby. However, the site of the Rose (a blue plaque at 56 Park Street – previously Maiden Lane – marks the site) became available for investigation in 1989 following the demolition of a 1950s office block, Southbridge House. Archaeologists from the Museum of London uncovered some two thirds of the ground plan of the Rose, which showed it as a relatively small, many-sided structure, based on the geometry of a fourteen-sided polygon. The yard of the theatre had a mortar floor that sloped down towards the stage to allow audiences at the back an unobstructed view and to help drain what was a naturally wet site. The excavation also revealed that the position of the stage was clearly marked whilst remains of a tiled floor from a smaller separate building were found in the south-west corner of the site. Over 700 small objects, including jewellery, coins, tokens and fragment of the moneyboxes used to collect entrance money from the audience, were also found on the site, and are now housed in the Museum of London.

However, the discovery of the site tended to raise the Shakespeare connection, as it fitted with the cultural capital of tourist Bankside, and played down the Marlowe association. Given that the life of the Rose was only eighteen years it was remarkable that 400 years later it could be unearthed by a six-month excavation in such good condition.

The site was bought in 1987 by the Heron Group, who applied to Southwark Council for planning permission to build a nine-storey office building. Heron Group then sold the site to Imry Merchant, who agreed to fund ten weeks of archaeological research. The excavation took six months, which meant a costly delay. In May 1989 all research had to stop and the tractors moved in. The Rose became a major international news story, and the site attracted many thousands of visitors. A campaign to 'Save the Rose' and protect it from redevelopment was launched with enthusiastic support from actors and archaeologists. The Rose Theatre Trust is engaged in raising funds to excavate the remaining third of the original foundations and to make the site a permanent display as an educational and historical resource for the public.

The Swan theatre seated 3,000 people and was built in 1595 and closed around 1637. The foundations of the Swan theatre were probably laid by November 1594, when John Spencer, the Lord Mayor, wrote a letter to William Cecil, Lord Burghley (advisor to Queen Elizabeth), in protest of the building of a theatre. It was named from a house and tenement called the Swan, mentioned in a charter of Edward VI. The Swan theatre was the most westerly of all the playhouses on Bankside. It was at the north-east corner of the Paris Garden estate that Francis Langley (1548–1602), a theatre builder and theatrical producer, had purchased land in May 1589, east of the manor house, and about 150 yards south of the Paris Garden Stairs at the river's edge. This location would be near the southern approach to Blackfriars Bridge, west of Hopton Street where the railway into Blackfrairs Station crosses Southwark Street. It was a large house and flourished for only a few years, being suppressed at the commencement of the Civil Wars and demolished soon afterwards.

Shortly after its opening the Swan was attended by a Dutch visitor, Johannes de Witt, who made a sketch of the interior of the theatre and a note describing the building. His diary notes, together with the picture, are probably the single most important source of information regarding the internal layout of London theatres. It is the only eye-witness view of the interior. It shows a large platform stage with doors and a balcony at the rear, a stage roof carried on elaborate pillars rising from the stage, a playhouse flag, a trumpeter announcing a performance, a yard and three-storey ring of gallery seating surrounding the performing area. Many features resemble the Globe.

An extract from the diary of De Witt noted,

There are four amphitheatres in London so beautiful that they are worth a visit, which are given different names from their different signs. In these theatres, a different play is offered to the public every day. The two more excellent of these are situated on the other side of the Thames, towards the South, and they are called the Rose and the Swan from their signboards ... The most outstanding of all the theatres, however, and the largest, is that whose sign is the Swan, as it seats 3000 people. It is built out of flint stones stacked on top of each other, supported by wooden pillars which, by their painted marble colour, can deceive even the most acute observers. As its form seems to bear the appearance of a Roman work, I have made a drawing of it.

The Hope Theatre was built in 1613–14 by Philip Henslowe and a partner, Jacob Meade, on the site of the old Bear Garden near to the Globe Theatre. In 1613 Henslowe contracted the carpenter Gilbert Katherens to tear down the Bear Garden and to build a theatre in its place, for a fee of £360. Construction took over a year. This was the same year that the Globe was being rebuilt after a fire had destroyed it. This may have been a factor in the slow progress of the building of the Hope.

The Hope was a more complex construction as it was designed as a dual-purpose building. The contract (which still survives) called for a 'Playhouse fit and convenient in all things, both for players to play in and for the game of Bears and Bulls to be baited in the same and also a fit and convenient tyre house [for actors to attire themselves, separated by a wall or curtain], and a stage to be carried and taken away and to stand upon trestles'.

The contract also tells us a good deal about the specifics of the construction. It states that the theatre must be built according to the pattern of the Swan, with two staircases on the outside, and the 'heavens' built over the stage, without posts or supports on the stage to disrupt the audience's view. The Hope was opened to the public in October 1614 and in the same month Ben Jonson's *Bartholomew Fair* was performed by the Lady Elizabeth's Men. Jonson was none too enamoured of the place. He described the Hope as being as dirty and stinking as Smithfield.

After Philip Henslowe's death the dramatist Philip Massinger (1583–1640), noted for his plays *A New Way to Pay Old Debts*, *The City Madam* and *The Roman Actor*, which are full of satire as well as political and social themes, died suddenly at his house near the Globe, and was buried in the churchyard of St Saviour's on 18 March 1640. Henslowe's son-in-law Edward Alleyn inherited his share in the Hope. The Hope continued to entertain audiences, but after 1617 it attracted no regular acting company and was used mainly for bear-baiting until it was closed down in 1656. After the Restoration Samuel Pepys recorded in his diary a visit he and his wife made to the Bear Garden on 14 August 1666. By 1714 a development called Bear Garden Square had been built on the site of the old Hope.

In an age when Puritan zeal threatened many types of entertainments and events, relationships between the theatres and the local authorities were strained. In Southwark the local Vestry complained about the Bear Garden in 1596 and the playhouses in 1598. In 1597 a performance of the lost play *The Isle of Dogs*, at the Swan, was ruled seditious and slanderous. The play was banned, arrest warrants were drawn up for everyone involved, and all London theatres were closed down for months. The Globe was one of those to be allowed to stay open but the theatres were carefully controlled for the rest of Elizabeth's reign. Puritan hostility towards the theatre had been a thorn in the side of actors for many years but even Jacobean dramatists could not have foreseen the closure of the playhouse by Parliament in 1642. The outbreak of Civil War in that year saw the Puritans ordering the suppression of all remaining playhouses. The Globe was closed down in 1644 and three years later JPs were given the power to demolish the stage, galleries and boxes of a theatre, whip the players and fine the audience 5 shillings each. The Hope, the last surviving Bankside playhouse, was demolished, marking the end to a glorious era in Bankside history.

Southwark often appears in the work of Charles Dickens (1812–70), whose early experience of his family being at the Marshalsea prison clearly had a particular influence. The idyllic childhood of Charles came to an abrupt end when his father, John Dickens (a clerk in the Navy Pay Office), had spent beyond his means in entertaining and maintaining his social position. In 1824 he found himself in the debtors' prison of Marshalsea. Shortly afterwards, the rest of his family, except Charles, joined him in residence. Charles was just twelve years old at the time and this was his worst memory, which was to haunt him for the rest of his life. Charles, who went to work at Warren's Blacking Warehouse, on Hungerford Stairs, near the present Charing Cross Railway Station, was put into lodgings in a 'back-attic … at the house of an insolvent-court agent', who lived in Lant Street in the Borough. The agent was described as a fat, good-natured, kind old gentleman, with a quiet old wife and a very innocent grown-up son. This family became the inspiration for the Garland family in *The Old Curiosity Shop* (1841). Bob Sawyer, a medical student at Guy's Hospital, and 'a carver and cutter of live people's bodies' had lodgings in Lant Street in *The Pickwick Papers*.

Dickens's experience of living in Lant Street was used to realistic effect in *The Pickwick Papers*:

> There is a repose in Lant Street, in the Borough, which sheds a gentle melancholy upon the soul. There are always a good many houses to let in the street: it is a by-street too, and its dullness is soothing. A house in Lant Street would not come within the denomination of a first-rate residence, in the strict acceptation of the term; but it is a most desirable spot nevertheless. If a man wished to abstract himself from the world—to remove himself from within the reach of temptation—to place himself beyond the possibility of any inducement to look out of the window—we should recommend him by all means go to Lant Street.

In this happy retreat are colonised a few clear-starchers, a sprinkling of journeymen bookbinders, one or two prison agents for the Insolvent Court, several small housekeepers who are employed in the Docks, a handful of mantua-makers, and a seasoning of jobbing tailors. The majority of the inhabitants either directed their energies to the letting of furnished apartments, or devote themselves to the healthful and invigorating pursuit of mangling. The chief features in the still life of the street are green shutters, lodging-bills, brass door-plates, and bell-handles; the principal specimens of animated nature, the pot-boy, the muffin youth, and the baked-potato man. The population is migratory, usually disappearing on the verge of quarter-day, and generally by night. His Majesty's revenues are seldom collected in this happy valley; the rents are dubious; and the water communication is very frequently cut off.

Dickens recalled that his usual journey home to Lant Street from the blacking factory was 'over Blackfriars Bridge, and down that turning in the Blackfriars Road which has Rowland Hill's chapel on one side, and the likeness of a golden dog licking a golden pot over a shop door on the other'. Thanks to this journey we have some idea of the variety of shops and other sites en route:

There are a good many little low-browed old shops in that street, of a wretched kind; and some are unchanged now. I looked into one a few weeks ago, where I used to buy bootlaces on Saturday nights, and saw the corner where I once sat down on a stool to have a pair of ready-made half-boots fitted on. I have been seduced more than once, in that street on a Saturday night, by a show-van at a corner; and have gone in, with a very motley assemblage to see the Fat Pig, the Wild Indian, and the Little Lady. There were two or three hat-manufactories there, then (I think they are there still); and among the things which, encountered anywhere, or under any circumstances, will instantly recall that time, is the smell of hat-making.

– John Forster, *The Life of Charles Dickens* (1875)

Blackfriars Bridge appears in *Bleak House* (1853): 'Jo moves ... down to Blackfriars Bridge, where he finds a baking stony corner wherein to settle to his repast. And there he sits, munching and gnawing, and looking up at the great cross on the summit of St Paul's Cathedral, glittering above a red-and-violet-tinted cloud of smoke.'

Dickens noted how, when he first visited his father in the Marshalsea, they 'cried very much'. John offered his son some financial advice, 'that if a man had twenty pounds a year, and spent nineteen pounds nineteen shillings and sixpence, he would be happy; but that a shilling spent the other way would make him wretched'. Years later Dickens, in his novel *David Copperfield* (1850), modelled Wilkins Micawber on his father. Micawber, like John Dickens, also ended up in a debtors' prison after failing to meet the demands of his creditors (this was King's Bench prison, which also appears in *Nicholas Nickleby* (1839) where Madeline Bray and her father lived in the Rules of the King's Bench). Micawber is famous for frequently asserting his faith that 'something will turn up'. He also offered similar financial advice:

Annual income twenty pounds, annual expenditure nineteen pounds nineteen and six, result happiness. Annual income twenty pounds, annual expenditure twenty pounds ought and six, result misery.

Dickens was clearly haunted by Marshalsea prison for the rest of his life. It dominates *Little Dorrit* (1857), a debtor's daughter born and raised within the confines of Marshalsea along with her family, old Mr William Dorrit, the 'father of the Marshalsea', and Amy, the 'Little Mother' – the 'child of the Marshalsea'.

Marshalsea prison first appears in the novel through recollection:

Thirty years ago there stood, a few doors short of the church of Saint George, in the borough of Southwark, on the left-hand side of the way going southward, the Marshalsea Prison. It had stood there many years before, and it remained there some years afterwards; but it is gone now, and the world is none the worse without it.

Saint George the Martyr church, built between 1734 and 1736, is also known as Little Dorrit's church and there is a depiction of Little Dorrit in the church's east window, behind the altar, on which her kneeling figure is shown wearing a poke bonnet. However it was the Marshalsea in which the life of Little Dorrit began:

> The baby whose first draught of air had been tinctured with Doctor Haggage's brandy, was handed down among the generations of collegians, like the tradition of their common parent ... Thus it came to pass that she was christened one Sunday afternoon, when the turnkey, being relieved, was off the lock; and that the turnkey went up to the font of Saint George's Church, and promised and vowed and renounced on her behalf, as he himself related when he came back, "like a good 'un."

The early years of Little Dorrit were spent between one end of the Borough and the other:

> Worldly wise in hard and poor necessities, she was innocent in all things ... This was the life, and this the history, of Little Dorrit; turning at the end of London Bridge, recrossing it, going back again, passing on to Saint George's Church, turning back suddenly once more, and flitting in at the open outer gate and little court-yard of the Marshalsea.

The area round London Bridge provides the setting for a number of scenes from Dickens's novels. *Our Mutual Friend* (1864–65), the last completed novel written by Dickens, is believed to be the most challenging that he produced. The novel is about the son of a tycoon who must marry a certain woman to inherit his father's fortune. However, he shuns this, leaves, and is presumed drowned. He returns under a new identity, gets hired at a company related to his father, marries the same woman on his own merit, not on his father's riches, and only afterwards assumes his original identity and inherits his fortune. The book opens with Gaffer and Lizzie Hexam, father and daughter, on the Thames and the unknown drowned man whose body they are towing to the shore.

Twenty-year-old Lizzie Hexam is appalled by the fact that her family depends on money and spoils scavenged from the river, and is determined that her brother Charlie gets an education and succeeds in life. Her father, Gaffer Hexam, is a waterman who makes a living by robbing corpses in the Thames along Bankside. In 1867 it was estimated by one newspaper that there were '100,000 persons' living by plunder in London. There were some 200 open sewers flowing into the Thames. Mains drainage was not introduced until 1865 so the water would not only be brown in colour but would contain untreated sewage that also formed into stinking cesspools around the houses and yards of the city.

In these times of ours, though concerning the exact year there is no need to be precise, a boat of dirty and disreputable appearance, with two figures in it, floated on the Thames, between Southwark Bridge which is of iron, and London Bridge which is of stone, as an autumn evening was closing in. The figures in this boat were those of a strong man with ragged grizzled hair and a sun-browned face, and a dark girl of nineteen or twenty, sufficiently like him to be recognizable as his daughter. The girl rowed, pulling a pair of sculls very easily; the man, with the rudder-lines slack in his hands, and his hands loose in his waistband, kept an eager look out ...

Trusting to the girl's skill and making no use of the rudder, he eyed the coming tide with an absorbed attention. So the girl eyed him. But, it happened now, that a slant of light from the setting sun glanced into the bottom of the boat, and, touching a rotten stain there which bore some resemblance to the outline of a muffled human form, coloured it as though with diluted blood. This caught the girl's eye, and she shivered.

At every mooring-chain and rope, at every stationery boat or barge that split the current into a broad-arrowhead, at the offsets from the piers of Southwark Bridge, at the paddles of the river steamboats as they beat the filthy water, at the floating logs of timber lashed together lying off certain wharves, his shining eyes darted a hungry look. After a darkening hour or so, suddenly the rudder-lines tightened in his hold, and he steered hard towards the Surrey shore.

Until now, the boat had barely held her own, and had hovered about one spot; but now, the banks changed swiftly, and the deepening shadows and the kindling lights of London Bridge were passed, and the tiers of shipping lay on either hand.

In *Oliver Twist* (1838) the old granite London Bridge is where Nancy,

Mr Brownlow and Rose meet to discuss Oliver. Noah Claypole hides near the stairs of the bridge and reports what he hears to Fagin.

> The church clocks chimed three quarters past eleven, as two figures emerged on London Bridge. One, which advanced with a swift and rapid step, was that of a woman who looked eagerly about her as though in quest of some expected object; the other figure was that of a man, who slunk along in the deepest shadow ... Thus, they crossed the bridge, from the Middlesex to the Surrey shore.

Dickens offers a description of a misty night along the river at Bankside with the shadows of small boats, wharves, warehouses and the shapes of the churches either side of the Thames.

> It was a very dark night. ... A mist hung over the river, deepening the red glare of the fires that burnt upon the small craft moored off the different wharfs, and rendering darker and more indistinct the mirky buildings on the banks. The old smoke-stained storehouses on either side, rose heavy and dull from the dense mass of roofs and gables, and frowned sternly upon water too black to reflect even their lumbering shapes. The tower of old Saint Saviour's Church, the spire of Saint Magnus, so long the giant-warders of the ancient bridge, were visible in the gloom; but the forest of shipping below bridge, and the thickly scattered spires of churches above, were nearly all hidden from the sight ...
>
> The hour had not struck two minutes, when a young lady, accompanied by a grey-haired gentleman, alighted from a hackney-carriage within a short distance of the bridge, and, having dismissed the vehicle, walked straight towards it ... 'Not here,' said Nancy hurriedly, 'I am afraid to speak to you here. Come away – out of the public road – down the steps yonder!' ... The steps to which the girl had pointed, were those which, on the Surrey bank, and on the same side of the bridge as Saint Saviour's Church, form a landing-stairs from the river ... These stairs are a part of the bridge; they consist of three flights. Just below the end of the second, going down, the stone wall on the left terminates in an ornamental pilaster facing towards the Thames. At this point the lower steps widen: so that a person turning that angle of the wall is necessarily unseen by any others on the stairs who chance to be above him, if only a step.

When Bill Sikes heard of what Nancy had done, he murdered her at his house in Bethnal Green, not on the steps of the bridge, as the plaque on the wall states.

Dickens referred to both the old London Bridge and sometimes to the 1832 reconstruction. In *Barnaby Rudge* (1841) Gabriel Varden, the locksmith, crosses London Bridge to visit Mrs Rudge in Southwark. In *David Copperfield* (1850) David recalls that he was 'often up at six o' clock bridge' and would visit his favourite lounging place on London Bridge, 'where I was wont to sit, in one of the old stone recesses watching the people going by, or to look over the balustrades at the sun shining in the water and lighting up the golden flame on top of the Monument'. In the quad of Guy's Hospital is a round-hooded Portland stone alcove from old London Bridge. It was taken down in 1831 and brought to the hospital in 1861. It was bought for ten guineas as a shelter for convalescing patients and moved to its present position in 1926.

With regard to the inns around Bankside and Borough in the mid-nineteenth century we have contemporary social accounts by Sala and Dickens, In *Gaslight and Daylight* (1859), journalist and writer George Augustus Sala (1828–95) tells us something about the inns of Bankside: 'the Surrey shore of the Thames, at London, is dotted with damp houses of entertainment' and the typical waterside public house, the Tom Tug's Head, is 'surrounded on three sides by mud, and standing on rotten piles of timber, and with its front always unwashed'. Dickens comments on the old inn the White Hart in *The Pickwick Papers*. Nothing exists today of the White Hart Inn, save the name of the yard. It was, until its demolition in 1889, the largest of the coaching inns that lined Borough High Street. It is where Pickwick meets Sam Weller and where Mr Pickwick and his friends depart on their own pilgrimage. However we are given a description of the inn by Dickens:

> A double tier of bed-room galleries, with old clumsy balustrades, ran around two sides of the straggling area, and a double row of bells to correspond, sheltered from the weather by a little sloping roof, hung over the door leading to the bar and

coffee-room. Two or three gigs and chaise-carts were wheeled up under different little sheds and pent houses; and the occasional heavy tread of a carthorse, or rattling of a chain at the further end of the yard, announced to anybody who cared about the matter, that the stable lay in that direction.

Across the road from White Hart Yard is Borough Market which was used by Dickens as a setting in *The Pickwick Papers*. A very drunk Bob Sawyer, in attempting to find his way home, 'double knocks at the door of the Borough Market Office' and takes 'short naps on the steps … under the firm impression he lived there and had forgotten the key'.

The workhouse, so vividly portrayed in *Oliver Twist* (1838), was an institution never far from the view of Victorian society. Near to where Dickens lived in Lant Street there was, in the parish of St George the Martyr, a workhouse on the north side of Mint Street, originally dating from 1729. A new building in Mint Street was erected in 1782, which was later taken over by St Saviour's Poor Law Union. In September 1865 the workhouse was the subject of an investigation by the medical journal *The Lancet*, which revealed a catalogue of appalling conditions.

This house is situated in Mint-street, Southwark, a densely crowded district on the S.E. of the Thames, with a population of 55,510 and is surrounded with every possible nuisance, physical and moral. Bone-boilers, grease and cat-gut manufactories represent some of them, and there is a nest of thieves, which has existed ever since the days of Edward III.

Commenting on the lavatory and water closet it said that 'the grossest possible carelessness and neglect were discovered'. In one case thirty men had used one closet, in which there had been no water for more than a week.

In an adjoining ward the drain smell from a lavatory was particularly offensive. *The Lancet* added,

For the last three years and a half this house appears to have suffered from various epidemics, and especially from typhus. Many cases are admitted into the house

from the neighbourhood; but many are developed in the house ... The tramp
ward for the women is a miserable room, foul and dirty, with imperfect light
and ventilation, the floor being simply bedded with straw. Into this open sty the
women are passed in, often with little or no clothing.

So bad were the conditions that the report said 'these poor outcasts'
would be better off sleeping in the streets and on doorsteps than
'entrapped into this manufactory of fever'. The conclusion was damning:
'From what has come within our knowledge here in connexion with the
creation of fever, we doubt whether a greater or more flagrant instance
of recklessness about human life could be pictured.'

The area around Borough had been noted in the report as being
overcrowded, impoverished and noxious. Social reformer Octavia Hill
commented in 1887 that much of Victorian Southwark was given to
crime, pollution and poverty. In Charles Booth's *Survey of Life and
Labour of the People in London* (1891) Southwark and Bermondsey
were identified as the only areas in London with over 50 per cent of the
population living in poverty. More specifically the area between London
Bridge and Blackfriars Bridge was viewed as 'the most serious blot to be
reformed'. The area stretching back to Mint Street was described as
being unrivalled in poverty, viciousness and crowding.

London shaped the novels of Dickens. We have, through his fiction, a
vivid description of a London that has largely gone. He bequeathed to
us imaginative scenes and characters in a way that no other writer did.
Years later he reflected on the pain of his early years and recalled, 'My
old way home by the Borough made me cry, after my eldest child could
speak.' He lived through a time when London was undergoing huge
changes and he chronicled many of those changes. Not surprisingly
he has been called 'the first great novelist of the industrial city'. The
1820s and 1830s still had much of eighteenth-century street life with
its almanacs and ballads, strolling peddlers, gin palaces, beer shops and
even the public executions in which the behaviour of the crowd horrified
Dickens when he attended a hanging at Horsemonger Lane Gaol in
Southwark. Coaching inns were a distinctive feature of the Borough

from earliest times to the end of the nineteenth century. However, the arrival of the railways in the 1830s removed much of their purpose, but some diversified into ticket agents and goods depots. In 1838 the first railway for the London area was created, around London Bridge, and the first deep-level London 'tube' underground opened in 1890, running from King William Street through Borough to Kennington.

Dickens reflected the vibrancy and disorder of the capital at a unique time in its history.

13

Industrial Development

Just as the City of London was content to have the locations for seedy, bawdy and boisterous pleasures comfortably out of sight in Southwark and Bankside particularly, so the dirty and polluting industries essential for the well-being of the Metropolis, many of which used coal as fuel, were likewise consigned to what was clearly thought of as the underbelly of the capital.

It is often forgotten that London has always been a centre of manufacturing, and previously it had heavy industries such as iron-founding and shipbuilding. The size and wealth of London's population has always provided a large market for a huge variety of industries. With the river and the sea nearby and the roads and later the railways converging on it, London could draw on fuel, especially coal and the raw materials needed for its industries. The good transport facilities made distribution of its finished goods easy.

There is some evidence that the Romans worked iron and bronze in Southwark. By the late fourteenth century, local industry was highly diversified. Clothing, textiles and leather-making were prominent and there was a fair sprinkling of the metal trades. What would now be called the 'hospitality industry' was a sizeable employer as might be expected and was supported by a substantial number of people in the victualling trade who probably also catered for the large market presented by the people of the City, just across the river. There were rich people living in the vicinity and they had domestic servants and others with specialised roles such as ostlers. The presence of the river and of shipping explains the presence of such trades as boatmen, coopers, porters and carters. The fact that Rotherhithe just down the river was a major shipbuilding centre accounts for Southwark having what can be described as 'ancillary' industries. These included ships' chandlers, sail-makers and also rope manufacture on the Thames foreshore.

Southwark has always been cosmopolitan and immigrants have long played a significant role in its industrial development. Flemish refugees set up breweries which produced beer as opposed to other local brewers who made traditional English ale. The latter was spoken about in complimentary terms by Chaucer and perhaps led to the ditty 'The nappy strong ale of Southwirke keeps many a gossip from the kirke'. The simplest distinction between ale and beer was that the former was un-hopped, dark and often flavoured with herbs while the latter contained hops, which gave it a distinctive bitterness and made it more thirst-quenching. Beer was also lighter in colour and essential oils in the hops helped to give it a longer shelf life. The indigenous population did not take readily to beer but it gradually increased its market share because it offered advantages to brewers and innkeepers. With the appearance of hopped beer came wholesale brewers who sold their products to inns and alehouses where previously brewing had been done on the premises, usually by the woman of the house (a 'brewster'). The Anchor Brewery in Park Street was the largest brewery in London. Hops were grown in huge numbers in Kent and the Hop Exchange Building off Borough High Street is evidence of how this fruit became such a valuable raw material. Flemings were also to the fore in the printing trade and in bringing the making of tin-glazed pottery to the district.

Other industries that developed were often serious pollutants and the processes employed and materials handled often presented a serious fire hazard in a closely packed district where industrial and domestic premises were frequently cheek by jowl. Hat-making was a long-lived industry and its processes involved the discharge into local watercourses of large amounts of poisonous mercury. Other polluting industries included leather-working and the manufacture of soap, glass and pottery. Close to Blackfriars Bridge were the late eighteenth-century Albion Flour Mills. Employing Boulton & Watt steam engines, it was a huge complex and very much state of the art for its time. It became what would now be known as a tourist attraction, but it seems that someone did not like it because it burned down, the cause almost certainly arson.

Glassmaking seems to have started in the seventeenth century. A cluster of glassworks was to be found close to the river in Bankside. Coal-fired furnaces were banned from the City. An early one was established on the site of a brewhouse in Winchester Palace, another was in Park Street and Stoney Street and one close to the Bear Garden. These two were run by John Bowles, and at the latter he made glass for windowpanes which became well known as 'Crown Glass' after his trade sign. Close by in Hopton Street the Falcon Glass Works was established in 1688. In the middle of the eighteenth century the works was taken over by Pellatt & Green, who went on to establish a formidable reputation over the next century. The curiously named Apsley Pellatt IV (1791–1863) served as a local MP and became a leading expert on all matters concerning glassware. Close to Blackfriars Bridge a firm called the British Plate Glass Company had a substantial warehouse. In Montague Close adjacent to St Saviour's church from the 1620s to the 1760s a company produced imitations in blue and white tin-glazing of Delft and Ming pottery.

In the nineteenth century, Bankside's industries became even more diverse, although what they all tended to have in common were noxious effluents. Some of these were substantial workplaces. They included Potts and Sarsons vinegar works, the pickle factory of Crosse & Blackwell, Epps Steam Cocoa mills and the shoe polish manufactory of Day & Martin. Heavier engineering could be found at the firm of Easton & Amos at Ewer Street, who, among other achievements, provided the hidden hydraulics for Trafalgar Square's fountains, and in Sumner Street, behind what is now Tate Modern, stood the crane works of Messrs Coles. Numerous iron foundries produced the million and one items eagerly devoured by the burgeoning Metropolis and the increasingly integrated national economy of the 'workshop of the world'. These included such items as diverse as coal-hole covers, cartwheels, boilers, pokers and railway equipment. Among other famous names with manufacturing premises in or close to riverside Southwark were Pearce Duff's, whose best-known product was custard, Hartley's jams, Peek Frean's, Oxo and Spillers. These were all major employers for much of the twentieth century. Nearly all of these companies have either closed or relocated. The raw materials for many of these industries were unloaded at the wharves just below London Bridge along Tooley Street. There was such a concentration of warehouses at this point that it was often referred to as 'London's Larder'. The best known of these premises was probably Hay's Wharf which opened in 1856. Pickford's had warehouses five storeys high in Clink Street. This part of the Surrey bank was a hive of activity.

All this meant that Southwark had a major concentration of manufacturing and processing industry, but rather than the medium to large-sized concerns mentioned above, most of Southwark's industries were of a workshop size. Hats had been made in Southwark for centuries. At the luxury end of the market, beaver hats, made of beaver fur or a high-class imitation, were superseded by silk hats in the 1830s and Southwark manufacturers ensured that they kept abreast of changing fashion. Hats of all kinds first saw the light of day in Southwark but perhaps the most famous was the 'Bowler'. This was named after Thomas Bowler, who had premises in Southwark Bridge Road. It was originally designed for hunting gentlemen as a more practical substitute for the 'topper' when engaged in the chase. It went on to enjoy widespread popularity. No fewer than 3,500 companies were engaged in the hat trade in Southwark in 1841 employing more than 23,000 workers, the vast majority of whom were women. Interestingly, many of them had migrated to London from textile-manufacturing districts.

Other industrial activity in the district included storage and distribution facilities. These sometimes handled materials which were then processed by local industry. Southwark had dealers in items as wide-ranging as pipe clay, slate, lead and alum. Manufacturers, some of them very small scale, produced goods as diverse as tarpaulins, ships' chronometers, and pet food. They also often had mutually dependent relationships with the riverside wharves that brought in their raw materials and took away their finished products. Likewise, numerous timber yards and sawmills had a symbiotic relationship with waterborne transport. Imported products arriving by water and being processed locally included fur, hair and tallow. Other manufactured products included oilcake, candles, whitelead and blacklead. No wonder the City and Westminster for that matter were happy to consume such products as long as they were made some distance away. Clearly a case of 'not in my back yard'!

Southwark, then, was a hive of industrial activity of a variety and complexity which was simply bewildering. Some of the businesses were highly specialised. The presence of Guy's Hospital probably accounts for a company making small enamel containers. One company produced webbing for the armed forces, a second made machinery for filling bottles with mineral water and a third specialised in Christmas cards. A company with the no-nonsense name of the 'American Cockroach and Black Beetle Solvent Company' had premises in Southwark Street. Presumably it did what it said on the label and found plenty of customers among the owners of the large number of warehouses and food-processing concerns close by.

Even though the district received more than its fair share of bomb destruction in the Second World War and some businesses closed and never resumed operations, in the 1950s and even into the 1960s Bankside and its surroundings largely retained the sights, sounds and smells of old-fashioned industry. The nature of the economy was changing rapidly and this was reflected locally. Just immediately west of Bankside, Sainsbury's, for example, had their headquarters. Consumerism was on the increase and firms in the area were still busy manufacturing but what was being produced was changing in response and now included office furniture, packaging, confectionery as well as lineal descendants of older local industries such as those making glue, paint, sacks and rubber boots. Internationally known products such as Collis Browne's Chlorodyne (this didn't necessarily do what it said on the bottle but it didn't half make you feel better) and Wright's Coal Tar Soap had their roots in Bankside and district.

Although it stood where a previous coal-fired establishment had been, a striking addition to the Surrey side of the river was Bankside Power Station. Unequivocally a building in a modern style, it perhaps does not have quite the dramatic impact of Battersea Power Station, which likewise was designed by Sir Giles Gilbert Scott. It was completed over a period from 1947 to 1963 and its most obvious feature is a single chimney which was kept to 99 metres in height so as not to overawe St Paul's or have too much of a harmful impact on the skyline. The power station stands on the site of the former Great Pike Gardens, which in the fourteenth century supplied fish to various religious houses in the area. It ceased operations in 1981 and stood semi-derelict, a symbol of de-industrialising Southwark until finding a new lease of life as Tate Modern.

Change came quickly to Bankside, Borough and Southwark. The wharves and warehouses closed in the 1960s and 1970s. Companies which were indelibly associated with the district closed their doors for the last time and their buildings were demolished or adapted for new purposes. These included Hayward Brothers, whose foundry had been turning out coal-hole covers since 1848. Demand for their products had dried up and the foundry closed down in 1976. The massive Park Street Brewery complex ceased to produce beer in 1982. Jobs in manufacturing, many of which employed people living in the more far-flung parts of the Borough of Southwark and nearby Lambeth, went into freefall. The industries of a post-industrial society moved in – infinitely cleaner and capital intensive, being based on the latest technologies. Business, finance, media, culture, consumerism, expensive apartments and tourism are the flavours of the age. As they advance so they ease out the last remnants of an age where production was based on labour-intensive muscle power and steam-driven coal-powered machinery. The result is a sanitised Southwark. It was glowingly described in recent (2010) publicity material as 'a very vibrant, wonderful area that is full of creative people and industries'.

Brewing was taking place in the Bankside area as early as the fourteenth century. Chaucer made complimentary comments about 'the ale of Southwark'. The Anchor Brewery at Deadman's Place, Park Street, is first found in records in 1633. In 1692 it is known that the owner was James Child, who, through marriage, was a prominent member of the influential 'beerocracy' which formed a powerful interest group in Parliament. In 1710 the owner is recorded as Edmund Halsey. Clearly a man to take every opportunity that came his way, his ability and diligence came to the attention of his boss, who kept promoting him and then allowed him to marry his daughter. When his father-in-law died, Halsey inherited the brewery and secured a lucrative contract supplying beer to the military. Halsey was a 'mover and shaker' of his time who enjoyed the good and expensive things of life but left money when he died to every one of his employees. The business was then acquired by Ralph Thrale from Streatham, who passed the business on to his son Henry. He was a close friend of Dr Johnson. Successful brewers were rich people and Henry Thrale lived in a substantial villa in salubrious Streatham, took expensive holiday and held social events which were patronised by the glitterati of the day. Regular visitors to these occasions were Sir Joshua Reynolds, Edmund Burke, David Garrick and Oliver Goldsmith. Thrale married a young Welsh woman of lively character called Hester Lynch Salusbury and in fourteen years she bore him twelve children, only four of whom lived beyond infancy. Thrale was not content with what he had, and although he managed to make the Anchor Brewery the fourth largest in London, his feverish drive to increase production and market share almost bankrupted him on two occasions. He was a *bon vivant* who was systematically unfaithful to Hester. She knew about his goings-on but did not make waves since he was the goose that laid the golden egg. She found solace in writing and the arts and in the company of Dr Johnson, who could have talked for England in the Olympics. There have always been many who could also have done that but few who, like Johnson, could be erudite, stimulating and witty. Anyway, Hester and Dr Johnson got on like the proverbial house on fire and Hester delighted in the celebrities from the world of the arts and literature who, while they undoubtedly came to see her and her husband, might have come with less frequency had Dr Johnson not been there as well. The good doctor managed to be friends with both Mr and Mrs Thrale though doubtless interacting with them in different ways. In fact, so well did he get on with them that not only did he frequently stay at Streatham but they also made a room available in the brewery where he is supposed to have written his dictionary. This seems to have become one of those urban myths. Yes, Dr Johnson may well have had a room in the brewery to do whatever he wanted to do in but the dictionary was published several years before he ever met the Thrales. He died in 1781 and the brewing business was then sold on to the Barclays, a well-known banking family. Dr Johnson acted as one of Thrale's executors. Everyday management of the business was placed in the capable hands of John Perkins. This arrangement was so successful that Perkins became a partner and the brewery came to be known as Barclay, Perkins & Co. After Thrale's death, Hester began to play the merry widow. She and Dr Johnson began to drift apart. Much to the good doctor's chagrin and against his advice, she then married an Italian piano master considerably younger than herself. It was a happy marriage.

Part of Thrale's success was that they invested heavily in the production of porter. This was a heavy, dark beverage using roast barley in the brewing process. It was invented in the eighteenth century and was especially suited to the local water supplies. It required longer maturing but could be stored in bulk. It was easy to handle and a cask once tapped had a longer shelf life than most other beers. It was cheaper to make than lighter beers and proved extremely popular especially with male working-class London drinkers. Although market porters did indeed drink this beer, there is no evidence that it was exclusively associated with them.

Earlier, in 1780, Bankside had found itself at the centre of the anti-Catholic Gordon Riots. The rioters had set fire to the Clink and released the prisoners from the Marshalsea and were torching and plundering more or less at random. They then headed for Thrale's Brewery because they thought that Thrale himself was a Catholic sympathiser. John Perkins, mentioned above, knew they were on their way and managed to head them off and cool their ardour by diverting them to a nearby pub where drinks and food were then on him. No wonder Perkins was Thrale's favourite.

The Anchor Brewery went from strength to strength and by 1810 was producing a formidable 235,000 barrels annually and keeping up with every innovation that would speed up production while minimising costs. The brewery suffered a serious fire in 1832 but was rebuilt so impressively that it became a major visitor attraction.

In 1850 the brewery again hit the news because of the treatment meted out on General Haynau by its draymen. Haynau was well known as the despotic and cruel dictator of Austria with a particular penchant for flogging helpless women. It could not last for ever and he was eventually forced into exile. He came to London and one of the places he wanted to see was the Anchor Brewery. The workers were incensed that the tyrant was on the premises and they attacked him and gave him a severe beating. With some companions, Haynau fled and was forced to hide in a dustbin in a pub yard while his pursuers searched in vain for 'Hyena' as they disparagingly called him. He was eventually smuggled away from the scene of his humiliation in a police boat. This episode in which freedom-loving Englishmen showed Johnny Foreigner what they thought of his tyranny struck a chord and *Punch* magazine contributed a little poem to the general air of merriment:

Our Baron bold, who wopp'd the fair,
Of hanging who had the knack, man.
Came over here to England, where
He could have no ladies to whack man.
For gibbet and halter in vain he sigh'd
At hanging unable op play, man,
So in quest of amusement, a visit he tried
To BARCLAY and PERKINS' draymen.

For over 170 years, railways have stamped their presence decisively on the northern parts of Southwark and they look set to do so even more in the foreseeable future. Without question their presence is obtrusive, and especially around Borough Market and in the neighbourhood of Southwark Cathedral, they define the townscape and set their stamp on it. The station at London Bridge is one of the largest and busiest in the UK and processes vast numbers of commuters every working day. The presence of the railway has had a major influence on the economic, social and cultural life of the district and has helped to ensure one continuity over time – that it remains a major transport hub.

The London & Greenwich Railway is the oldest in London. That in itself bestows historical significance but it is also important because it set something of a pattern for the extraordinarily complex network of lines that came to serve London south of the river. After it had issued a prospectus in September 1832, the L&G was surprised by the lukewarm response that it generated, especially given the huge success of the Liverpool & Manchester Railway, opened just two years previously. A fast rail link to Greenwich would benefit not only that village but Bermondsey and Deptford where intermediate stations were planned. Commuters (the word had not yet been invented) who lived in leafy Greenwich could get into London in half the time it took by river steamer. The prospectus listed fifteen reasons why the projected line made sound sense.

In the event, the company had some difficulty raising the money it needed, the eventual cost being almost £1 million rather than the initial estimate of £400,000. The reason that the line proved difficult and expensive to build was largely that nothing similar had previously been attempted. The problems lay with the fact that the railway had to traverse a district that, although it was not continuously built up, was intensively utilised. It was low-lying, flat country with a high water table, many roads and lanes to cross as well as the Deptford Creek and large numbers of market gardens and smallholdings. The decision was taken to build the line on a continuous viaduct which would be 3¾ miles long and have an unprecedented 878 arches! The company hoped to recoup some of the costs of the promotion and construction of the line by letting the arches as dwelling houses or, failing that, as stables or workshops. This idea did not catch on. Potential residents shied away from the noise, headaches and general disturbance that would be the inevitable concomitant of having a bedroom only a few feet below a railway on which the company originally proposed to run a service every ten minutes in either direction. That the trains would not run all night was a minor point. Many of the arches, however, went on to house small businesses and later on lock-up garages. Those arches that were untenanted quickly acquired the reputation of being places where ladies of the night hawked their wares or the homeless and others of the disfranchised found some shelter. For this reason many such arches were bricked up. It is worth mentioning that the entire length of the viaduct was lit up with gas lights during the hours of darkness. This line, the first of many running into London on low viaducts, caught the public imagination. It was not, however, a huge financial success.

The line opened in February 1836 from Deptford to a station at Spa Road, Bermondsey. The line through to London Bridge opened on 14 December. London Bridge, therefore, is the oldest of London's permanent terminus stations. There was the usual pompous opening ceremony attended by a variety of bigwigs and their hangers-on. A sense of rejoicing usually accompanied such ceremonies and on this occasion the inaugural train had a group of players dressed as beefeaters riding, one would think rather hazardously, on the roof of one of the carriages and providing a musical accompaniment to the journey. It took another two years for the line to be opened throughout to Greenwich. London's first railway was then complete. The L&G had a more harmful effect on parallel horse bus routes than on the competing steamer services.

This initial station was a spartan affair reflecting the company's poor financial situation, and there was a minor scandal caused by the low platforms. Ladies had to climb down from the carriages and in so doing frequently exposed what they regarded as unacceptable quantities of ankle and, dare we say it, even leg. They had to do this under the lascivious gaze not only of railway workers but male passengers and even some base loafers who seemed to haunt the platforms for no other reason than to catch quick glimpses of such womanly flesh. A number of letters appeared in local newspapers taking the railway company to task for its low platforms and for allowing such opportunist undesirables to hang about and use them to titillate their lusts. At the same time there were also complaints that some of the railway servants abused their trust when helping ladies in and out of carriages. Some of them held the ladies' hands too long while others took the opportunity of staring at them too closely.

The country was moving into the period known as 'railway mania' and it was not long before lines were built by other companies who were granted running powers over the L&G metals into London Bridge Station. The first was in 1839 and was the London & Croydon Railway, which joined the L&G at Corbett's Lane. Before long, trains were running over this line from as far away as Brighton on what was to become the London, Brighton & South Coast Railway. In 1842 trains of the South Eastern Railway also shared the tracks into London Bridge. The two tracks into that station proved inadequate and in 1840 another two tracks were authorised to extend the south side of the viaduct. Tolls were levied on the trains of these other companies and these were sufficiently burdensome to persuade the Croydon and South Eastern Companies to set up a station of their own at Bricklayers Arms. This opened in 1844 and avoided the viaduct of the Greenwich Company and its tolls. It proved to be inconvenient and was short-lived as a passenger station. The companies had the effrontery to describe the Bricklayers Arms during its short life as a 'West-end terminus'.

The viaduct into London Bridge went on to be widened several times to carry eleven tracks out as far as Spa Road. The final widening took place around the end of the nineteenth century. Traffic had built up to levels that could not possibly have been foreseen and as a result the station at London Bridge also expanded. The original station consisted of a three-storey block doubling as a station building and the company's administrative headquarters. In 1844 the Croydon Company opened three platforms for its trains and in 1850 a new grander joint station was built catering for the Brighton and South Eastern Railways as well. The Croydon and Brighton Companies amalgamated in 1846. The intention was to impress since London Bridge was the gateway to the European Continent. It had a wide frontage and an eye-catching campanile of Italian style. Relations between what became just two companies, the SER and the LB&SCR were poor and before long a wall was erected to separate their respective parts of the station.

It was not long before both companies operated what were virtually separate stations alongside each other with the South Eastern occupying the northern part. In the late 1850s London Bridge was enjoying the peak of its prestige before the opening of Charing Cross and Cannon Street Stations diminished its importance. In 1858 the *Illustrated London News* sent its man down to London Bridge to gather material for an article which duly appeared on 24 July 1858. What seems to have impressed him most was the fact that the whole station complex rested on arches and was 'suspended in mid-air, more wonderfully than the Hanging Gardens of Babylon, looking down from an altitude of seventy feet upon Tooley Street and sending forth its convoys along an elevated route which lifts them above the chimney pots of Bermondsey'. Few people would have thought to bring together the Hanging Gardens of Babylon and Tooley Street in one sentence. We must allow for a little exaggeration as regards the height of the station and assume that he was having a rush of blood, not necessarily to the brain. Next he becomes excited about the station roof, which he claims was 'unmatched in the world until the new Paddington Station was built'.

A hotel was built at the front of that part of the station serving the trains of the LB&SCR. It abutted onto St Thomas and Joiner Streets. Called the 'Terminus Hotel', it was seven storeys high, had about 150 bedrooms and was never very successful. It closed in 1893 when the LB&SCR bought it and converted it into offices. It was destroyed by enemy action in the Second World War and its remains demolished in 1941.

What had started off as two platforms in 1836 became twenty-one platforms and the huge station evolved into a rambling, unattractive and awkward-to-use complex, damaged by bombing in the Second World War but, until its extensive rebuilding in the 1970s, still bearing considerable resemblance to photographs taken around 1900. What was impressive about the station was its sheer size as well as the huge number of trains that used it. As early as 1854, 10 million passengers were using London Bridge Station annually. As the volume of traffic increased, seemingly exponentially, such intensive services could only be handled safely and efficiently by large-scale electrification and the use of power signalling. The first electric trains to use London Bridge began to run in 1909 and by 1929 virtually all the services that could be described as 'suburban' were electrified with multiple units that could be driven from either end, which greatly simplified station working and shortened turn-round times.

For anyone who is fond of grubbing about in London's nether regions and likes to combine this activity with a bit of nineteenth-century industrial archaeology, a visit to the old streets below the station is rewarding. Joiner Street, Stainer Street, Weston Street and Bermondsey Street are aligned much as they were before the railway was built. Variations in the brickwork give clues to the successive widenings that have taken place. These seemingly subterranean, Stygian and even threatening streets are stark evidence of how the railway viaducts penetrated, dominated and then destroyed the cohesiveness of the communities over which and through which they passed, creating new divisions as they did so and establishing this gloomy and depressing no man's land. Part of the frontage of the L&C station can still be made out in Joiner Street.

London Bridge was reasonably placed for those daily business travellers in the easterly parts of the City who could walk or take a bus over the bridge. It was not so convenient for the Blackfriars, Fleet Street, Strand areas or for the West End. Having arrived at London Bridge Station, they were then faced with slow horse bus or cab rides onwards and, of course, in reverse when they made their way home later. The South Eastern became convinced that it needed at least one station in the City and one, serving the West End, in the Charing Cross area.

Parliamentary approval was received in August 1859 for an extension westwards from London Bridge to Charing Cross. A difficult task lay ahead because the act stipulated that the new line must not block the approaches to London Bridge, that it must avoid St Saviour's Church and that the bridge across the Thames must be high enough not to provide an obstacle to shipping. There was also a myriad of legal problems and financial costs given the almost Byzantine complications of land ownership along the route, the authorities that needed to be negotiated with including those that ran St Thomas's Hospital and Borough Market. Large amounts of working-class housing had to be demolished and, with there being no legal requirement for the company to house those who were displaced, the occupants were simply decanted and often finished up in other poor-quality and then overcrowded accommodation in the locality. Not the least of the difficulties was that presented by the College Burial Ground, which lay athwart the proposed route. An extraordinary total of 7,950 bodies was disinterred and taken away. The architect responsible for this project wrote to Samuel Smiles, Secretary of the SER, 'Each body has cost us less than three shillings. It was fortunate that such reasonable terms could be made at Woking Cemetery. A more horrible business you could not imagine; the men could only continue their work by the constant sprinkling of disinfectant powder.'

The extension was carried on a viaduct and immediately on leaving London Bridge Station it passed onto a large iron girder bridge across the approaches to London Bridge itself. This quickly elicited splenetic criticism:

Nothing uglier, nothing more objectionable in an artistic point of view, could possibly have been designed. It is a pity that there should exist such an utter disregard among our railway authorities ... for anything which is not strictly utilitarian. A few hundred pounds, and how many are wasted annually in civic feasts and ceremonials, could have given us a bridge which would have been an ornament to this approach to London ... its ugliness serves, however, to set off the architecture of the fine church of St Saviour, whose tower may be seen standing above it.

The line opened in 1864 with an intermediate station at Great Surrey Street, which gave access to the western part of the City via Blackfriars Bridge. A proposed station at Southwark Bridge was not proceeded with. In 1861 parliamentary powers had been obtained to build a line from the Charing Cross extension across the river to a terminus at Cannon Street, very central for the City. On the south side of the river there was a triangular bridge which allowed trains to run to and from both Charing Cross and Cannon Street Stations. In 1878 a spur was put in from the London Bridge to Charing Cross section of line which allowed trains to cross the river and gain access to yet another terminus in the City, this time at Blackfriars. In 1901 a depot for continental goods traffic was opened at Ewer Street and this remained open until 1960.

A final line that skirts the western edge of the Bankside part of Southwark is that which crosses Blackfriars Railway Bridge. This had its origins in the London, Chatham & Dover Railway Company. It managed to obtain parliamentary authority in 1860 for a line from Herne Hill and Elephant & Castle across the Thames and penetrating the very heart of the City. This line, like the others in Southwark, ran over brick viaducts to reach the Bankside area in 1864 where it opened a station called 'Blackfriars'. Shortly afterwards, the bridge across the Thames opened, as did a temporary station at Ludgate Hill.

Thameslink was inaugurated in 1988. This was a short but imaginative railway link which, once put into place, enabled a substantial number of new through journeys to be made that previously would have required one or more changes and the time and inconvenience that went with that. Thameslink involved reopening the long-disused Snow Hill Tunnel in the Holborn area which then allowed the operation of through services from Bedford, Luton and St Albans to Gatwick Airport and Brighton via St Pancras and London Bridge and also to the Wimbledon area via Elephant & Castle. The new services were hugely successful in terms of usage, which meant that trains, especially at peak times, could become grossly overcrowded.

The Thameslink Project is a £5.5 billion investment to upgrade services and increase capacity, focusing particularly on the worst bottleneck on the whole of Britain's railway system, which is in the Borough Market area just west of London Bridge. A new viaduct will be built over the Borough area, allowing Thameslink trains to pass over the lines to Charing Cross and Cannon Street. Part of the existing viaduct will be widened. Controversially, Borough Market will be affected. New developments will take place in the Market and its Victorian roof will be refurbished. The through part of London Bridge Station will be rebuilt with improved track layout and increased capacity. The station at London Bridge will effectively become a podium from which the Shard of Glass will thrust its way into the sky and large parts of it are going to be rebuilt to provide the right kind of launch pad. A dive-under at London Bridge will allow Thameslink trains to follow their route without impeding other lines into and out of London Bridge Station.

The viaducts are such a feature of this part of South London that it is easy for us to forget that under the Borough there once ran a railway of immense historical importance. It was the world's first deep-level tube railway and also the first major electric railway. In 1884 parliamentary powers were obtained for the City of London & Southwark Subway. The intention was for it to be a cable-operated railway running between the Monument near the north end of London Bridge and Elephant & Castle. This was a distance of about one and half miles. Work commenced in October 1886.

Burrowing deep had certain advantages for anyone wanting to build a transport system under London's streets. The London clay, bane of many a gardener's life, is actually comparatively easy to bore through with modern tunnelling machines. Tube lines mostly avoid the complex network of pipes and cables that provide many of London's vital services. They also avoid the costly and complicated legal and financial negotiations that need to be solved where railways are built on or above the surface.

In 1887 legal sanction was given to extend the line southwards to Stockwell via Kennington. This would mean that the entire line would be about three miles long, a fact which cast doubts on whether cable traction would be viable on a line of this length. The decision was taken to use electricity despite doubts about its reliability. A third rail laid alongside the running lines would supply the power and it was decided to employ locomotives. The gauge was to be that which was standard on the main line railway system, although with the tunnels only being 10 feet 6 inches in diameter, the rolling stock was considerably smaller.

The line was opened in November 1890 by the Prince of Wales, who seemed rather confused by the large lift in which he descended to platform level at King William Street Station as the northern terminus of the line in the City was known. Perhaps he had never come across such a contraption before. The Prince made a stirring speech in which he expressed his hopes that the new line would help to tackle the appalling traffic congestion that was bedevilling so much of inner London. Since the average speed over the line, including stops, was over 11 mph, the line must have made some kind of contribution to lessening the burden on the roads along its route because it was markedly faster than the speed any road vehicles could achieve under normal circumstances.

The locomotives were strange-looking little machines but the carriages were even odder. They had no windows that passengers could use, the company arguing that there was nothing to see anyway. Very quickly these carriages gained the not-very-affectionate nickname 'padded cells'. The trains gave a rough ride and in the absence of straps to hold on to, standing passengers were frequently flung around the claustrophobic little cabins on wheels. The electricity supply was at the southern end of the line and was not always sufficient to power trains up what was admittedly a steep incline into King William Street Station. Sometimes the lights went very dim and the train ran back down the incline before stopping and trying the climb again. All this sorely tried those passengers of a nervous disposition but was regarded as great value for money. A conductor rode on the platform of each carriage and was required to bellow out the name of the stations as the train arrived. A fitful electric light illuminated the interior of the carriages and the platforms and passages were gas lit. In the absence of escalators, still to be invented, large hydraulically powered lifts were employed. Altogether, the City & South London was a quirky little line which was unusual by the standards of its time in having only one class and also at first a flat fare of two pennies, on submission of which an operator opened a turnstile. Each train contained a smoking carriage to which lady travellers were not allowed admittance. Although there was a station in Borough High Street, very oddly there was not one at London Bridge, which could have been expected to generate a lot of traffic.

Despite the snags already mentioned and various other teething problems, the line was soon dealing with more passengers than had been anticipated and the locomotives proved grossly underpowered, often failing in service. Despite transporting passengers in unexpectedly large numbers and providing only a poor return for those who had invested in the company, it quickly spawned imitators. The first of these was the Central London Line, which obtained parliamentary approval in summer 1891.

The City & South London, despite some of its oddities and shortcomings, was a success as a deep-level tube electric railway and it undeniably proved the efficacy of using the Greathead tunnelling shield and of the method of constructing the tubes in which the trains ran. Improved locomotives and rolling stock were introduced but in the event were rendered superfluous when a decision was taken to extend the line northwards to the Angel at Islington. This involved abandoning the section from just north of Borough to King William Street completely and driving new tunnels under the river. At last a station was to be built at London Bridge and, on the City side, a station at Bank would replace King William Street. The first portion of line opened to a temporary terminus at Moorgate Street on 25 February 1900. This line has been further extended and now of course forms the City branch of the Northern Line with its southerly terminus at Morden.

The Northern Line under the Thames between London Bridge and Bank was closed on 7 September 1939 shortly after the start of the Second World War and not reopened until 1945. The old tunnel of the original City & South London Railway was eventually brought into use as a deep-level air-raid shelter. That part of Southwark which included London Bridge, Borough and Bankside with its mixture of industry, warehouses, wharves and working-class housing was heavily bombed during the Blitz, and this put a great strain on the local population. Much has been written about the 'shelterers' and the strange nocturnal world that was created down there deep below the streets. M. Panter-Downes wrote fulsomely that 'the courage, humour and kindliness of ordinary people continued to be astonishing'. This was unquestionable. She was fascinated by the nightly descent of so many people into the depths below London. She continued, 'If history is being torn up by the roots in London, history is also being made. The new race of tube dwellers is slipping a fresh page into the record; nothing has ever been seen like the concourse of humanity that camps underground every night ... by five, when the homeward rush hour is in, one walks between double rows of men, women, and children – eating, drinking, sleeping, reading newspapers, and just sitting; all part of the most extraordinary mass picnic the world has ever known.' This roseate view had much truth in it but it told only part of the story. It did not mention the titanic struggle ordinary people had had to fight in order to force the authorities to allow them to shelter in the first place. It did not mention the fear of emerging on the morrow to see what further horrific destruction and chaos had been rendered by bombing overnight. It did not mention the sleeplessness and consequent incapacity to face the following day's challenges for those kept awake for hours on end by the snoring around them or the sheer squalor of the conditions. She says nothing about the sexual promiscuity, the thieving and the fights that took place among the 'shelterers' and the bugs, lice and contagious diseases that thrived in the humid, airless, overcrowded conditions far below ground. The King and Queen visited a number of shelters including that at the Borough in the disused tunnel. This was supposed to be for the purpose of boosting morale. Many Londoners, however, knew that the Royal Family also had their night-time shelter but that the conditions in that shelter would have borne no resemblance whatever to those endured night after night by the people who actually kept London going throughout the war.

The abandoned tunnel housing the original line from Borough to King William Street slumbers on, an eerie place whose only denizens are rats and ghosts.

14

The Twentieth Century

Bankside and Borough were affected by some momentous events and changes during the twentieth century. St Saviour's became Southwark Cathedral in 1905, old industries declined and disappeared, the area was subject to bombing, notably in the Second World War, traditional communities experienced upheavals and changes, people from the Caribbean settled in Southwark and were followed later by immigrants from West Africa, South America and Eastern Europe. Towards the end of the century Bankside would see a huge regeneration that would have been unimaginable even twenty years previously. In addition there were changes in local government. In 1900 the century began with the creation of twenty-eight metropolitan boroughs. The metropolitan borough of Southwark included the areas now known as the Borough, Bankside, Elephant & Castle, Newington and Walworth. This came to an end on 1 April 1965 when the London Borough of Southwark was formed by the amalgamation of the three metropolitan boroughs of Southwark, Camberwell and Bermondsey.

The Boer War (1899–1902) had served to highlight the poor health of the British working class when up to 40 per cent of recruits were deemed unfit for military service with many suffering from problems such as rickets, which is symptomatic of malnutrition, and other poverty-related diseases. Attempts to improve this situation saw the introduction of medical inspections of children in schools and the provision of free school meals for the very poor. The pattern of disease in the capital fifty years earlier was dominated by fevers and was associated with poverty, hunger, vice and dirt. Hospitals and workhouses had to be content with dealing with the consequences of the conditions around them; hospitals for those who were proper objects of charitable relief and the workhouses for the destitute. Even though high infant mortality rates pushed up the age of deaths in Southwark in the mid-1840s the average age of death was twenty years for artisans and forty-six for the gentry, well below that for most of London.

In 1917 during the First World War only 36 per cent of men examined were suitable for full military duties, and 40 per cent were either totally unfit or were classified as unable to undergo physical exertion. Southwark had been viewed by late Victorian poverty surveys as suffering from a high degree of poverty and overcrowding. Nonetheless when war broke out in 1914 there was a surge of patriotism among men from the area who volunteered to fight. In South London tens of thousands of men enlisted for service and many women entered the workforce in the absence of men who were fighting on the front. The war took a tragic toll with nearly 350 men from St Saviour's parish alone losing their lives.

A blackout of London began in autumn 1914. However German airships, mainly Zeppelins, did not begin to bomb the capital until 31 May 1915. Some 600 Londoners died from German bombing raids. The only notable air raid in the Bankside area was in 1917 when three people were killed at Bennington (Blue Cross) Tea Co. in Southwark Street. In Borough High Street a war memorial, designed by P. Lindsey Clark and erected in 1924, commemorates the 'men of St Saviour's, Southwark who gave their lives for the Empire 1914–1918'. A bronze figure of a soldier with tin hat and rifle marches through mud, with figures of a knight in armour and a weeping woman and child. One bronze panel depicts battleships and the other biplanes in aerial combat. Nearby is a large wall-mounted bronze memorial with sprays of hops to the hopmen of London killed in the First World War.

The end of the First World War brought with it demobilisation, unemployment and demonstrations. Some years later in the 1926 General Strike battles were fought with striking workers against scab labour, notably Oxford undergraduates, and police to prevent unloading at Hay's Wharf. Labour MPs were critical of police violence against strikers in Southwark.

Observations of Bankside and the area were made between the wars by author and illustrator Grace Lydia Golden (1904–93), who was born in East London to a working-class family then moved to the City end of Southwark Bridge Road at the age of five where, from the top window of a five-storey house, she could observe the working Thames river. Grace became an artist and depicted an extraordinary range of London life in her work and particularly the working life of the Thames. From childhood she had witnessed the lives of the industrious people who were employed near and on the river. This fascination led to her producing her *Old Bankside* (1951) book. Her descriptions of places along Bankside reveal an insight into the lanes, alleys and houses. Describing Skin Market she wrote of a 'row of two-storey, jerry built houses ... the crumbling brickwork of half demolished dwellings'. She observed children with 'bare feet and matted hair' and the gas-lit interiors of the houses revealing a 'broken brass bedstead and tumbled bedding'. Between 1936 and 1940, she was exhibited at the Royal Academy, working in both water colour and oils and a number of her paintings are held by the Tate and the National Archives. Years later, Sam Wanamaker invited Golden to become an honorary archivist to the Bear Gardens Museum project.

The Second World War took a huge toll on London, destroying well-known landmarks, irreplaceable historic buildings as well as homes, shops, offices and factories. The loss of life and the number of serious injuries were considerable with almost 30,000 people killed during the war in London and a further 50,000 seriously injured. Docklands was particularly vulnerable as it became a major target for the Luftwaffe. The government delivered Anderson shelters to house people in their own back gardens and railway arches were converted into shelters but these were the places where bombs could be expected to fall. Southwark suffered during the Second World War as a consequence of German bombing. Most of the windows of the cathedral were blown out and the organ was put out of action. In Sumner Street, named after John Sumner, there stood St Peter's church (consecrated in 1839), which had been built on ground leased from the Bishop of Winchester by Messrs Potts, the vinegar distillers. In 1940 it fell victim to German bombs and was completely destroyed.

One of the worst nights was 17 February 1941. Heavy bombing raids took place across London, with thirty-four incidents occurring in Southwark. This was the night of the tragic Stainer Street bombing. Some 300 people were taking shelter at the arch near London Bridge Station, which had been converted into a shelter containing a medical aid post. At each end of the shelter was a pair of 10-ton steel doors. It was at 10.25 p.m. that a high-explosive bomb burst into the shelter and exploded in the medical aid post hurling the steel doors into the shelter. To add to the mayhem the water and hydraulic mains burst which contributed to 68 people being killed and 175 injured. Many had been crushed by the steel doors and were beyond recognition. A plaque at the St Thomas Street end of Stainer Street commemorates the bombing.

Business continued as best it could in places such as Borough Market and other makeshift spaces. Growers from farms in Kent and Essex made their pitches and did business by the light of oil lamps in one particular area which backed onto Southwark Cathedral. Breakfasts could be had at small cafés nearby where a cup of tea and a sausage sandwich were a welcome relief. The area around Borough High Street, London Bridge Station and St Thomas Street was busy. Guy's Hospital suffered some bomb damage, but still operated and remained open treating over 3,000 air-raid casualties throughout the war.

On Borough High Street a post office was demolished and a little further south Great Dover Street, Swan Street and the surrounding area were badly damaged. A three-floor building collapsed and about 200 houses and other buildings were damaged in Blackfriars and neighbouring roads. When high explosives fell near a school betwe en Copperfield Street and Union Street, the school was fortunately empty, thus sparing any casualties. The evacuation of these children had been successful. On 22 January 1945 there was a serious V2 Rocket incident in Borough High Street near the junction with Southwark Street. Major destruction was caused to the area with thirty-five people killed in the offices and workshops that occupied the site.

Wartime bombing had been something of a mixed blessing for Southwark. It left much of the local population homeless, but it also forced change and Southwark became a major focus for redevelopment. After the war, the new Bankside Power Station, conceived by Sir Giles Gilbert Scott, was constructed. However by the 1970s changes in oil prices and technology meant that the power station gradually slipped into obsolescence as did much of the surrounding area, and Bankside soon became cut off from the mainstream of London. This situation had been made worse by the decline of the docks and the food and manufacturing industries in the 1970s and 1980s, which in turn had brought further unemployment and poverty to many local people. Bankside had been, from the mid-eighteenth century, active in trade, commerce and industry. During the nineteenth century there was a gasworks, an iron foundry, glassmaking, a coconut fibre works, a boiler works, a vinegar distillery, breweries and wharves that lined the river. There were some 90,000 people in the Bankside ward alone. After the Second World War the area became impoverished, tightly packed with alleyways, factories and slums.

Town planner Sir Leslie Patrick Abercrombie (1879–1957) is best known for the post-Second World War re-planning of London. He created the County of London Plan (1943) and the Greater London Plan (1944), commonly referred to as the Abercrombie Plan. The Plan had proposed that Southwark's population should be half of what it was before the war, although bombing had already meant many people were unable to return to their homes. The post-war intention to revitalise London through such planning had failed by the 1960s. Population declined even below the intended target as people left the Borough because of council building schemes.

Much of Docklands had been destroyed during the war and the following decade saw a reconstruction of the industry and its working practices. However, by the late 1960s changes in goods transportation, notably the development of large container ships, contributed to the end of the industry and the jobs that accompanied it. Major local manufacturing factories followed this trend by the 1980s, leaving empty wharves from Blackfriars Bridge to Rotherhithe. The knock-on effect was seen in the closure of local shops, clubs and cinemas.

Southwark has a long history of immigration, with Flemish emigrants arriving from the fifteenth century. During the mid-nineteenth century a new influx of immigrants from Ireland fled the Potato Famine of the 1840s to work on the new London & Greenwich railway. To help with Britain's post-war recovery, people from the Caribbean settled in Southwark from the 1950s. During the 1970s and 1980s political refugees from Vietnam came to live in Southwark and further refugees from Cyprus also settled in the 1970s. In recent years people from various West African countries such as Sierra Leone, Liberia and Somalia who were escaping war and conflict have come to live in the area. There is also a growing Latin American community as well as people from Poland and other Eastern European countries who have came to find employment.

The London Borough of Southwark was formed in 1965 out of the local metropolitan councils of Bermondsey, Southwark and Camberwell. There had been proposals to rebuild local industries and to develop Bankside as a cultural centre and area for offices. However, this would also mean decreasing the population. The attempt to rebuild industries did not last, and by the 1980s they began to disappear. Sainsbury's, whose food-processing site was in Bankside for years, moved away in 1973; the hop trade with its long history went as did the Bankside

Power Station, which closed in 1981; the London Hydraulic Power Works next to the power station went in 1977; the City Lead Works near Southwark Bridge was demolished in 1981. Others followed. Hay's Wharf, near London Bridge, bought up land between London Bridge and Tower Bridge in the 1950s, which became very lucrative by the 1970s. In 1971 over 200 wharf workers protested about the activities of property companies buying land and industries in the borough. It was all to no avail as a £300 million plan for the development of shops, offices, hotels and homes was put forward. The following year local tenants' associations began to oppose the Hay's Wharf plan. This action at least delayed developments for about four months, but land and property speculation in the area soared. In a five-year period shops and homes were turned into office developments.

Once there had been cranes, barges, timber yards, tanning yards, warehouses, a large vinegar manufacturer, at least two large breweries, hatters, hawkers, drapers, porters, labourers, a 'skin market', factories that made soap, lead, and patent medicines and of course the variety of river occupations. These are gone along with the two-way traffic that had run along Bankside for three centuries. Skin Market Place, which was demolished to make way for the Globe Theatre, was once an island that yielded Neolithic pottery and centuries later showed evidence of timber-revetted seventeenth-century fish ponds on the King's Pike Garden. By the nineteenth century it contained a jam factory and a number of small, cramped houses that once accommodated workers who laboured on the barges. Between the wars those old houses were replaced by a factory that made soap and perfume. Some of the spaces along and behind Bankside have been made into community areas such as the Community Garden Space on the front of the landscape of Tate Modern, which was formally opened in June 2007.

From the 1990s Bankside went through a huge regeneration turning it from a run-down and forgotten area overlooking the City to one of London's main tourist spots. This is the subject of out next chapter.

15

Re-inventing Bankside

Following industrial decline after the Second World War, Bankside remained largely derelict and neglected. By the millennium it was one of London's main tourist attractions. With the establishment of attractions such as the Globe Theatre, Tate Modern, Millennium Bridge, Clink Prison, Bankside Gallery, replica of the *Golden Hind*, restaurants, and the adjacent Borough Market, the changes in Bankside have been amongst the most dynamic in London.

By the 1950s Docklands had fallen into terminal decline, as a result of greater overseas competition and outdated port facilities. Twenty years later the Docklands were virtually derelict. The developments within the former docks of East and South East London were the first stage of the regeneration of the riverside. One has only to see the huge changes that have taken place between Tower Bridge and the Isle of Dogs over the past three decades to appreciate the scale of development. From 1981 the London Docklands Development Corporation (LDDC – an urban development corporation that operated between July 1981 and March 1998 to secure the regeneration of the London Docklands) was invested with a large degree of planning. They had extensive powers to purchase and sell land compulsorily, as well as 'vesting' (transfer of land from the local authorities). Much of the land they gained, which had previously been public properties, was sold to private developers at knockdown prices. Vast amounts of speculative capital and developers competing in prestige constructions led to a transformation of the landscape around Docklands as huge expanses of mud and concrete were turned into a high-rise skyline of glass and steel. A huge inflation in land prices followed, soaring from £70,000 per acre in 1981 when the LDDC was set up to around £4 million within six years. Little wonder that areas such as north Southwark became a dream for property developers.

In 1987 Nicholas Ridley, then Minister for Environment, could boast:

> Take a trip around London Docklands and see what has happened. In five years it has been transformed from a desert of dereliction to a showpiece of British building, design, architecture and business. It has created thousands of jobs by stimulating private enterprise. Homes have been built and refurbished.
>
> – *Listener*, 3 December 1987

The Dockland area on both sides of the river witnessed the transition of wharves into apartment blocks, disused jam factories (Hartley's Jam Factory off Tower Bridge Road) into converted chic, riverside loft-living accommodation along with restaurants and huge office complexes. These developments reflected a stark contrast between those who occupied these conversions and locals living in the social housing of the old London County Council flats that remained. Much of the criticism of the LDDC has been levelled at its failure to bring about social change, particularly for the lower social classes. The Docklands were regenerated economically, but not socially. A 1996 survey found at least half of the population did not reap any benefits from the millions poured in. Traditional working-class areas such as the Borough saw the local community destroyed in a short period as local shops and homes along Borough High Street were turned into office developments. Throughout most of the 1990s no council housing was built in Southwark. Regeneration, it seems, often led to gentrification.

With the inevitable closure of the docks the London Boroughs needed to replace them with alternative planning ventures but there were often conflicts of interest between the boroughs and some of the ideas put forward for regeneration. For example there was disagreement between Southwark Council regarding permission for the building of the Globe Theatre. The *Independent* (8 December 2003) commented that Southwark claimed that the site 'was the only place that it could store municipal dustcarts'. Of particular note was Greenmoor Wharf on Bankside, which was the site of Southwark Corporation's rubbish depot. Refuse was once transported by horse and cart then loaded into these barges by chutes and hydraulic cranes. The barge's loaded with refuse would head downriver to the estuary.

In the late 1980s Southwark Council drew up a regeneration strategy aimed at developing Bankside into a vibrant area which would provide a new cultural focus for London. This regeneration has no doubt been helped, particularly in the planning stages, by the presence of the LDDC, which acted as a catalyst by allowing and encouraging architectural projects and making available sites around Butlers Wharf.

An important factor in the regeneration of Bankside was the transformation of the redundant Bankside Power Station into the Tate Modern Art Gallery. Disused, derelict and dreary, the original Bankside Power Station stood as the polar opposite of the tourist draw it has now become. It showed great perception and commitment to convert a disused power station into an attraction that would draw 5 million visitors a year, even exceeding the initial expectations for annual visitor numbers of 2 million. It is a testimony to the hard work and planning that Tate Modern is now one of the UK's top tourist attractions.

The original Bankside Power Station dates from the late nineteenth century and was coal-fired. The Electricity Act of 1947 nationalised the industry and created twelve area boards from the existing proliferation of power supply and distribution companies. The London Electricity Board (LEB) took over responsibility for Bankside and a new oil-fired plant was commissioned. Bankside Power Station, designed by Sir Giles Gilbert Scott, was built in two phases between 1947 and 1963. The western half of the structure, which included the chimney, replaced an earlier coal-fired power station, in 1952. The eastern half of the building was brought into commission in 1963.

However, by 1981 the power station closed and for many years was at risk of being demolished by developers eager to buy this desirable riverside location. Campaigners fought for it to be declared a 'listed' building, although not everyone agreed that it was a particularly attractive building. In fact when the power station was built, many thought that such a large building at Bankside was hardly in keeping with any idea of post-war regeneration and there was huge local opposition. Questions were raised in the House of Commons (10 June 1947) about the noise and sulphur or other noxious fumes. In addition the power station was considered architecturally incongruous with St Paul's Cathedral on the opposite side of the river.

After just twenty-nine years of electricity generation the station closed as a result of the increase in oil prices, which meant that other forms of electricity production became more cost effective. Bankside Power Station remained empty for thirteen years until Tate Modern acquired the site in 1994. Transforming Sir Gilbert Scott's power station into Tate Modern was never straight forward, particularly in light of conservationists who campaigned to have the building listed. The then curator of the Tate Gallery, Nicholas Serota, had listened to suggestions that the building would be a good place for a new gallery of modern art. Serota became a convert and enthusiast for the idea and invested much of his energy into planning and raising money for the site as well as overcoming opposition from certain quarters including some sections of Southwark local council. Nonetheless, the gallery was given support from the people of Southwark when they were asked.

The Tate Gallery at Millbank had begun to outgrow its collection, and in December 1992, the Tate Trustees announced their intention to separate the display of the Tate Collection in London between two sites. The original Millbank gallery, which became Tate Britain, would show British art from 1500 to the present day, while a new national gallery of international modern and contemporary art would be created at a separate site. Three years later in 1995 the leading Swiss architects

Herzog & de Meuron were appointed to transform the Bankside Power Station into an art gallery. Bankside Power Station proved an inspired discovery with its proximity to the Thames, St Paul's, Globe Theatre and a panoramic view across the river. In 1995 Tate received £52 million towards the conversion of the former power station to create Tate Modern. The final cost was £135 million; Serota managed to secure the funds to make up the shortfall from a range of private sources. The £135 million conversion to Tate Modern started in June 1995 with the removal of all the power station machinery, the roofs of both the old boiler house and the turbine hall, the demolition of a number of outbuildings and sandblasting and repainting of the remaining steelwork. On 11 May 2000 Tate Modern opened (with free admission) to the public.

The power station consisted of a substantial central chimney which stands at 99 m (320 feet) and a huge turbine hall, five storeys tall with 3,400 square metres of floor space, which once was home to the giant electricity generators of the old power station. Parallel to the turbine hall was the boiler house, which became the Tate Modern galleries. The turbine hall at 500 feet long by 100 feet high provided a dramatic entrance area, with ramped access, as well as a large display space for specially commissioned works by contemporary artists. A 35-foot-high giant bronze spider by Louise Bourgeois provided the inaugural exhibition at Tate Modern.

The Tate Collection of modern art is displayed on two of the gallery floors and the third is devoted to temporary exhibitions. The top level houses a café-restaurant with stunning views of the river and the City.

Since it opened the Tate Modern galleries were not displayed in chronological order but were arranged thematically into four broad groups:

– History/Memory/Society
– Nude/Action/Body
– Landscape/Matter/Environment
– Still Life/Object/Real Life

In May 2006 Tate Modern rejected the thematic groupings in favour of pivotal moments of twentieth-century art. The layout is now as follows: Level 3 'Material Gestures', which is devoted to painting and sculpture from the 1940s and 1950s, and how new forms of abstraction and expressive figuration emerged in post-war Europe and America. The 'Poetry and Dream' gallery looks at how contemporary art provides fresh insights into the art of the past and includes a wing devoted to Surrealism. Also on Level 3 is a gallery called 'Scale Experimentations' which is intended to encourage new views of the familiar. On Level 5 the two galleries are 'Energy and Process', which looks at artists' interest in transformation and natural forces, and 'States of Flux', which is devoted to the early twentieth-century art movements Cubism, Futurism and Vorticism. Tate Modern now stands as Britain's national museum of modern and contemporary art displaying the works of famous twentieth-century artists such as Cézanne, Bonnard, Matisse, Picasso, Rothko, Dalí, Pollock and Warhol.

The Millennium Bridge was designed by Norman Foster, Anthony Caro and Ove Arup to link Tate Modern with St Paul's Cathedral, just across the Thames. There is also a 'Tate-to-Tate' catamaran service (with interiors and exteriors designed by British artist Damien Hirst) for visitors operating during gallery hours linking Tate Modern with Tate Britain.

In a period of eight years Tate Modern has revitalised Bankside, transformed an underdeveloped area of London and has become a key London landmark. Further expansion of the building is planned. Tate has embarked on a £215 million development to create a spectacular new building designed by architects Herzog & de Meuron, with the aim of completing in time for the London Olympics in 2012.

In March 2009 it was reported that the remains of Shakespeare's first theatre had been found in Shoreditch, East London. Archaeologists from the Museum of London unearthed what they believe to be part of the original curved wall of the first Globe Theatre built outside the City in 1576. They also uncovered the Tudor structure's gravel surface, the area where the audience would have stood that sloped down towards the stage, as well as a fragment of pottery of a man with a beard that resembles Shakespeare. However, the stage itself is thought to be buried under a housing development.

What do we know about the seventeenth-century Globe? Although its actual dimensions are unknown, its shape and size can be approximated from much scholarly inquiry over the last two centuries. According to Dr John Orrell, who became involved with the Globe project in 1979, it was a three-storey, open-air amphitheatre approximately 100 feet (30 m) in diameter and could house up to 3,000 spectators. The actual location of the theatre remained unknown until a small part of the foundations, including one original pier base, was discovered in 1989 beneath the car park at the rear of Anchor Terrace on Park Street, a short walk from the site of the rebuilt Globe Theatre. The site on Park Street is marked by a plaque and some information boards as well as a useful granite line showing the original theatre location.

In 1949 the American-born actor-director-producer Sam Wanamaker came to London looking for the site of the original Globe and was disappointed not to find a more lasting memorial to Shakespeare and his theatre. As a first step in bringing Shakespeare back to the bank of the Thames, Wanamaker acquired some rights to property in Emerson Street and persuaded the Southwark Borough Council to allow him to operate a tent theatre in which he mounted Shakespearean and contemporary dramas. Sam also began a Shakespeare museum and a small theatre in a warehouse just around the corner. By 1970, from these beginnings, the International Shakespeare Globe Centre project emerged. In 1987 building work began on site, and in 1993 the construction of the Globe Theatre began, after twenty-three years of fundraising, research into the appearance of the original Globe and planning the reconstruction with the Trust's architect Theo Crosby. Sam Wanamaker died on 18 December 1993.

Research for the design of the Globe was based on contemporary evidence, including a drawing by artist Wenceslaus Hollar around 1638 in preparation for his later etching 'Long View of London'. Hollar's drawing, as well as other sources, gave clues to the Globe's exact appearance, for example the seating arrangements and capacity. However, the building of the present Globe had to make some compromises, because, for example, modern audiences consist of people substantially larger, on average, than Elizabethans.

The Globe was not a truly circular building and the excavation of the Rose theatre in 1989 confirmed what most scholars had long suspected – that the Elizabethan playhouses were polygonal buildings. Great pains were taken to ensure that the reconstruction of the theatre was accurate. For example, 'green' oak was cut and fashioned according to sixteenth-century methods; oak laths and staves, which support lime plaster, were mixed according to a contemporary recipe and the walls were covered in a white lime wash. The water reed thatch roof is based on samples found during the excavation. The stage was the most difficult as nothing survives from the period to give any clues, thus this had to be conjectural. As information for the Globe Theatre itself states, 'the new Globe is designed with the 21st century in mind. An additional exit, illuminated signage, fire retardant materials and some modern backstage machinery are all concessions to our times. The reconstruction is as faithful to the original as modern scholarship and traditional craftsmanship can make it.'

The present Globe Theatre has a capacity for more than 1,500 people, 500 of them standing in the yard at the actors' feet, many of them close enough to reach out and touch. During the 5½-month theatre season in 2009, over 345,000 theatre-goers experienced a play at the Globe.

A replica of Sir Francis Drake's famous ship the *Golden Hind* (or *Golden Hinde*), painted in black, red and yellow, is berthed in St Mary Overie Dock, Pickfords Wharf, only a short walk from Southwark Cathedral.

The original *Golden Hind* became famous as the flagship of Sir Francis Drake during his three-year voyage around the world between 1577 and 1580. It was originally known as the *Pelican*, but was later renamed by Drake mid-voyage. In 1577 Drake and his crew left Plymouth with the intention of becoming the first Englishmen to circumnavigate the globe. Queen Elizabeth I granted Drake a charter allowing him to attack and loot enemy ships, which effectively meant the Spanish. Drake, who captured much treasure from Spanish ships, saw himself as acting as a privateer, but the Spanish viewed his actions as piracy.

Drake intended to pass around South America through the Strait of Magellan and to explore the coast that lay beyond. He set sail in December with five small ships, manned by 164 men, and reached the Brazilian coast in the spring of 1578. He returned across the Pacific, reaching the Cape of Good Hope in June 1580. On 26 September 1580, Drake arrived into Plymouth Harbour with only fifty-six of the one hundred original crew. Drake's exploits made him both rich and famous as well as a favourite of Elizabeth. She visited the *Golden Hind* and Drake was knighted on the deck of the ship.

The *Golden Hind* became Britain's first museum ship when Elizabeth decreed that it should be preserved at Deptford in order that the general public could visit the ship and celebrate Drake's success. The ship remained there for nearly 100 years before she eventually rotted away and was finally broken up.

The replica of the *Golden Hind,* which stands at Bankside, is a fully working ship that was launched in Devon in 1973. It has sailed over 140,000 miles, and in 1979–80, it retraced Drake's around-the-world route. Between 1984 and 1985, it circumnavigated the British Isles and then sailed to the Caribbean. The following year it sailed through Panama Canal to Canada for the World's Fair in Vancouver. It sailed on further voyages between 1987 and 1992, including the United States and the Gulf of Mexico. It has also featured in the films *Swashbuckler* (1976), *Shogun* (1979) and *Drake's Venture* (1980). Since 1996 it has been berthed at Pickfords Wharf in Bankside. Another replica of the *Golden Hind* has been permanently moored in the harbour at Brixham in Devon since 1963.

Given the notorious history of Bankside and Southwark, as well as the number of prisons boasted by the area, it's not surprising that a number of tourist attractions were quick to cater for this darker and grisly history. These have proved enormously popular over the years and include the London Dungeon, the more recent London Bridge

Experience/London Tombs on Tooley Street and the Clink Prison Museum on Clink Street.

A short walk from London Bridge and situated near the remains of the fourteenth-century Palace of the Bishop of Winchester is the Clink Prison Museum on Bankside. A gibbet-hung skeleton suspended high on the outside wall offers a portent of what is in store. Clink Museum is built on the foundations of one of the original prisons once owned by the Bishops of Winchester. The word clink is believed to have derived from the clinking of the manacles, fetters, chains and bolts as well as meaning 'in prison'. The Clink was in use from the twelfth century until 1780. Life in the prison was grim and the prisoners were treated badly with beatings and torture as common practice. In 1485 Bishops were ordered by Henry VII (r. 1485–1509) to incarcerate priests in the Clink for adultery, incest and fornication whilst Queen Mary I (r. 1553–58) used the Clink to imprison and starve Protestants. Queen Elizabeth (r. 1558–1603) continued to use the prison for religious persecution, but this time it was mainly Catholics who were on the receiving end. The present museum, which was refurbished in 2007, attempts to recreate the conditions of the prison with a series of cells, a whipping post, torture chair, foot crusher, and other torture instruments.

The London Dungeon is located in Tooley Street, near London Bridge Station. It opened in 1976 as an elaborate chamber of horrors but the Dungeon has evolved to become an actor-led, interactive experience that draws visitors from far and wide. The visitor can expect to see and be scared by various tortures throughout history. The Dungeon recreates various gory historical events in a gallows humour style by using a mixture of live actors, special effects and rides. It is operated by Merlin Entertainments, which also operates Madame Tussauds and London Eye.

The cellars of the Dungeon are located under London Bridge Station and contain such ghoulish pleasures as the mirror maze, the Great Plague and Great Fire of London (which includes smells and cries of agony), the Boat Ride to Hell, the Sweeney Todd Show, the Drop Ride to Hell and a Jack the Ripper Exhibition.

Across the road from the London Dungeon are two recent tourist attractions: the London Bridge Experience and the London Tombs. Located under the streets, the London Bridge Experience, which officially opened in February 2008, is geared towards family entertainment. It displays a 2,000-year history of London Bridge complete with haunted tunnels. During the excavation and construction of the London Bridge Experience workers came across a large collection of buried bones. Some of the skulls had holes through the top of their craniums. One theory suggests that they might have been the heads of executed criminals and traitors that were placed on London Bridge as a warning to others. The London Tombs is for the brave-hearted and is designed to scare those who enter with its haunted catacombs, zombies and other unsavoury creatures that leap from the darkness.

Anyone looking for a wine-tasting experience might want to pay a visit to Vinopolis which is built into massive Victorian railway arches and is located between London and Southwark Bridges next to Borough Market. Vinopolis was developed by a wine merchant called Duncan Vaughan-Arbuckle and launched in 1999. It has a mini amphitheatre for wine-tasting sessions, and visitors proceed to other rooms that are spread out deep in the cavernous confines of the Vinopolis complex.

The business started as a four-hour-long guided tour through static wine displays with tastings, but gradually evolved over time. In September 2005 the Whisky Exchange set up a retail shop in the complex and in 2008 Vinopolis opened the Authentic Caribbean Rum Experience where visitors are taken on a journey through the rum production process and allowed to sample a diverse selection of Caribbean rums. There is also an attached restaurant, Cantina Vinopolis.

With its railway arches, narrow streets and riverside location, Bankside has provided an ideal location for a number of well-known films. The area around Borough Market became the setting for a few scenes in *Bridget Jones's Diary* (2001, dir. Sharon Maguire) and *Bridget Jones: The Edge of Reason* (2004, dir. Beeban Kidron). A flat above the Globe pub on Bedale Street near Borough Market was where the eponymous heroine lived her single life. Across from Bedale Street the shops were transformed into the cab office, the newsagent and the Greek restaurant where Daniel Cleaver (Hugh Grant) and Mark Darcy (Colin Firth) fight during a birthday party. Bridget walks despondently through Borough Market after discovering Cleaver with Lara (Lisa Barbuscia) and the Clink Wharf Apartments on Clink Street were used as Cleaver's flat.

Nearby Stoney Street can claim to be the location for a number of film scenes. The triple-decker Knight Bus in *Harry Potter and the Prisoner of Azkaban* (2004, dir. Alfonson Cuaron) trundles along the street whilst the pub the Market Porter was the setting for the 'Third Hand Book Emporium' and next door became the 'Leaky Cauldron'. Also on Stoney Street Harvey Keitel, who plays a US cop (John Harris), sees his British counterparts incinerated in their car in *The Young Americans* (1993, dir. Danny Cannon). Green Dragon Court in Borough Market was used in the filming of the fantasy film *The Imaginarium of Dr. Parnassus* (2009, dir. Terry Gilliam) and also *The French Lieutenant's Woman* (1981, dir. Karel Reisz), where Charles (Jeremy Irons), the Victorian gentleman, searches for Sarah (Meryl Streep) among the whores.

Winchester Walk became the grubby little side street in *An American Werewolf in London* (1981, dir. John Landis) where the werewolf is finally cornered. Also on Winchester Walk is a bar called the Rake, which provided a scene for Mike Leigh's *Naked* (1993). Park Street has been frequently used for film scenes, which include *Keep the Aspidistra Flying* (1997, dir. Robert Bierman), *Howards End* (1992, dir. James Ivory) and *Lock Stock and Two Smoking Barrels* (1998, dir. Guy Ritchie). In *Lock, Stock* the gang's hideout is 15 Park Street. Park Street provides a scene in *Entrapment* (1999, dir. Jon Amiel) starring Sean Connery and Catherine Zeta-Jones as well as David Cronenberg's *Spider* (2002), in which it is the site of Spider's (Ralph Fiennes) childhood. The historic Anchor Tavern is a place where Ethan Hunt (Tom Cruise) relaxes on the terrace in *Mission Impossible* (1996, dir. Brian de Palma), a far cry from the days when Samuel Pepys watched the Great Fire in 1665 from the Anchor.

Tate Modern makes appearances in *Bridget Jones's Diary* and *Agent Cody Banks 2: Destination London* (2004, dir. Kevin Allen). It is also where Chris Wilton (Jonathan Rhys Meyers) bumps into Nola (Scarlett Johansson) in the gallery in *Match Point* (2005, dir. Woody Allen) while the Turbine Hall appears in *Children of Men* (2006, dir. Alfonso Cuaron). During the transition from Bankside Power Station to Tate Modern in 1995 the building served as the Tower of London in *Richard III* (1995, dir. Richard Loncraine). Next to Tate Modern is Hopton Street, where incriminating evidence is thrown into the Thames beneath Blackfriars Bridge in *Match Point.*

One particular vision of the future is Shard London Bridge, also known as London Bridge Tower, which will be the first building in the UK to break the 1,000-foot barrier. When completed in 2012 it will be the tallest building in the UK, nearly twice the height of the Gherkin, and one of the tallest buildings in Europe. It will consist of seventy-two floors, plus fifteen further radiator floors in the roof. The architect is Renzo Piano, who compares his design to a 'shard of glass'.

The project will mean major improvements to London Bridge Station and the surrounding area, such as a new concourse and public piazza, affordable housing, a new museum and regeneration programmes.

In September 2007, preparations for the demolition of Southwark Towers had begun, but instability in the financial markets put the construction phase of the project into jeopardy. New owners promised to provide finance, which meant construction of the tower could begin. In early 2009, demolition of Southwark Towers was complete, and site preparation began for construction.

By October 2009, steel beams began to appear and by mid-spring 2010 the building was progressing well with final completion planned for May 2012. It is intended that the 'Shard at London Bridge Quarter' will combine a mix of office residences, hotel, restaurants and public viewing platforms. The Shard will be open to the public, who can visit the viewing platforms on floors 68–72. London Bridge Quarter will include a new public square for art installations, cafés and places for visitors to the area to relax.

A project designed to guide visitors on foot around London is the Jubilee Walkway, the capital's premier walking trail and one of

London's seven designated Strategic Routes. It was designed to connect the majority of London's key attractions and was first developed for the Queen's Silver Jubilee in 1977. The Jubilee Walkway Trust was then set up in 1978 as a charity to look after its interest in partnership with strategic and local authorities. Its purpose is to 'provide an opportunity for visitors to experience the variety of London life'. To that end the Jubilee Walkway enters Southwark from Lambeth, runs along the south bank of the Thames and leaves Southwark crossing the Thames on Tower Bridge. Another service that facilitates tourists is the Bankside Pier, a stop on the river bus service. It is located on the Thames, close to Tate Modern.

Regeneration and the issues of preserving the past led in the 1980s to many debates around the idea of 'heritage' as distinct from history. Heritage was initially motivated by the principles of an 'enterprise culture' and critics argued that the so-called 'heritage industry' contributed to creating a false past which could be packaged and sold. According to this view, it became difficult to tell the difference between history and a romanticised, sanitised construction of it. Heritage itself is a large and clumsy term that has on the one hand been instrumental in providing a good deal of important historical preservation and in stimulating an interest in history. On the other hand there have been some spurious projects more concerned with money making than providing a faithful representation of the past. The development of Bankside provides an interesting mirror for these debates.

What now stands as penthouse accommodation and shopping centres with names such as Tea Trade Wharf was once part of the great larder of London. Advertisements which promote the properties, and by doing so attempt to define the commercial potential and nature of Bankside, state,

To truly absorb Shad Thames unique environs perhaps one should step back 50 years and relive the grand heydays of 'the Empires Warehouses' – then return to the present, blend in fabulous international al-fresco eateries, specialty and haute couture boutiques, showcase arts and more.

The tea trade was once worth millions of pounds a year, and tea was one of the main consumer goods brought to Britain from the East. For 200 years the East India Company sailing ships returning from China would unload their cargoes on the Thames with some Clipper sailing ships coming as far as London Bridge in the 1860s. The trade expanded rapidly between 1750 and 1900 and tea-drinking began as an expensive and fashionable pastime in Britain. But as tea became cheaper, more people could afford it. The Bramah Museum, at 40 Southwark Street, is the world's first museum devoted entirely to the history of tea and coffee. Bramah's tells the 400-year-old commercial and social history of tea and coffee, two of the world's most important commodities since their arrival in Europe from the Far East and Africa. As the British played a key role both in the China trade and development of production in India, Ceylon and Africa, the museum naturally tells the story from a British perspective. Unfortunately, the museum closed down for refurbishment and at the time of writing shows little sign of reopening.

As part of a seasonal tourist attraction Southwark Council in 2003 recreated the Frost Fair, which dates back hundreds of years to when the Thames used to freeze over and Londoners took to the ice for fun and games. The last Frost Fair was held in 1814, almost 200 years ago. However, in an age conscious of Health and Safety, the reinvented Frost Fair did not include skating on the ice (should there be any ice). Instead it substituted this with a 'spectacular 40 metre real ice slide'. In addition there were riverwalks outside Tate Modern and the Globe, lantern processions, marquees, beer tent, street entertainment, ice sculpting, stalls selling festive food, children's activities, street theatre and choirs singing Christmas carols.

As with many parts of London, the deindustrialisation of factories, warehouses and offices saw the abandonment of many areas. On Bankside old warehouses were converted into flats, penthouses and shops and, as we saw, the power station into an art gallery. A middle-class shift to the area followed from the 1990s as *The Times* commented in 1998: 'Five years ago, hardly anyone lived between Waterloo and Tower Bridge except council tenants.'

Bankside to Tower Bridge was once known as London's larder. The larders now are in the form of the fresh produce of Borough Market and the wealth of eating places and pubs surrounding it. As with much of the south bank of the Thames, the Borough has seen extensive regeneration in the last two decades. Declining light industry and factories have given way to residential development, shops, restaurants, galleries and bars. With the establishment of the Globe in 1993 and Tate Modern in 2000, Bankside became an increasingly attractive place and inevitably new lofts and warehouse refits appeared in the backstreets of Bankside and Borough. In addition to facilities such as Glaziers Hall, a conference and banqueting venue, there are many building projects such as NEO Bankside (which completes a first phase of development in 2010). NEO Bankside states that it is 'poised to become one of the most desirable residential addresses in the world' with '197 stunning, luxury apartments and penthouses, designed by the international, award-winning architects Rogers Stirk Harbour + Partners'. 'Bankside Lofts' are advertised as a group of 'idiosyncratic buildings where the oldest is an Italianate red brick mill which supplied cocoa to the Empire'. Keeping up the Empire theme, it adds that the new 'glassy penthouse floors add the equivalent of froth on top of the cocoa'.

To see the development of shops, restaurants, offices and residential flats, one has only to walk along Southwark Street and some of the streets that run between there and Bankside, such as Canvey Street. Reminders of older places remain but one gets a feeling of the area being swallowed up by such development. There are schemes to address the environment and public spaces such as Bankside Urban Forest, a landscaping programme stretching from the riverside to the Elephant & Castle, and between Blackfriars Road and Borough High Street. Public art projects have appeared in the area, such as the statue at the back of Tate Modern known as the 'Monument to the Unknown Artist', which is a piece of interactive public art created by Greyworld. Their website states that this large sculpture 'seeks inspiration from passers-by, inviting them to strike poses which he copies.' The statue stands in front of the Blue Fin Building designed by architects Allies & Morrison and occupied by the magazine publisher IPC Media. It stands on the site of the former St Christopher House. 'Poured Lines' on Southwark Street is one of the longest pieces of public artwork in the world (48 m long and 3 m tall – 157 x 10 feet). It is a multi-coloured painting by Turner Prize-nominated artist Ian Davenport. The £290,000 project was funded largely by Land Securities and Southwark Council. A council spokesman said that public art plays a vital role in regenerating the area and 'helps to reinforce the emergence of Bankside as the leading cultural quarter of London'.

Continued expansion of Bankside is planned, with a number of large-scale schemes approved such as the Shard of Glass, New London Bridge House, Tate Modern extension, Thameslink Programme, London Bridge Station master plan, Project Bankside, More London, and Bankside Mix. Business developments are organised through groups such as Better Bankside, an independent business located on Great Guilford Street which is owned, funded and led by employers in the Bankside area. Southwark Council states that it is important that the 'construction of these developments are undertaken in a manner that protects as far as possible the safety, environment, health and well being and livelihoods of existing residents and businesses'. Such developments are hoped to create 30,000 new jobs and 2,500 additional homes between 2001 and 2026.

Bankside has a rich and diverse history and has, over the centuries, reinvented itself on many occasions. It changed from the early residential area of ecclesiastical houses and mansions to brothels, bear-baiting and theatre, which in turn gave way to the many bustling activities including lime-burning, tanning, breweries, wharves, ferry services, printing, engineering railways, docks, foundries, and countless small industries. Bankside has provided hospitals for the poor, the inspiration for literature and has one of the finest medieval buildings in London. After the Second World War the area became impoverished and the industries declined along with the tightly populated alleyways. A major regeneration came during the 1990s which transformed Bankside into one of the capital's main tourist destinations as well as one of the most desirable residential locations in London. Much has been lost whilst there have also been gains. Peter Ackroyd wrote, 'London has always been rebuilt, and demolished, and vandalized ... one of the characteristics of London planners and builders, over the centuries, has been the recklessness with which they have destroyed the city's past.' Bankside echoes Ackroyd's description of London as a 'living organism, with its own laws of growth and change'.

Bibliography

Ackroyd, P. (2000). *London: The Biography*. London: Vintage.

Andrews, W. (1887). *Famous Frosts and Frost Fairs in Great Britain*. Hull.

Anon. (1661). *Sad and wonderful newes from the Faulcon at the Bankside: Being a … relation of the strange visions … and apparitions in the house … of Mr. Powel a baker, lately deceased*. London: Horton.

Berry, G. (1978). *Taverns and Tokens of Pepys' London*. London: Seaby Publications.

Boast, M. (1985). *The Story of Bankside: from the River Thames to St George's Circus*. Council of the London Borough of Southwark, Neighbourhood Histories, No. 8.

Boger, C. G. (1881). *Southwark and its Story*. London: Simpkin, Marshall & Co.

Bowsher, J. (1998). *The Rose Theatre: an archaeological discovery*. Museum of London.

Bowsher, J., & Miller, P. (2009). *The Rose and the Globe: Playhouses of Tudor Bankside, Southwark Excavations 1988–91*. Museum of London Archaeology Service.

Brimblecombe, P. (1987). *The Big Smoke. A history of air pollution in London since medieval times*. London: Routledge.

Browner, J. A. (1994). *Wrong Side of the River: London's disreputable South Bank in the sixteenth and seventeenth century*. Essays in History 36: 34–72. University of Virginia.

Burford, E. J. (1976). *Bawds and Lodgings: A History of the London Bankside Brothels c. 100–1675*. London: Owen.

Burford, E. J. (1977). *In the Clink, The Story of London's Oldest Prison*. London: New English Library.

Calder, A. (1991). *The Myth of the Blitz*. London: Pimlico.

Carlin, M. (1996). *Medieval Southwark*. London: Hambledon Press.

Cavendish, W., 1st Duke of Newcastle (1667). *The Humorous Lovers*. London.

Concanen, M., & Morgan, A. (1795). *The history and antiquities of the parish of St Saviour's, Southwark*. London.

Corner, J., & Harvey, S. (eds) (1991) *Enterprise and Heritage*. London: Routledge.

Course, E. (1962). *London Railways*. London: Batsford.

Croome, D. F., & Jackson, A. A. (1993). *Rails through the Clay, A History of London's Tube Railways*. 2nd edition. London: Capital Transport.

Currie, I. (2001). *Frosts, Freezes and Fairs*. Coulsdon: Frosted Earth.

Davis, R. (1996). *Southwark at War: A Book of Memories*. London Borough of Southwark.

Forster, J. (1875). *The Life of Charles Dickens*. London: Cecil Palmer.

Golden, G. (1951). *Old Bankside*. London: Williams & Norgate.

Golding, B. (1819 & 2008). *An Historical Account of St Thomas's Hospital, Southwark*. London: Bibliofile.

Goodman, N. (1632). *Hollands leaguer: or, an historical discourse of the life and actions of Dona Britanica Hollandia the arch-mistris of the wicked women of Eutopia*. London.

Gregg, J. (2001). *The Shelter of the Tubes*. London: Capital Transport.

Hare, Augustus J. C. (1901). *Walks in London*. 2 volumes. London: George Allen.

Home, G. (1931). *Old London Bridge*. London: The Bodley Head.

Horne, M., & Bayman, B. (1999). *The Northern Line, An Illustrated History*. 2nd edition. London: Capital Transport.

Jackson, A. A. (1985). *London's Termini*. 2nd edition. Newton Abbot: David & Charles.

Kent, W. (ed.) (1937). *An Encyclopaedia of London*. London: J. M. Dent & Sons.

Kingsford, C. L. (1920). 'Paris Garden and the Bear Baiting'. *Archaeologia 70*.

Lupton, D. (1632). *London and the countrey carbonadoed and quartred into seuerall characters*. London.

Merritt, J. F. 'The creation of Strype's Survey of London', in Strype, *Survey of London* (1720), [online] (hriOnline, Sheffield).

Norman, P. (2009). *The Accounts of the Overseers of the Poor of Paris Garden, Southwark: May 17, 1608 to September 30, 1671* (1901). Kessinger Publishing.

Oudney, J. (1972). *Crossing London's River*. London: J. M. Dent & Sons.

Panter-Downes, M. (1972). *London War-Notes 1939–45*. Harlow: Longman.

Phillips, G. (1981). *Thames Crossings*. Newton Abbot: David & Charles.

Pierce, P. (2002). *Old London Bridge: The Story of the Longest Inhabited Bridge in Europe*. London: Headline Review.

Reily, L., & Marshall, G. (2001). *The Story of Bankside*. London Borough of Southwark, Neighbourhood History, No. 7.

Rendle, W., & Norman, P. (1888 & 2009). *The Inns of Old Southwark and Their Associations*. Kessinger Publishing.

Rex, R. (1995). *"The sins of Madame Eglentyne", and other essays on Chaucer*. University of Delaware Press.

Roberts, H., & Godfrey, W. H. (eds) (1950). *Southwark Street, Survey of London: volume 22: Bankside (the parishes of St Saviour and Christchurch Southwark*. London County Council.

Sabbagh, K. (2000). *Power into Art: Creating Tate Modern, Bankside*. London: Allen Lane.

Seeley, D., Phillpotts, C., & Samuel, M. (2007). *Winchester Palace: Excavations at the Southwark Residence of the Bishops of Winchester*. Museum of London Archaeology Service.

Shelley, H. S. (1909). *Inns and Taverns of Old London*. London: Pitman.

Stevens, T. P. (1931). *Southwark Cathedral, 606–1931*. London: Sampson Low, Marston & Co.

Stow, J. (2005 ed.). *A Survey of London: Written in the Year 1598*. Stroud: The History Press.

Strype, J. (1720). *A Survey of the Cities of London and Westminster*. *[online] (hriOnline, Sheffield)*.

Tames, R. (2001). *Southwark Past*. Historical Publications Ltd.

Tindall, G. (2007). *The House by the Thames*. London: Pimlico.

Thornbury, W., & Walford, E. J. (1896). *Old and New London*. London: Cassell.

Tyler, F. E. 'The bear gardens at Southwark and old Bank-side'. *Home Counties Magazine*, vol. 12, pp. 199–206.

White, J. (2008). *London in the Twentieth Century: A City and Its People*. London: Vintage.

Wallington, N. (2005). *In Case of Fire: The Illustrated History and Modern Role of the London Fire Brigade*. Huddersfield: Jeremy Mills Publishing.

Weightman, G. (1990). *London River. The Thames Story*. London: Collins & Brown.

Weightman, G. (2004). *London's Thames*. London: John Murray.

Weinreb, B., Hibbert, C., Keay, J., & Keay, J. (2008). *The London Encyclopaedia*. 3rd edition. London: Macmillan.

Withington, J. (2003). *Capital Disasters. How London has survives Fire, Flood, Disease, Riot and War*. Stroud: Sutton Publishing.

Wolmar, C. (2004). *The Subterranean Railway*. London: Atlantic Books.

List of Illustrations

27. The Shakespeare memorial in Southwark Cathedral. Author's collection.
28. The rose window in the remains of Winchester Palace. Author's collection.
29. Southwark Cathedral. Author's collection.
30. Portrait of Chaucer, *c.* 1412. © Jonathan Reeve JR991b1p2 13001400.
31. A selection of Canterbury Pilgrims from an early edition of Chaucer's *Canterbury Tales* which first appeared in 1387. © Jonathan Reeve JR331b11p429 13001400.
32. Plaque commemorating the site of the Tabard Inn. Author's collection.
33. Southwark Bridge opened in 1921. Author's collection.
34. Tate Modern, previously Bankside Power Station. Author's collection.
35. Shard London Bridge, March 2010, on its way to becoming the tallest building in Europe. Author's collection.
36. The houses in Southwark, close to the south end of London Bridge. © Stephen Porter.
37. Ferryman's seat at the corner of Bankside and Bear Gardens. Author's collection.
38. Medieval wooden roof bosses. The one at the top is the Devil devouring Judas Iscariot. Author's collection.
39. An execution at Horsemonger Lane Gaol in the nineteenth century. Author's collection.
40. The site of Horsemonger Lane Gaol today. Author's collection.
41. The church of St Mary Overy, Southwark, and London Bridge. Note the spiked heads of executed felons in the right foreground.© Jonathan Reeve JR1077b3fp174 16001650.
42. Among the many entertainers operating on Bankside were conjurors. © Jonathan Reeve JR1086b3p497 15501600.
43. The Albion Flour Mills at Bankside. Author's collection.
44. Christ Church as it looked in 1817. Author's collection.
45. The pamphlet *News from Holland's Leaguer* – named after a famous Bankside stew. Author's collection.
46. An illustration of the London & Greenwich Railway, 1836. Author's collection.
47. *Southwark Fair*, by William Hogarth, 1743. Author's collection.
48. The Manors of Southwark by the sixteenth century. Author's collection.
49. Fish Pond Houses. These houses in Shakespeare's time stood adjacent to the Royal Fish Ponds on Bankside. © Stephen Porter.
50. Bankside as depicted on the plan of London included in Georg Braun and Franz Hogenberg's *Civitatis Orbis Terrarum* (1572). The bull- and bear-baiting arenas are shown; the first playhouse in the district was built later. That was the Rose, erected in 1587 by Philip Henslowe and John Cholmley. © Jonathan Reeve JR1107b21p429 15501600.
51. Bear-baiting. Londoners flocked to Southwark for such 'entertainments'. © Jonathan Reeve JR1053b4p494 13501400.
52. Bankside. A very early plan of the site on which the Elizabeth playhouses were subsequently built. © Stephen Porter.
53. The engraved portrait of William Shakespeare on the title-page of the First Folio of 1623, by Martin Droeshout.
© Stephen Porter.
54. The Globe Theatre on Bankside, home of Shakespeare's company. © Stephen Porter.
55. The Bankside area of Southwark, shown on Wenceslaus Hollar's *Long View of London* of 1647. © Jonathan Reeve JR1119b67pxvi 16001650.
56. Warrant of James I dated at Greenwich on 17 May 1603, ordering the issue of Letters Patent authorizing the king's servants, including William Shakespeare, Richard Burbage, John Hemming and Henry Condell, to play 'comedies, tragedies, histories, enterludes, pastoralls & stage plaies... within their now usuall house called the Globe'.© Jonathan Reeve JR1111b22p1487 16001650.
57. William Shakespeare's signature on a page of his will. © Jonathan Reeve JR1067b5fp306 16001650.

List of Illustrations

58. Richard Burbage (1568–1619), the leading man in Shakespeare's company, the Chamberlain's Men formed in 1594. Richard and his brother erected the Globe playhouse on Bankside in 1599. © Jonathan Reeve JR113ob40p204 15501600.

59. The title page of the First Folio edition of Shakespeare's plays. © Stephen Porter.

60. The Swan theatre, redrawn from Visscher's view of 1616. © Jonathan Reeve JR110b22p1486 15501600.

61. The interior of the Swan Theatre on Bankside, built in 1595. © Jonathan Reeve JR1080b3p299 16001650.

62. John Norden's plan of London of 1593, showing the city. © Jonathan Reeve JR1074b3fp156 15501600.

63. Rogues and vagabonds. © Jonathan Reeve JR1085b3fp492 15501600.

64. Costumes of the Elizabethan period. © Jonathan Reeve JR1073b3fp108 15501600.

65. An apothecary's shop. Bankside was 'full of apothecaries' shops'. © Jonathan Reeve JR1069b5p429 15501600.

66. This section of Anthonis van den Wyngaerde's pen-and-ink drawing of c.1544 shows Southwark with the frontage of two-storey houses in its High Street broken by the Earl of Suffolk's house Southwark Place. © Jonathan Reeve JR1095b20p952-3 15001500.

67. Card games were a popular form of recreation in the many inns on Bankside. © Jonathan Reeve JR1083b3fp472 15501600.

68. Winchester Palace after Wenceslaus Hollar, 1660. Author's collection.

69. A convivial marriage festival at Horsleydown, east of Southwark, on the south side of the Thames. © Jonathan Reeve JR1070b3fpiii 16001650.

70. In very cold winters the Thames above London Bridge froze over, sometimes so deeply that a frost fair could be held on the ice. © Jonathan Reeve JR520b24p1430 16501700.

71. St Saviour's church, Southwark. William Shakespeare was a parishioner for a time and in 1911 a memorial was erected to him, with a reclining effigy in alabaster. His brother Edmund was buried here in 1607. © Jonathan Reeve JR112ob67pxxx 16001650.

72. This section of Hollar's view of London from Bankside of 1647 shows a part of Southwark in the foreground, with London Bridge and the City. The buildings along the river came right down to the waterside, with occasional quays. © Jonathan Reeve JR1925b67pxix 16001650.

73. Hollar's view has the crowded roofs of Southwark in the foreground, with the gables of the buildings facing the High Street that were to be destroyed in the fire of 1676. St Olave's church, dedicated to the king of Norway, who died in 1030, was rebuilt in 1740 and demolished in 1928. © Jonathan Reeve JR1926b67pxix 16001650.

74. & 75 The Great Fire, which began in the early hours of 2 September 1666 and continued to burn for four days. The first is from the viewpoint to the south of St Mary Overy's church in Southwark. The second shows the western edges of Southwark © Jonathan Reeve JR446b8fp108 16501700. and © Jonathan Reeve JR1893b8fp84 16501700.

76, 77, 78 & 79. Street sellers also sold useful household items such as fine lace and pots and pans, and second-hand clothes, while the chimney-sweep and his boy went around the streets to attract business. © Jonathan Reeve JR1972b24p1588B 16501700, JR1973b24p1589B 16501700, JR1970b24p1587T 16501700 & JR1966b24p1579 16501700.

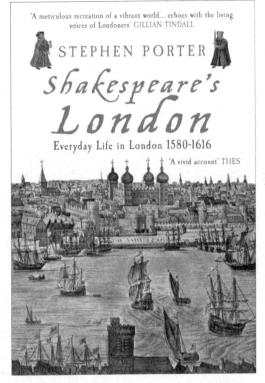

Also available from Amberley Publishing

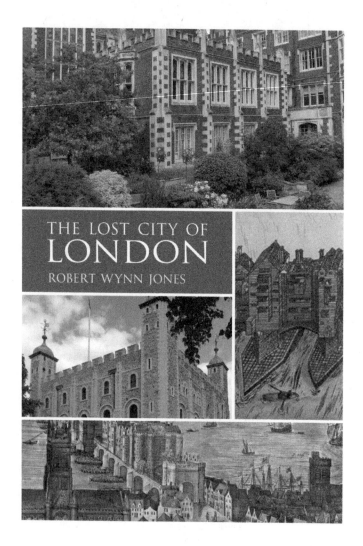

THE LOST CITY OF
LONDON
ROBERT WYNN JONES

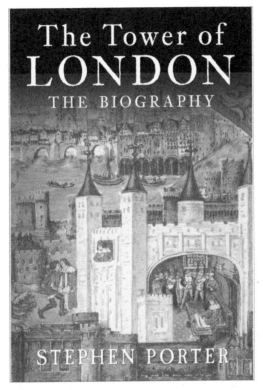

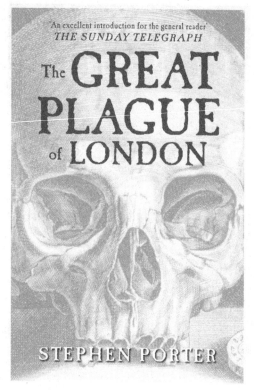

Also available from Amberley Publishing

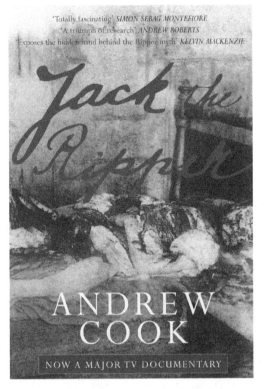

Finally lays to rest the mystery of who Jack the Ripper was

Also available from Amberley Publishing

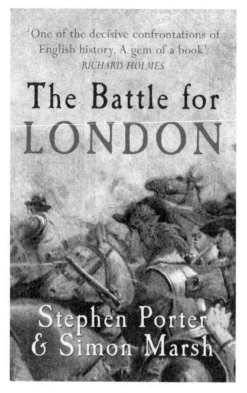

The story of the battle of Turnham Green and how 'the sack of London' was prevented by Londoners

'One of the decisive confrontations of English history. A gem of a book' RICHARD HOLMES.

At Turnham Green the Civil War that had pitched Englishman against Englishman came to London. On 13 November thousands of volunteers streamed out of the city to join the army and the most ferocious battle in London's long history began. The outcome would mark a turning point in the conflict that had split the nation.

£12.99 Paperback
43 illustrations (15 col)
176 pages
978-1-4456-0574-6

Available from all good bookshops or to order direct
Please call **01453-847-800**
www.amberleybooks.com

Also available from Amberley Publishing

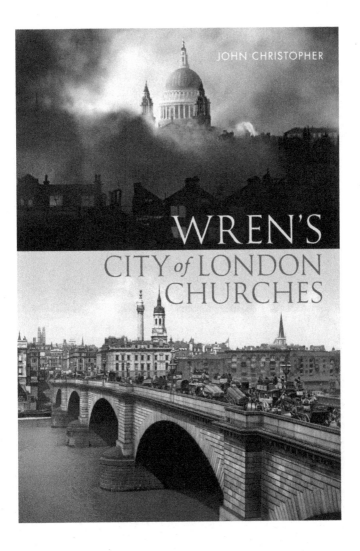

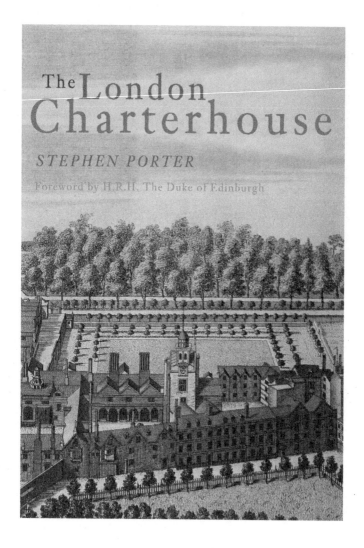

Also available from Amberley Publishing

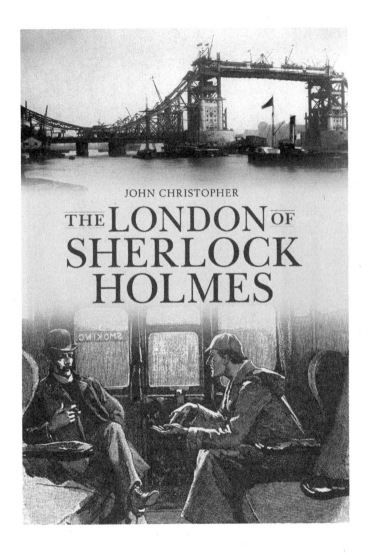

JOHN CHRISTOPHER

THE LONDON OF
SHERLOCK
HOLMES

Also available from Amberley Publishing

Available from all good bookshops or to order direct
Please call **01453-847-800**
www.amberleybooks.com

Index